# Using Internet Primary Sources to Teach Critical Thinking Skills in Mathematics

# Using Internet Primary Sources to Teach Critical Thinking Skills in Mathematics

## Evan Glazer

Greenwood Professional Guides in School Librarianship
*Harriet Selverstone, Series Adviser*

**GREENWOOD PRESS**
Westport, Connecticut • London

**Library of Congress Cataloging-in-Publication Data**

Glazer, Evan, 1971–
    Using Internet primary sources to teach critical thinking skills in mathematics /
    Evan Glazer.
        p.  cm.—(Greenwood professional guides in school librarianship, ISSN 1074–150X)
    Includes index.
    ISBN 0–313–31327–X (alk. paper)
    1. Mathematics—Study and teaching (Secondary)—Computer network resources.  2.
    Internet in education.  I. Title.  II. Series.
    QA11.5.G54  2001
    510'.71'2—dc21        00–052137

British Library Cataloguing in Publication Data is available.

Library of Congress Catalog Card Number: 00–052137
ISBN: 0–313–31327–X
ISSN: 1074–150X

First published in 2001

Greenwood Press, 88 Post Road West, Westport, CT 06881
An imprint of Greenwood Publishing Group, Inc.
www.greenwood.com

Printed in the United States of America

The paper used in this book complies with the
Permanent Paper Standard issued by the National
Information Standards Organization (Z39.48–1984).

10 9 8 7 6 5 4 3 2 1

I dedicate this book to Ken Travers, whose vision, excitement, and support have given me, and countless others, opportunities to excel in technology-enhanced mathematics education. His outstanding care for and attention to his students have made him a teacher of teachers, and a leader of leaders. Dr. Travers, you are my hero.

# Contents

# Acknowledgments

I wish to thank Amy Hackenberg and Chad Galloway for the countless hours of editing and viewing Web sites. Their invaluable support and suggestions have created an efficient and improved production. I would like to thank Jim Wilson and Mary Ann Fitzgerald for their insightful expert critique from their respective fields of mathematics education and instructional technology. They are, of course, not responsible for any misconceptions presented in this book. I wish to thank my colleagues at Glenbrook South High School in Glenview, Illinois, for their continual dedication towards innovation and excellence in teaching and learning. I am grateful to John McConnell in Glenview, Illinois, and George Magdich in Rutherford, New Jersey, for giving me opportunities to contribute to their vision and leadership of outstanding technology-enhanced education. I wish to thank the production editor Rebecca Ardwin and copy editor Lynne Goetz of this book for their highly professional assistance. Last, and certainly not least, I thank the many teachers and students that have devoted time and energy towards using the Internet as a resource and tool for learning mathematics. The progress I have witnessed in this domain since 1993 has been remarkable.

# Introduction

The activities in this book have been generated based on my experiences as a high school mathematics teacher, scholar, and Web surfer. They represent an effort to promote students' use of critical thinking by constructing knowledge through conjecturing, experimentation, and argumentation. Implementation and modification of these resources should involve thoughtful attention to students' needs, students' prior knowledge, use of cognitive strategies, and the classroom environment. Links to all of the URLs in this book have been posted and will be updated at http://www.greenwood.com/glazer.htm. Please do not hesitate to contact me at evanmglazer@yahoo.com to share your thoughts, questions, and experiences so that future revisions and development of curricular resources will best serve students' learning.

## RATIONALE

### Purpose

This book provides examples of instructional and learning opportunities that use Web sources in order to promote critical thinking in the high school mathematics classroom. As a tool for collecting data and experimenting in microworlds, the Web generates active learning situations where students construct mathematical representations. The activities in this set of instructional resources focus on learning opportunities that would be impossible, unmanageable, costly, or inefficient without the Web. Consequently, I do not utilize Web sources that can be found in a book or mathematics lessons. I find sites like these useful, and some of them probably include critical thinking, but I feel that they do not make best use of the Web as a tool that promotes learning *with* technology. When students learn with technology, they use it as a cognitive tool that helps them to construct meaning based on their prior knowledge and conceptual framework.

## Significance for Developing Educational Materials

The growth rate of Web users and developers has increased exponentially recently, at least doubling each year (Klotz, 1997). Publishers, curriculum specialists, mathematicians, teachers, and students have placed a great deal of mathematics and mathematics-related information and activities on the Web. There is a need to consolidate these Web pages and applications so that students can access a greater range of learning opportunities, and teachers can have a stronger sense of the Web's utility and connection to learning outcomes. Many Web pages are unrealized instructional resources and tools because they have been developed by people who have different interests and use different Web publishing standards. Furthermore, many pages have been developed to share information or to illustrate an idea, but they are not necessarily intended for educational purposes. For example, a mathematician may create a Java applet without describing its purpose or providing exploratory questions, or a government agency may display a set of data without discussing suggestions for analysis. Consequently, there is a need for curricular materials to support these sites in order to better promote learning opportunities with the Web.

## The Need for Technology in a Changing Curriculum

The National Council of Teachers of Mathematics (NCTM) Standards (1989, 2000) is a driving force behind the K–12 mathematics teaching community. The purpose of the Standards is to establish new curricular and learning goals in order to empower students with mathematical skills that will enable them to participate in a changing society centered around managing, using, and manipulating information. Curricular standards include familiarity with numbers and operations, algebra, geometry, measurement, data analysis, and probability. Learning standards emphasize problem solving, reasoning and proof, communication, connections, and representation. Throughout this framework, NCTM has deemphasized memorization and skills and has placed increased emphasis on higher-ordered and critical thinking skills.

Even though technology can influence what is taught, teachers need to be mindful of designing instruction and environments that promote these content and learning standards. According to NCTM, technology supports learning standards when it is used "as a tool for processing information and performing calculations to investigate and solve problems" (1989, p. 8). In 2000, NCTM emphasized that technology enhances learning opportunities because it can efficiently support graphing, visualizing, and computing. Moreover, the Standards advised that the Web be used as a medium to provide resources and learning situations that would otherwise be unrealistic or impossible to create.

## Other Technologies That Promote Critical Thinking

Technology has been recognized as a tool for exploring and developing mathematics in new ways. "Changes in technology and the broadening of the areas in which mathematics is applied have resulted in growth and changes in the discipline of mathematics itself" (NCTM, 1989, p. 7). In fact, more than half of the recorded mathematical principles discovered in history have occurred since World War II (Davis & Hersh, 1981). Seeley (1995) argued that "some mathematics now becomes possible because technology allows it. . . . students can model and solve problems inaccessible to them, using mathematics previously above their level" (p. 251). Heid and Baylor (1993) found that technologies used as a tool, such as the graphing calculator, symbolic manipulator, simulations, and dynamic geometry software, offer opportunities for advancements in conceptual development and higher-order thinking. A specific tool may be more advantageous to use depending on the learning context. For example, a simulation would be a useful way to illustrate how the probability of an event and the number of trials influence the shape of a binomial probability distribution.

In an ideal setting where schools could provide unlimited resources, teachers and students could select which tool(s) they would like to use when exploring specific concepts. Realistically, teachers and students try to make best use of the tools that are available to them, and they do not always have the most current resources from which to select. A great benefit of the Web is its ability to offer many of the features of these tools without added software costs. Function graphers, simulations, symbolic manipulators, and dynamic geometry tools are all available, to some extent, in Java or Shockwave environments on the Web. However, disadvantages of using the Web are its lack of hardware mobility and the user's dependability on a reliable network. In the future, these limitations will likely be reduced due to advances in portable and wireless technologies. Some calculators already have a built-in spreadsheet, text editor, dynamic geometry software, graphing capability, and symbolic processor; it is possible to think that one day a student in math class may also have Internet access from the calculator that she stores in her backpack.

## Advantages to Using the Web versus Other Technologies

Information and tools on the Web are similar to the features of many calculators and software packages. As the Web evolves, the capabilities of the interactive elements of the Web will probably not differ much from other technologies currently used in the classroom. More important, the Web creates possibilities for new and different learning opportunities because it provides efficient and convenient access to large sources of information, real time data collection capabilities, collaboration and contribution capabilities, and a diverse array of interactive environments.

Information can be shared more effectively via the Web than by conventional paper means. When a user accesses an organized database on the Web, she can use hypertext to sift through information quickly and identify what she needs. A textbook or library is not only physically restrictive, but it also contains a miniscule portion of information compared to the content available on the Web. Moreover, information from the Web can be viewed on multiple computer screens simultaneously, so the school is not restricted to limited copies of a book or software package.

The Web provides opportunities for real time data collection. Real time data sets are unique and useful for instructional purposes because they provide opportunities to predict outcomes and to model real world phenomena. Local temperatures, stock prices and volumes, and currency exchange information are examples of information that is updated instantly in various locations on the Web. Public opinion polls, where an individual has the opportunity to answer a question and contribute to a data source, are also updated once a response is submitted.

Collaboration via the Web can occur from multiple locations around the world. Teachers are no longer confined to the isolated environment of their classroom and can participate in a larger community of teachers with common goals. Furthermore, collaborative efforts give students an opportunity to learn about people and properties from different physical and social environments. Students can post questions and analyses on the Web in order to build their own representation of their learning experiences. Global School House (http://www.gsh.org) is a location with numerous unique collaborative efforts in individual and multidisciplinary environments.

Interactive learning environments on the Web offer an array of styles, features, and representations. Students can form conjectures by modifying mathematical objects, running a simulation, and performing an experiment. This diversity is likely a result of the broad range of people from various educational domains who generate resources for the Web.

In contrast, a textbook often exposes the perspectives of an author or group of authors who may or may not consider and foster multiple learning environments and multiple representations of knowledge.

## The Evolving Nature of the Web

The World Wide Web is an evolving system with expanding information and enhanced capabilities. The Web was first used to transmit data and display information in a text-based environment. Since the multimedia browser Mosaic was developed in 1993, many people have found new uses that incorporate images, sound, and video. Since that time, programming and scripting languages created opportunities for dynamic interaction on the Web, such as Java, Java Script, and the Common Gateway Interface (CGI). Users now had opportunities to search databases, customize information, obtain instant feedback and live interaction, and manipulate a simulated object. Consequently, new experiences and learning opportunities have developed outside of the physical time and place of the typical classroom environment.

In the future, more information will be posted to the Web and new uses of the Web will be developed. The number of Internet hosts and Web sites has been increasing exponentially since 1993 (Zakon, 2000), and we should expect that educational materials will follow a similar pattern. In the past, familiarity with programming languages such as HTML and Java was necessary to post static and dynamic resources to the Web. However, the recent development of Web authoring tools has made programming practically obsolete. As a result, teachers and students can develop Web pages and Java applets more easily. We may also see more opportunities to use the Web as a tool to construct ideas. For example, teachers and students can share dynamic geometry templates that they have constructed through a software package or Java. When viewing these templates, the user can manipulate the objects on the screen and view predetermined measurements but cannot add anything to them. The constructions that users manipulate in most cases are dynamic, but finite. However, there are some instances where providing opportunities to learn by construction is under development. For example, at the MathsNet Dynamic Geometry site (http://www.anglia. co.uk/education/mathsnet/dynamic/cindy/index.html), various geometric figures can be constructed in a set of "Exercises." School Geometry in Java has also created a similar cognitive tool (http://mathsrv. kueichstaett.de/MGF/homes/grothmann/Java/zirkel/zirkel102/Zirkel. html). The addition of construction tools will be a significant enhancement to the Web and will provide even more learning opportunities.

Resources on the Web have unforeseen potential to influence learning.

Advanced computing such as virtual reality systems and artificial intel-ligence, along with advanced technological breakthroughs such as port-able technologies and wireless communication, are powerful resources that will likely affect the future development and learning opportunities with the Web. The merger of media powerhouses Time Warner and America Online may blend technologies and create new environments that present the Web as a more dynamic and active resource that em-phasizes creating and communicating information instead of receiving information.

## USING THE ACTIVITIES IN THIS BOOK

### Assumptions and Biases

Some schools have limited access to computers, the Internet, and high speed connections. I assume that these capabilities will improve over time, so I have designed several lessons and activities using powerful features of the Web that I believe will foster critical thinking opportu-nities in mathematics. However, right now these features may not be universally available. Many of these activities have been designed so that students interact with computers using them as tools to discover, make conjectures, and construct mathematics. Teachers can use many of these activities using only one computer connected to an overhead display and access to the Internet. However, in order to take advantage of the full potential of the Web and what I believe is an effective learning environ-ment, I assume that these activities will be used in a computer lab setting with at least half as many Internet-capable computers as students.

Many of these activities take advantage of the dynamic capabilities of Java and Shockwave applets. If you have a slower Internet connection, then I strongly recommend you download the page for the activity be-fore using it in your class so that the applet is stored in your browser's cache. This means that the page will be stored locally, so the next time you access the applet, it will take less time to appear on the screen. I was able to download and use all of these applets efficiently while using a cable modem and the browser Internet Explorer. One current disad-vantage with most versions of Web browsers is that they cannot read all forms of Java. I assume the development of Web browsers will improve so this problem will not exist in the future and may not exist by the time the activities in this book are in use.

I believe activities geared towards critical thinking can be used at all levels of instruction and with all students. Many teachers might argue that critical thinking is only intended for gifted students because they have mastered basic skills and lower-ordered thinking questions. I be-lieve technology creates opportunities so that mastery learning of basic skills is not an essential requirement for critical thinking. Students can collect data and generalize a new concept, explore an extension of a familiar concept, or engage in a realistic problem solving situation without being predisposed to extensive symbolic manipulations and algorithmic operations.

## Required Software

A Java-capable Web browser is the only necessary software to engage in the activities in this book. Some of the interactive activities have been created by Macromedia products that require a plugin. You can see if you have the Shockwave plugin, or download it, at http://www. exploremath.com/about/shockerhelp.cfm. Since critical thinking depends on cognitive strategies, you may give students the option to use additional technologies, such as software or calculators, if they are available. However, you will not find any investigations that depend on mathematical software or calculators. For example, I do not make use of Web sites that house explorations that depend on the TI Graphing Calculator, Geometer's SketchPad, Cabri, Mathematica, or Microsoft Excel templates. View the following URLs if you are interested in these types of resources:

TI Graphing Calculator:
   http://www.ti.com/calc/start/teachers-math-high.htm
Geometer's SketchPad:
   http://www.keypress.com/sketchpad/sketchlinks.html
Cabri:
   http://forum.swarthmore.edu/cabri/cabri.html
Mathematica:
   http://www.mathsource.com/Content/Applications/Education
Microsoft Excel:
   http://curry.edschool.virginia.edu/teacherlink/math/interactiveexcel. html

You might need to set the preferences of your Web browser so that it can read these types of templates.

## Finding Activities Appropriate for a Specific Class and Concept

The Appendix in this book is an organization of all of the highlighted Web sites by mathematics courses from prealgebra through calculus, including probability, statistics, and math history. A teacher can use this listing to get a sense of which Web resources can be used throughout the year in a given course. In addition, a teacher can use the Index to locate activities that incorporate a specific concept. For example, a geometry teacher looking for an activity that incorporates slope would probably find an activity by looking in the Index under "slope." However, if the geometry teacher wants to find an activity that can be used for a fourth quarter project, he may want to look at the list of resources in the Appendix.

## These Are Not Typical Textbook Problems

Mathematics textbooks are often filled with problems that require the student to apply only one step or process. In these situations, the problems are geared towards mastery in performing algorithms and manipulating symbols. If a student has mastered a particular algorithm, then he will likely be able to know how to do the remaining problems in the section without much thought. Consequently, students can often complete several dozen problems in a relatively short time frame, without always understanding the purpose of the algorithm or how it fits into the larger picture.

In contrast, the investigations and activities in this book are intended to rely on constructing solutions based on mathematical reasoning. Thus, the emphasis switches from recall, comprehension, and application, to analysis, synthesis, and evaluation. The activities in this book are intended to stimulate thinking about and reasoning in unfamiliar situations. Students are expected to construct mathematical understanding based on their own mathematical framework, instead of receiving prejudged information from the teacher. The teacher may also be a learner if she has never encountered a certain simulation or a particular solution generated by the students. Consequently, the reasoning skills used in exploring, conjecturing, and developing arguments may significantly extend the time it takes to answer a single question. Without practice, this experience can be frustrating to some students who are accustomed to skipping a question if they do not know an immediate solution.

Since mathematical understanding depends on a student's prior knowledge, some of the questions and activities in this book will be of lower-order thinking to students who have been previously exposed to similar situations or concepts. For example, investigating the relationships within and between rows of Pascal's triangle can be a critical thinking task when students are making and testing unfamiliar conjectures. However, once students have learned these concepts, the investigation may just be a matter of recalling knowledge. If a student is familiar with an idea, then a more appropriate investigation would be an extension that the student has not seen before. For example, after a student has incorporated properties of Pascal's triangle into his mathematical framework, a teacher might pose the investigation of different coloring patterns of multiples and remainders or quotients within the triangle. Since critical thinking opportunities depend on a student's prior knowledge and experiences, the teacher needs to select questions in this set of instructional resources that will challenge the learner to experiment and explore different ideas, and not those that will provoke an immediate, simplistic, or automatic answer.

## Related Internet Sites

The related sites after each activity are intended to act as a replacement or supplement for the activities addressed in the lesson. These sites can be useful if the main URL at the top of the page is no longer available, or if the instructor decides the URL does not sufficiently meet his needs. If this situation occurs, you will probably need to revise the questions, but the concepts addressed will likely be similar. In a lab setting, you can create questions that use these related sites in order to challenge students who finish ahead of others. You can also use the additional resources as an extension or a means for a project related to the ideas addressed in the lesson.

## Generation and Limitations of These Activities

This group of lessons has been created based on mathematics-related sites on the Web through August 2000. Consequently, any data sources, Java applets, or investigations posted on the Web after that date are not included in this edition. Since there are millions of pages on the Web, it is realistic to assume that my own searching strategies are limited. I found most of my references using libraries of links and data, such as the Math Forum (http://forum.swarthmore.edu/library/) and Mathematics Resources on the Internet (http://www.abc.se/m9847/math. html). I also used search engines, such as Alta Vista (http://www.av. com). As a search query, I would often enter a concept and the word Java or data. For example, if I were looking for a site that had an interactive pendulum, I would type +Java +pendulum in the search field. Often I would find one or two useful sites with this method, as well as information that was not useful.

According to Papert (1993), constructionism is the active construction and representation of knowledge by creating and designing something new. The resources in this book do not provide many opportunities for students to learn through constructionism by constructing objects on the screen or building their own microworlds. Instead, the learning goals in these resources are more aligned with a constructivist model, where students are expected to build their knowledge base and develop arguments through their own cognitive representations. Learning outcomes occur as a result of testing hypotheses and manipulating objects on the screen. The primary distinction between constructionism and constructivism is the opportunity to learn in the process of designing something. Additional software, such as a dynamic geometry tool, would be necessary to foster a constructionist environment. Students can use such tools to create their own complex designs that incorporate elementary definitions. However, the advanced capabilities and evolving technologies on the Web indicate possibilities for future incorporation of learning tools with a constructionist philosophy.

These resources do not represent materials for a comprehensive curriculum. Even though I have selected a broad range of topics from pre-algebra through calculus, these activities do not address all of the mathematical concepts used in a high school mathematics curriculum. In addition, some of the concepts, such as linear functions, have been highlighted in these resources because they are well represented on the Web. Consequently, these resources should be used to supplement and enhance classroom teaching. They should not drive instructional strategies because learning and mathematical reasoning should stem from a variety of concepts and forms of thinking.

## Locating Sources

Occasionally Web pages will be removed from a site and placed in another location. Most often this occurs when an individual responsible for developing the site has left a school or corporation. In some instances, the host computer will provide a friendly forwarding note indicating that the page has been moved. However, if you are unable to find the page, I recommend any of the following strategies:

1. Access a page with updated URLs from this book at http://www. greenwood.com/glazer.htm

2. Notify me at evanmglazer@yahoo.com, and I will often reply in a day's notice with the new location or an alternate site that provides similar capabilities.

3. Remove the file and folder names from the end of a URL to see if the file has been moved to a different location on the server.

For example, suppose you want to access a Web page at http:// www.criticalthinking.com/mathematics/algebra/example.html. In the third instance, the URL indicates that there is a file named example.html located in a folder titled "algebra" on the Internet computer domain www.criticalthinking.com. If the example.html file is not available, you can check to see whether the contents of the algebra folder are available by deleting example.html from the URL. That is, enter the URL http://www.criticalthinking.com/mathematics/algebra/. If a page appears, then you may be able to determine if any links exist relating to the page you were trying to access. For instance, in some cases the content may still be there, but the file name was changed. If a page does not appear in this case, then you can move up one more folder and look in the "mathematics" folder by deleting algebra/ from the URL and entering http://www.criticalthinking.com/mathematics/. If this effort is not successful, then try the machine's domain name at: http://www.criticalthinking.com/. If you are still unable to find the information, you can try to email someone at that domain and ask where the page has been moved. You will often find a link for contact information at the bottom of a page.

## REFERENCES

Davis, P. J., & Hersh, R. (1981). *The mathematical experience*. Boston: Houghton Mifflin Co.

Heid, M. K., & Baylor, T. (1993). Computing technology. In P. Wilson (Ed.), *Research ideas for the classroom: High school mathematics* (pp. 198–214). National Council of Teachers of Mathematics: Research Interpretation Project. Reston, VA: National Council of Teachers of Mathematics.

Klotz, G. (1997). *Mathematics and the World Wide Web*. Swarthmore, PA: The Math Forum. [Online]. Available at http://forum.swarthmore.edu/articles/epadel/index.html.

National Council of Teachers of Mathematics. (1989). *Curriculum and evaluation standards for school mathematics*. Reston, VA: National Council of Teachers of Mathematics.

National Council of Teachers of Mathematics. (2000). *Principles and standards for school mathematics*. Reston, VA: National Council of Teachers of Mathematics.

Papert, S. (1993). *The children's machine*. New York: Basic Books.

Seeley, C. (1995). Changing the mathematics we teach. In I. M. Carl (Ed.), *Prospects for school mathematics* (pp. 242–260). Reston, VA: National Council of Teachers of Mathematics.

Zakon, R. H. (2000). Hobbes' Internet timeline v5.1. [Online]. Available at http://info.isoc.org/guest/zakon/Internet/History/HIT.html.

# USING CRITICAL THINKING SKILLS IN MATHEMATICS

**1**

## CHARACTERISTICS OF CRITICAL THINKING

Scholars have varying definitions of critical thinking, and some suggest that we generate a math-specific description because the domain "has different criteria for good reasons from most other fields, because mathematics accepts only deductive proof, whereas most fields do not even seek it for the establishment of a final conclusion" (Ennis, 1989, p. 8). I will state a working definition of critical thinking in mathematics based on a synthesis of general definitions, as well as those that relate and apply to mathematics. The purpose of this working definition is to provide a framework and common understanding of the ideas and activities presented in this book. *Critical thinking in mathematics is the ability and disposition to incorporate prior knowledge, mathematical reasoning, and cognitive strategies to generalize, prove, or evaluate unfamiliar mathematical situations in a reflective manner.* Figure 1 is an illustration that describes the general connection between each of these components, yet keep in mind that this process can be more complex. I will elaborate on each of the components of this working definition with examples and connections to the World Wide Web and then conclude with strategies that promote critical thinking in the mathematics curriculum and classroom. An illustrated classroom experience using Internet primary sources is described at the end of the primary sources chapter.

### Ability and Disposition

*Ability* refers to a skill or power to demonstrate something. Abilities used in critical thinking are *support, inference, clarification,* and *strategies*

**Figure 1**
**The Relationship Between Critical Thinking Criteria in Mathematics**

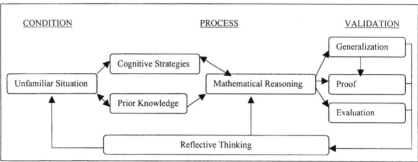

(see Ennis, 1987, for a detailed taxonomy). *Support* refers to examining, observing, and judging the credibility of a source, such as the level of expertise used in or created by the source. For example, the validity of information on a Web page may be questioned if that person's work is unfamiliar. Consequently, additional sources would need to be examined to verify the information. *Inference* involves the process of deducing and inducing information, such as logic or forming a generalization. For example, after experimentation with a dynamic kite, a student may hypothesize that its area is dependent on the length of its diagonals. With further exploration, and perhaps a proof, he can validate this conjecture. *Clarification* relates to questioning, analyzing, classifying, and defining arguments that develop or support your reasoning. For example, in a forest fire simulation, a student may develop conditional reasoning about when a fire will spread, depending on the wind direction, the probability that the fire will spread, and the type of trees in the forest. Last, *strategies* are the decisions used with an action and tactics employed when interacting with others. For example, suppose a student is asked to predict the temperature in your hometown six months from now. Strategies may revolve around how and where she will find historical data and how she will model the data to form a prediction.

*Disposition* refers to the willingness and open-mindedness to use an ability. It relates to a combination of attitudes and a tendency to think and act in positive ways. Examples of disposition include the display of interest, curiosity, reflection, confidence, values, and appreciation. These actions strongly influence the way students reason, ask questions, solve problems, and approach learning new mathematics. For example, a student who enjoys mathematics may believe there is only one way to solve a problem, and thus not show flexibility or open-mindedness in seeking alternate solutions that would supply a more comprehensive view of a mathematical situation. Without disposition, a student may have difficulty understanding the purpose and multiple interpretations of information from the Web. This type of student just wants to know how to get to "the" answer, thinking that only one solution is possible and relying on the credibility of only a single source.

## The Mathematical Situation

Critical thinking occurs in an unfamiliar situation where an individual does not immediately understand a mathematical concept or know how to determine the solution of a problem. Too often in textbooks we find exercises where students are asked to practice an algorithm for multiple problems. In essence, if they follow the steps in the algorithm, then they will likely be able to solve most of the problems. In contrast to this situation, a critical thinking experience relies on the ability to suspend judgment about how to solve the problem. After the students read a critical thinking investigation, they should not recognize the situation as repeating or practicing a skill, nor should they instantly apply a specific method that leads to a solution. Instead, students should first make sense of the problem, address how they can start the problem, how they will organize their ideas, and how they will test conjectures. For example, suppose a student finds an automobile blue book on the Web that describes the price of a specific car model over the last five years. She finds an advertisement for a six-year-old car of that model with 120,000 miles, a new stereo, and leather interior. The student's task is to determine if the car is a good buy, and if not, to produce a reasonable counteroffer. In this case, first the student needs to generate ideas on how to predict an appropriate price of the car, as well as determine a set of criteria to judge the factors that influence what constitutes a good buy.

## Processing Information

Critical thinking involves a student's ability to exercise prior knowledge, mathematical reasoning, and cognitive strategies. Students will develop strategies to solve problems based on the mathematical experiences with which they are familiar. For example, suppose a student is presented with a Java applet that simulates walking from home to school. As the walker is guided along a path, the applet simultaneously generates graphs for position vs. time and velocity vs. time. A student in algebra may associate the walker's average speed with the slope of a position vs. time graph, but a calculus student might examine the ratio of the area beneath a velocity vs. time graph and the time covered over a certain distance. There are multiple activities in this book that can be used at different levels of mathematical understanding.

Mathematical reasoning refers to the processes used to investigate a mathematical situation. When a student solves a problem, the student's ability to justify why an answer is correct involves mathematical reasoning. Thus, how a student arrives at an answer can be viewed to be of equal or perhaps even greater importance than the answer. With this in mind, critical thinking should include the process by which students develop patterns, construct arguments, validate ideas, draw logical conclusions, and recognize counterexamples.

Cognitive strategies are mental tools that help students process information, organize thoughts, and reason through mathematical situations. In many mathematics classrooms, the teacher often guides students to predetermined responses through questions that break up a complex task into smaller and simpler tasks. In critical thinking situations, the students have control of creating, selecting, and applying their own cognitive strategies. For example, students may establish a problem solving method to coordinate their ideas and understanding, such as to explore, form a hypothesis, test the hypothesis, and then develop an argument. In a simulation, students may choose to select the number of data collection trials in an experiment, choose a means of organizing their data, and then validate their arguments based on patterns, logic, and theory associated with their findings.

## Validating Information

Critical thinking also involves the validation of information or an idea with either a generalization, proof, or evaluation. Generalizations are developed through pattern recognition when a mathematical phenomenon occurs consistently within certain conditions. The generalization is not considered a proof because it cannot verify every possible case, yet it can be used to develop hypotheses and support mathematical reasoning. The presence of one counterexample will refine or refute this generalization, so the student should be prepared to defend and justify generalizations by analyzing a variety of possible situations. For example, a student using a Web-based function plotter can hypothesize that a function is reflection symmetric over the y-axis if all of its variables contain even exponents. The student tests this conjecture by examining multiple cases of functions that include combinations of exponents and by varying the number of terms in a polynomial. The student forms the generalization when she is confident that a pattern exists, without counterexample, and is prepared to defend her claim. A proof sometimes follows a generalization when a student can show that a certain condition exists for all possible cases. In this situation, the student needs to recognize that every function that is reflection symmetrical with the y-axis maintains the property $f(-x) = f(x)$. That is, the y-coordinate on this type of function will be the same for any point with opposite x-coordinates. Consequently, a student can test and prove this symmetry with any function if she can show that $f(-x) = f(x)$. This property will be true for every function with variables that contain only even exponents because any negative number raised to an even power is always equal to its opposite raised to that same power.

While generalizations and proofs are generative means of validating ideas, evaluation is the process of determining the quality of an existing idea, product, or resource. Based on criteria, choices and decisions are made to distinguish the best resource from a good resource. For example, a student may determine that the function tools on a specific Web page are most useful because they connect representations of equations, tables, and graphing; adjustments in one of these features will simultaneously alter the other features, illustrating the connections between these representations. Evaluation can also be used to judge students' reasoning when they determine that one method or medium for solving a problem is better than another, perhaps because it is more efficient or strengthens connections that are made between concepts.

## Reflective Thinking

Reflective thinking involves making sense about the reasonableness of an answer or an argument, determining alternate ways to explain a concept or solve a problem, generating extensions for further study, and communicating a solution thoughtfully. It is easy for students to focus on completing a problem and moving on to other exercises without thinking much about what their answer means. For example, one student may conclude that an account at a local bank will yield $213,526 on a $100 investment after five years. Most of us would invest our life savings if we knew that we would accrue that much interest! To avoid this sort of error, students need to be encouraged to examine their answers and to look back at the problem posed to determine if their conclusions make sense. If an answer does not make sense, then they should examine and correct possible errors or flaws in argumentation until their answers appear more appropriate.

Reflective thinking also includes the ability and disposition to understand a problem in multiple ways. Along with understanding the reasonableness of an answer, students should reflect on their solution and determine alternate ways to support their arguments. For example, suppose students are asked to determine the dimensions of a rectangular fence that would produce a maximum area. One idea would be to use a spreadsheet to generate a list of possible areas based on various rectangle dimensions. To enhance this argument, the student could consider an alternate representation, such as a graph of the function to highlight a maximum point. The additional perspective can help generate additional ideas, such as illustrating why there is a maximum point and how to find it from the equation. Thus, critical thinking also engenders opportunities to generate questions that extend beyond the scope of the problem.

The "What if?" scenario can be applied to a problem when the context or conditions in the problem are slightly altered. For example, suppose a student generalizes a linear pattern from a data set that describes the speed of the men's 100 meter dash over various years at the summer Olympics. The student may wonder if this pattern exists between women's times, or question if and when women may start running faster than men. Communicating a solution invokes reflective thinking because students need to consider and understand the knowledge, ability, and disposition of their audience. The presentation of a solution should describe approaches and clear reasoning. Students need to determine when their solutions involve too little or too much information so that readers or listeners can understand the flow and justification behind the logic used in the solution process. Students can gauge the level of explanation needed in a solution by framing their analysis to a peer to receive feedback.

## CRITICAL THINKING IN THE CLASSROOM

### Establishing a Critical Thinking Environment

Even though we can be independent critical thinkers, there are advantages to creating an environment that encourages free thought and collaboration. Both teachers and students have responsibilities to support and maintain an atmosphere for critical thinking. The teacher should foster disposition among students so they feel comfortable to inquire, share, and challenge ideas. The epistemological framework of classroom instruction is often seen as objectivist, where the teacher directs the students to understand a body of knowledge that has been developed external to the learner. For example, the teacher may set a series of objectives that elicit responses from students that demonstrate an understanding of a particular concept. In this case, the dependency on the teacher's delivery of knowledge influences how students think and learn. As the teacher directs a lesson, she calls on students to elicit correct thinking and redirects incorrect thinking until students have developed an idea or process according to the teacher's standards. Not only does this method of inquiry emphasize the teacher's knowledge as the source for learning and correct thinking, but it also may inhibit ideas, suggestions, and thoughts from the students in the classroom.

In contrast, in a critical thinking environment, the students exercise more control over their learning by constructing their own representation of knowledge. The teacher facilitates a discussion or manages an activity where students develop arguments and rationale based on their own analyses. For example, movie theater managers make decisions about when to remove a particular movie from a theater as it loses popularity. A challenge is to predict when a movie might lose popularity based on the number of theaters showing the film and the amount of revenue they obtain each week. In this scenario, a teacher needs to suspend judgment about how to arrive at an answer and to consider the possibility that there may be more than one method to represent an answer. Consequently, the teacher's role is to support and promote the student's development of analysis methods, rationales, and argumentation. Students have more control over the direction of their learning, while the teacher becomes a learner and coach. This process can be difficult for teachers and students, especially if they are taking on unfamiliar roles. Thus, questioning strategies can help elicit students' construction of ideas, methods, and mathematical reasoning. For example, the teacher can encourage the development of cognitive strategies by continually asking, "What are you doing?," "Why are you doing it?," and "How does it help you?" (Schoenfeld, 1989). The teacher can also promote reflective thinking by asking, "Is there another way?," "Can you convince a friend?," and "What if . . . ?" (Burton, 1984).

The student's responsibility in a critical thinking environment centers on his disposition to engage in an activity. While some students maintain this willingness to learn independently, others may need encouragement from peers and teachers. Students are more likely to have this disposition if they believe that their ideas contribute to the welfare of a group. Consequently, small groups are often a useful means to structure a learning environment because students may feel more comfortable expressing ideas, drawing from other students' talents, and making a larger contribution to the success of the group. Small group interaction can also raise student interest in challenging tasks because the student-controlled learning environment supports risk taking, developing and defending arguments, and utilizing alternate representations or methods to solve a problem. The small group setting also allows students to agree on a common analysis that will not isolate the efforts of a single individual. As a consequence, incorrect solutions will less likely inhibit individual contribution, and correct solutions will promote feelings of ownership and success.

## Integrating Critical Thinking into the Curriculum

The mathematics curriculum in the United States varies among schools and teachers. However, most teachers use segmented units from a textbook to drive what they teach and how they teach (Brown, 1974). An advantage to this instructional strategy is that topics can be taught within a class period, making them easier to understand with more apparent success (Skemp, 1978). A disadvantage to this style is the lack of relational understanding. That is, it is more difficult to form connections within mathematics and between concepts.

I believe students need to experience a variety of learning approaches so they realize that there are multiple ways of representing and understanding mathematics. In some cases, students may only understand mathematics as a means of using formulas or algorithms to efficiently find answers, while other situations create the need to explore and understand how a concept relates to a larger scope of mathematics. Consequently, many of the activities in this book have been designed to target segmented topics that connect to other mathematical concepts. For example, an activity geared towards slope may also address ratios, angles, graphs, intercepts, and equations. I recommend that activities are introduced based on the primary concepts listed, but mindful of using questions that rely on prior knowledge and building mathematical connections. Students who are not familiar with conceptual reflection and integration will likely have difficulty making connections at first. The teacher must carefully work through these investigations before they are used in class in order to detect potential questions and difficulties. As students familiarize themselves with more activities that utilize relational understanding, they will likely feel more comfortable integrating their conceptual knowledge and constructing mathematical connections. Fostering these connections within the curriculum helps students realize that mathematical concepts are not independent entities that are used only to pass an exam or class. Instead, they are building blocks that form cohesive links in an effort to broaden their overall understanding of mathematics.

Many mathematics curricula focus on students' acquisition of predefined objectives. In these cases, assessment is based on the ability to demonstrate knowledge and skills in order to find "the" answer. In many critical thinking situations, there may not be one correct answer to an unfamiliar situation. For example, if a student is asked to determine the best player in baseball, you would not expect everyone to respond with the same name. Consequently, mathematical reasoning and performance is not primarily based on answers, but instead on the quality of the criteria and justification used to develop an argument. In addition, there may be critical thinking situations in which the same answer may result, but through different means. For example, a variety of methods can be used to prove an important relationship between the sides of a right triangle, yet the outcome should always be that the sum of the squares of the legs of a right triangle is equal to the square of its hypotenuse. Students who are not familiar with the possibility of multiple methods or answers to a mathematical situation will likely feel uncomfortable because there is not a definitive algorithm that will solve the problem. However, if students are provided with more opportunities to engage in open-ended investigations, they are likely to have an increased disposition towards critical inquiry.

## Using the Activities in Your Classroom

I believe that pedagogical methods are based on unique strengths of the teacher and characteristics of the learning environment. Consequently, instructional resources such as the activities in this book should be used to support, not drive, teaching and learning. Many of the activities can be used for classroom demonstrations, group discussions, activities, labs, explorations, or projects. In my teaching experience, I have found that explorations are useful for introducing a concept, and projects are helpful to extend or think more deeply about a concept. Most important, these investigations should be modified to fit each teacher's needs because every teacher has a unique style of pedagogy and emphasizes different ideas. Since the factors that influence critical thinking are not the same for all students, I encourage teachers to rephrase questions or activities so that their students will be challenged, but so that they will not feel lost. The teacher's role as a facilitator and moderator can greatly influence the progress of the student in the critical thinking process. An ideal learning situation involves placing students in an environment where they need to generate questions, manage strategies, and generalize a pattern or solution. To foster this environment, I suggest that the teacher create an open forum for students to practice reflective inquiry, take risks, and challenge ideas. This discourse will likely promote students to critically investigate the mathematical situations represented in the activities in this book.

These resources are not intended to be "teacher proof" worksheets. I do not endorse giving these questions to students without the teacher's understanding of the potential challenges and support needed for each activity. The teacher needs to be aware of the variety of concepts and levels of understanding necessary for each investigation. Some of the questions can be used to introduce a concept, while others are an extension of the concept. Consequently, an activity may not encourage critical thinking if not carefully selected and modified for the teacher's needs. Several of the activities rely on a variety of mathematical abilities that draw on connections from multiple concepts. In some instances, a prealgebra student can answer a few of the questions, while other questions are more appropriate for precalculus students. In sum, I encourage teachers to work through activities so they can understand how to carefully select and modify questions to best serve their students' needs.

The questions in the activities often take different amounts of time to answer. In some cases, a question can be answered in a couple of minutes; in other cases, a question can take as long as a classroom project. If you would like to discuss the applicability of a specific Web page for your own instructional needs, feel free to contact me at evanmglazer @yahoo.com. I may not necessarily have an answer to your question, but raising my awareness of an instructional need for a specific Web site will help me revise and improve the activities in this book. Moreover, I encourage you to send me an email message after you have tried an activity in your classroom. Your analysis and feedback about what was helpful and what could be revised will enhance learning opportunities in subsequent editions.

## Assessing Critical Thinking Activities

Mathematics has been often thought of as an objective subject, with little deviation in grading procedures. In essence, students' grades have been based on their ability to demonstrate specifically defined objectives and predetermined solutions. In contrast, an English paper is graded more subjectively, where the teacher judges a student's performance based on predetermined criteria. In a subjective situation, the teacher is likely to focus on a larger holistic system that includes goal-based criteria. These criteria may include the format of the paper, amount of evidence provided, validity of information, writing style, defense of an argument, grammar, and spelling. The teacher will also likely select how each of these criteria is weighted, perhaps devoting 35 percent of the grade to the student's defense of an argument and 10 percent to grammar and spelling. Based on this system, students are given greater flexibility to represent their knowledge since there is not one way to fulfill many of these criteria.

The open-ended nature of many of the investigations in this book suggests that a subjective and organized grading procedure should be applied to questions that have more than one possible method or correct answer. A mathematics teacher can develop a grading rubric that will define characteristics of and standards for the student's product. A sample rubric is provided in Figure 2. The rubric should probably be more specific to a particular situation or assignment, especially if the teacher has expected outcomes, such as the inclusion of a table or graph, or the use of a particular method.

Students' awareness of this type of grading scheme before beginning an assignment gives them a sense of the teacher's expectations and values. The rubric also communicates to students that their work is based on a partially subjective and partially objective scale. If students are working on a group project, a teacher may want to modify the rubric to include an evaluation of each member's participation. Even though

**Figure 2**
**Grading Rubric for a Project That Promotes Critical Thinking**

| Criterion | Excellent | Fair | Poor | Points |
|---|---|---|---|---|
| Correct Reasoning and Justification | 15  12 | 9  6 | 3 | _____ |
| Appropriateness of Mathematical Techniques | 10  8 | 6  4 | 2 | _____ |
| Thoroughness of Solution | 5  4 | 3  2 | 1 | _____ |
| Organization of Solution | 5  4 | 3  2 | 1 | _____ |
| Demonstration of Reflective Thinking | 5  4 | 3  2 | 1 | _____ |
| | | | TOTAL | _____ |

group tasks are intended to be divided evenly among members of the group, students often claim the contrary. Teachers may want to allow students to assess the individual participation of each member of their group, as well as the productivity of their group. Not only are these comments useful for assessing student participation, but they also provide teachers feedback about group dynamics and about the particular task.

## REFERENCES

Brown, J. K. (1974). Textbook use by teachers and students of geometry and second-year algebra. *Dissertation abstracts international, 34,* 5795A–5796A. (University Microfilms No. 74–5534).

Burton, L. (1984). Mathematical thinking: The struggle for meaning. *Journal for Research in Mathematics Education, 15*(1), 35–49.

Chancellor, D. (1991). Higher-order thinking: A "basic" skill for everyone. *Arithmetic Teacher, 38*(6), 48–50.

Cognition and Technology Group at Vanderbilt. (1993). Toward integrated curricula: Possibilities from anchored instruction. In M. Rabinowitz (Ed.), *Cognitive science: Foundations of instruction* (pp. 33–55). Hillsdale, NJ: Erlbaum.

Confrey, J., Piliero, S. C., Rizzuti, J. M., & Smith, E. (1990). High school mathematics: Development of teacher knowledge and implementation of a problem-based mathematics curriculum using multirepresentational software. *Apple classrooms of tomorrow* (Report #11). Cupertino, CA: Apple Computer Inc.

Dugdale, S. (1987). Pathfinder: A microcomputer experience in interpreting graphs. *Journal of Educational Technology Systems, 15*(3), 259–280.

Ennis, R. H. (1987). A taxonomy of critical thinking dispositions and abilities. In J. B. Baron & R. J. Sternberg (Eds.), *Teaching thinking skills: Theory and practice* (pp. 9–26). New York: W. H. Freeman.

Ennis, R. H. (1989). Critical thinking and subject specificity: Clarification and needed research. *Educational Researcher, (18)*3, 4–10.

Farrell, A. (1989). Teaching and learning behaviors in technology-oriented precalculus classrooms. *Dissertation abstracts international, 51A,* 100 (University Microfilms No. AAD 90–14417).

Fraser, R., Burkhardt, H., Coupland, J., Phillips, R., Pimm, D., & Ridgway, J. (1988). Learning activities and classroom roles with and without computers. *Journal of Mathematics Behavior, 6,* 305–338.

Grabinger, R. S. (1996). Rich environments for active learning. In D. H. Jonassen (Ed.), *Handbook of research for educational communications and technology* (pp. 665–692). New York: Simon & Schuster Macmillan.

Grassl, R., & Mingus, T. (1997). Using technology to enhance problem solving and critical thinking skills. *Mathematics and Computer Education, 31*(3), 293–300.

Heid, M. K. (1988). Reseqencing skills and concepts in applied calculus using the computer as a tool. *Journal for Research in Mathematics Education, 19*(1), 3–25.

Jonassen, D. H., & Reeves, T. C. (1996). Learning with technology: Using computers as cognitive tools. In D. H. Jonassen (Ed.), *Handbook of research for educational communications and technology* (pp. 693–719). New York: Simon & Schuster Macmillan.

Kuhn, D. (1999). A development model of critical thinking. *Educational Researcher 28*(2), 16–26.

Martin, L. M. (1987). Teachers' adoption of multimedia technologies for science and mathematics instruction. In R. D. Pea & K. Sheingold (Eds.), *Mirrors of minds: Patterns of experience in educational computing.* Norwood, NJ: Ablex Publishing Corporation.

Mason, J., Burton, L., & Stacey, K. (1982). *Thinking mathematically.* London: Addison-Wesley.

McPeck, J. E. (1981). *Critical thinking and education.* New York: St. Martin's Press.

Nickerson, R. (1988). On improving critical thinking through instruction. In *Review of Research in Education* (pp. 3–58). Washington, DC: AERA.

Norris, S. P. (1985). Synthesis of research on critical thinking. *Educational Leadership, 42*(8), 40–46.

O'Daffer, P. G., & Thornquist, B. A. (1993). Critical thinking, mathematical reasoning, and proof. In P. S. Wilson (Ed.), *Research ideas for the classroom* (pp. 39–56). New York: Macmillan.

Orton, R. E., & Lawrenz, F. (1990). A survey and analysis of factors related to the teaching of critical thinking in junior high mathematics classrooms. *Journal of Research and Development in Education, 23*(3), 145–155.

Paul, R. W. (1993). *Critical thinking: How to prepare students for a rapidly changing world.* Santa Rosa, CA: Foundation for Critical Thinking.

Polya, G. (1945). *How to solve it.* Princeton, NJ: Princeton University Press.

Romberg, T., & Carpenter, T. (1986). Research in teaching and learning mathematics: Two disciplines of scientific inquiry. In M. Wittrock (Ed.), *Handbook of research on teaching* (3rd ed.) (pp. 850–873). New York: Macmillan.

Rosebery, A. S., & Rubin, A. (1989). Reasoning under uncertainty: Developing statistical reasoning. *Journal of Mathematics Behavior, 8,* 205–219.

Schoenfeld, A. H. (1989). Teaching mathematical thinking and problem solving. In L. Resnick (Ed.), *Toward the thinking curriculum: Current cognitive research* (pp. 83–103). Alexandria, VA: ASCD Yearbook.

Skemp, R. R. (1978). Relational understanding and instrumental understanding. *Arithmetic Teacher, 25*(8), 9–15.

Thomas, E. J., Jr. (1990). A study of the effects of a computer graphics problem-solving activity on student achievements, attitudes, and task motivation (doctoral dissertation, Georgia State University, 1989). *Dissertation abstracts international, 51,* 102A.

Thompson, A. (1985). Teachers' conceptions of mathematics and the teaching of problem solving. In E. A. Silver (Ed.), *Teaching and learning mathematical problem solving: Multiple research perspectives* (pp. 281–294). Hillside, NJ: Lawrence Erlbaum.

# USING PRIMARY SOURCES

**II**

## INTERNET PRIMARY SOURCES

### What Are Primary Sources?

Primary sources typically refer to original documentation or artifacts that illustrate a particular idea or source. For example, an examination of Euclid's elements may help us understand why he did not prove his fifth postulate. In addition, quotations from mathematicians may help us to better understand their work and the times in which they lived. A secondary source is an interpretation of a primary source. An analysis of census data is a secondary source because it is based on an individual's perspective of that data.

Most of the primary sources referenced in this book are interactive microworlds, data sets, and mathematical procedures. Interactive microworlds are dynamic self-contained systems that allow the user to manipulate objects on the screen in order to recognize patterns and discover mathematical properties. They provide nondirective simulations that allow the user to generate questions, form hypotheses, and test multiple cases in order to better understand mathematical phenomena. Some microworlds, such as a flight simulator, are arguably secondary sources because they have been created to represent an actual phenomenon. However, realistically we cannot ask students to take data by flying real airplanes or by digging underground to see an entire train system in motion. Thus, I include these types of experiences in this book because they provide students new learning opportunities that would otherwise be impossible or unrealistic to attain.

**Figure 3**
**Classification of Mathematics Web-Based Sources**

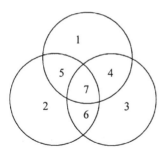

1 Databases
2 Classroom Lessons
3 Primary Sources
4 Primary Source Databases
5 Classroom Lesson Databases
6 Primary Source Lessons
7 Primary Source Lesson Databases

Data sets provide numerous opportunities for critical thinking because they are often multidimensional and can be interpreted differently. Students need to make decisions about selecting data that are important to analyze, rationalizing discrepancies in data, developing generalizations or models, and then forming an argument to support their conclusions. Real world data are often complex and messy, allowing greater flexibility for investigations that depend on interpretation, reasoning, and validation. For example, a 1993 Senate election in Philadelphia resulted in a narrow margin of victory in favor of the Democratic candidate, even though he received fewer votes on election day. This unusual instance was a result of a rather large number of absentee votes placed in favor of the Democratic candidate. Based on a data set that describes the number of absentee votes throughout different state districts, was the election fraudulent?

Mathematical procedures are descriptions or tools that produce a specific outcome. For example, a ruler and tape measure can be used to determine the height of a tree if certain prescribed methods are followed. These types of sites promote critical thinking when students evaluate the steps to determine if and why that method would appropriately measure the tree's height. Moreover, critical thinking skills are applied when students are asked to reflect upon the procedures and search for alternate methods based on different conditions or assumptions. A proof is another example of a mathematical procedure because a student is asked to judge the appropriateness of a particular step or the connection between steps in a mathematical argument.

## Mathematics Learning Opportunities with the Web

Databases, instructional lessons, and primary sources represent the mathematics and learning content on the Web. Most often Web resources do not include all of these intended purposes.

Figure 3 illustrates how mathematics resources on the Web are organized. Regions one, two, and three relate to Web resources that contain only one of these elements. Region one represents databases of information that are not related to teaching or primary sources. An example of this region is a bulletin board or electronic community where teachers can ask questions to one another, such as Teacher2Teacher at the Math Forum (http://forum.swarthmore.edu/t2t/). Region two represents independent lessons that teachers have created for their classroom, but do not necessarily rely on the Web for their use. Examples of this include Pi Mathematics (http://www.ncsa.uiuc.edu/Edu/RSE/RSEorange/buttons.html) and Sorting Quadrilaterals: Defining Parallelograms (http://www.cbv.ns.ca/sstudies/activities/math/2.html). Region three represents primary sources, such as factual information, a data set, or Java applet, that are not organized into a database or instructional activity. Examples include a BART Schedule Animation (http://www-itg.lbl.gov/vbart/) and National Average Maximal Temperatures (http://www.nws.mbay.net/maxtemp.html).

Regions four, five, and six represent a combination of two of these elements, but lack the third one. Region four describes databases of primary sources without questions for student exploration or investigation. Examples include the Journal of Statistics Data Archive (http://www.amstat.org/publications/jse/archive.htm) and Open Teach Simulations and Tools (http://www.openteach.com/list/index.html). Region five represents databases of lessons that do not rely on Web-based sources. Examples include a collection of secondary math units (http://forum.swarthmore.edu/workshops/sum98/participants/sinclair/contents.html) and SMILE lessons (http://www.iit.edu/~smile/fullinde.html#m0). Region six encompasses independent lessons that use Web resources. Examples include the cereal box problem (http://www.mste.uiuc.edu/users/reese/cereal/) and What a Steal! Or What a Rip-Off? (http://www.glenbrook.k12.il.us/gbsmat/car/intro.html).

This book is an effort to combine these three purposes in region seven, a database of resources that promote lessons which use primary sources on the Web. The primary focus is to use resources from region three as tools for an instructional setting that stimulates critical thinking. A database of instructional resources that use primary sources on the Web is not exclusive to this book. Examples on the Web include Exploremath.com (http://www.exploremath.com/activities/index.cfm), Shodor Foundation activities (http://www.shodor.org/interactivate/activities/), and MSTE Java Lessons (http://www.mste.uouc.edu/tutorials/default.html).

## Additional Sources

Providing mathematical content and sharing classroom lessons on the Web can broaden one's mathematical, curricular, and pedagogical understanding, as well as illustrate some exciting ideas. Even though these types of resources are not emphasized in this book, I leave a few URLs related to this use of the Web that you may wish to visit:

## Lesson Database Examples

### SMILE Lessons
http://www.iit.edu/~smile/fullinde.html#m0

This resource contains several hundred lessons related to geometry and measurement, patterns and logic, probability and statistics, recreational and creative math, practical and applied math, arithmetic, graphs and visuals, algebra and trigonometry, and miscellaneous topics.

### Explorer (Choose Mathematics Lessons)
http://explorer.scrtec.org/explorer/

This K–12 lesson database offers ideas for teaching a broad spectrum of mathematics from elementary to high school. Each lesson includes an abstract along with connections to school standards.

### Apple Learning Interchange (Choose Resources)
http://ali.apple.com/ali/

This search engine will find lessons posted to the Web on most K–12 mathematics topics. You can specify searches by subject, keyword, topic, level, and content type.

### Teachers.net
http://www.teachers.net/cgi-bin/lessons/sort.cgi?searchterm=Mathematics

This K–12 lesson database includes several hundred teaching ideas covering a multitude of concepts. You also have the option to add your own lessons to the database.

### The Gateway to Educational Materials
http://www.thegateway.org/

This lesson database includes highly selected resources in a broad range of content and grade levels.

## Mathematics Database Examples

### Eric Weisstein's World of Mathematics
http://mathworld.wolfram.com/

This mathematics encyclopedia at Wolfram Research includes an extremely large range of mathematics including history, recreational mathematics, and many other areas. You can search the site, browse by subject, or view an alphabetical index.

### The MacTutor History of Mathematics Archive
http://www-groups.dcs.st-and.ac.uk/~history/

This site includes a wealth of information about famous mathematicians throughout history. You can browse through biographical, topical, and famous curve summaries.

### Word Problems for Kids
http://www.stfx.ca/special/mathproblems/welcome.html

You will find over forty problems for each of grades 4 through 12 that ask students to solve various word problems. Each question provides a hint and answer for students to check.

## USING INTERNET PRIMARY SOURCES IN THE CLASSROOM

### Critical Thinking with the Web

The activities in this book focus on critical thinking with primary sources on the Web. In each instance I provide a URL to find information on a page, a context in which this information could be useful in a mathematics curriculum, and then a series of questions to help stimulate critical thinking. Teachers should not feel restricted to these resources as their only means to promote critical thinking with the Web. The content on the Web continues to grow each day, so there will likely be sites that supplement the sources and concepts illustrated in this book. In these situations, the teacher's task is to pose questions that will promote critical thinking. Based on my teaching experience and the methods I have used to pose problems in this book, I encourage teachers to write questions that

- cannot be immediately explained with a particular concept or cannot be solved using a practiced algorithm;
- promote exploration of unknown mathematical patterns;
- elicit a level of analysis that would necessitate reasoning with a generalization, proof, or evaluation;
- can be solved or represented in multiple ways.

Keep in mind that every critical thinking question may not include all of these characteristics. The appropriateness of a critical thinking question can be determined by a combination of consultation with a colleague and testing the question with a group of students. Following implementation, revision to the question could be made based on feedback and student performance. If the students immediately determine a solution, then the question probably needs to be a little more ambiguous. If the students do not know how or where to begin, then the question either needs more classroom discussion or direction.

Another type of critical thinking activity would be to ask students to determine the accuracy of information by checking multiple Web sources. In addition, students could research a specific topic by using search engines and subject trees as methods to retrieve information. The searching process itself involves cognitive strategies that place students in an evaluative position. In this situation, students need to determine what to search for, how to find useful information, and how they will determine what information is useful. On a similar note, teachers can also generate explorations that encourage students to use the Web as a tool to find information. For example, suppose a family wanted to buy a new car and had to trade in their old car. How much money should they expect to get for the car if they offer it for sale in an advertisement? To address this question, a student needs to locate and sift through car advertisements and sources that give estimates for the price of a car before any mathematical analysis can take place. This process of finding and selecting information can influence the level of analysis employed in a critical thinking task.

## Using Internet Primary Sources to Teach Critical Thinking Skills—A Case Study

Margaret Harrison has just completed a unit on functions in her advanced algebra class. She finds a few real estate Web sites that list a variety of homes for sale around the country. Each site lists information about the house, a floor plan (or room dimensions), and a sale price. She asks her class to determine a relationship between the cost of a house and its floor plan area. Ms. Harrison assigns the following series of questions as a group project:

• Is there a particular function that best describes this relationship?

• What additional factors affect the sale price of a house?

• What should be the current sale price of your house, or your friend's house?

• What comparisons and conclusions can you make about the additional data that describe the houses?

• Explain the criteria, procedures, data analyses, and reasoning when producing your results.

Ms. Harrison places the students into groups of three and asks them to address each of these questions for a class project that will be due in three weeks. She informs the students that points will be awarded on the quality of the students' reasoning, mathematical methods, accuracy in solutions, and presentation of work. She tells the class that reasoning represents how well the students justify their work; mathematical methods are the descriptions of the procedures and analyses used to produce or defend an answer; accuracy reflects the computations used throughout the investigation; and presentation is the organization, thoroughness, legibility of the work, grammar, and spelling. A participation grade will be determined by each group member to describe each student's contri-

**Figure 4**
**Grading**

| Criterion | Reasoning | Methods | Accuracy | Presentation |
|---|---|---|---|---|
| Best Function | 13 | 9 | 9 | 9 |
| Additional Factors | 8 | 5 | 5 | 5 |
| Predicted Sales Price | 5 | 3 | 3 | 3 |
| Additional Comparisons | 8 | 5 | 5 | 5 |

Participation = 20

Total points possible = 120

bution to the group effort. Figure 4 shows the maximum number of points that can be obtained for each component of the project.

The students spend the first day of class working in their groups to discuss how they would like to approach these questions, as well as how to divide responsibility among the group. Ms. Harrison has reserved the computer lab for the next two class periods. When the students browse the Web sites given by Ms. Harrison, they begin to raise additional questions about the data. Will the results depend on the type of house for sale, its location, the amount of property on the lot, or the realtor selling it? Ms. Harrison tells the students that they have raised interesting issues that she has not thought about before. She encourages each student in the group to collect data from a different perspective and then compare or contrast the data when performing the analysis. She emphasizes that there may not be one particular correct answer and reiterates that the students' reasoning is primarily valued in this investigation.

Most of the students finish collecting data after one class period, so they use the next class to analyze the data and discuss their findings. Ms. Harrison rotates around the class, listening to student ideas and asking "why" and "what if" questions. She uses Socratic questioning by redirecting student questions to other group members. Sometimes the questions prompt students to return to the computers and collect more data. Ms. Harrison encourages each group to design a plan before the end of the class that will involve everyone's participation to complete the project. Ms. Harrison has also asked that the groups prepare a rough analysis of their preliminary work due after three class periods.

Three class periods later, Ms. Harrison opens a topic of discussion about the group projects. She gets a sense of what the students have accomplished and where they are having difficulty. Groups share experiences, observations, and hypotheses with the entire class. Ms. Harrison collects the students' work and provides feedback the next day. Two weeks later when the projects are due, Ms. Harrison has each group present its findings. She points out differences in the groups' functions, and has the students debate over which group's function best models the situation. Ms. Harrison collects the students' work and has them provide a participation rating for each person in the group with an explanation next to each score. After grading the student projects, Ms. Harrison points out similarities and differences in the projects and results, brings closure by reflecting on the mathematics used in the investigation, and raises additional questions that can be considered when buying a house.

## Reflections on the Case Study

This vignette emphasizes certain characteristics about the nature of the mathematical task, the representation of knowledge, the suggested classroom environment, and the role of primary Internet sources involved in critical thinking. In this setting, the students were given an unfamiliar situation that required use of prior knowledge and the development of strategies to answer a set of complex questions. Once the students started collecting data, they developed questions about the situation because they realized that more variables than the price and area were involved. The ambiguity of the original question placed the students in a position where they had to rethink their initial problem solving strategy.

As the investigation became more complex, the teacher reassured the students that their reasoning would be the strongest factor when generating their conclusions. Ms. Harrison could not predict all of the possible challenges and variables involved in the situation, illustrating that one specific answer or method is not necessarily the expected result of a given problem. Ms. Harrison's role in the classroom was to facilitate ideas, moderate discussion, and coordinate the learning environment. She asked questions, provided ideas, offered advice, and gave feedback, but never acted as the source of knowledge. In fact, Ms. Harrison probably learned new ideas from the students because they had discovered unexpected variables. Furthermore, Ms. Harrison created a student-centered environment where students were producing the ideas and determining the direction of their study. This environment is seen when the groups presented their findings and debated discrepancies in their results. Their production of a model to describe the data was an effort to generalize a complex situation that required a high cognitive level of analysis, reasoning, and justification. In addition, Ms. Harrison reinforced the validation component of the critical thinking process when she asked students to evaluate the other groups' solutions and to judge which model was the best representation for the situation.

This specific activity would not be possible without Internet sources. In paper form, the data would be costly to provide, accessible to fewer individuals, probably outdated, and more difficult to manage. The Web-based searchable real estate listings allowed students to obtain updated information efficiently using a nationwide data set. Multiple Internet sources provide students the opportunity to gather and validate additional data, as well as to obtain documentation to help support their arguments. The multiple variables in the data prompted students to raise additional questions and reevaluate their strategies and hypotheses.

This classroom example is one illustration of the many possible ways to foster critical thinking in the mathematics classroom. The Internet could have been used to investigate an interactive microworld in a single class period. However, this case study provides an indication of how Internet primary sources can stimulate opportunities for a critical thinking community.

## REFERENCES

Day, R. (1998). An experiment in using the Internet in teaching and learning mathematics. *Journal of Science Education and Technology, 7*(3), 249–258.

Fetterman, D. M. (1998). Webs of meaning: Computer and Internet resources for educational research and instruction. *Educational Researcher, 27*(2), 22–30.

Follansbee, S., Hughes, R., Pisha, B., & Stahl, S. (1997). *The role of online communications in schools: A national study.* Peabody, MA: Center for Applied Special Technology. [Online]. Available at http://www.cast.org/publications/stsstudy.

Gerber, S., Shuell, T. S., & Harlos, C. (1998). Using the Internet to learn mathematics. *Journal of Computers in Mathematics and Science Teaching, 17*(2), 113–132.

Huff, D. (1954). *How to lie with statistics.* New York: W. W. Norton & Company, Inc.

Johnson, D. (1995). Student access to the Internet: Librarians and teachers working together to teach high level survival skills. *Emergence Librarian, 22*(3), 8–12.

Oppong, N. K., & Russell, A. (1998). Using combinations of software to enhance pre-service teachers' critical thinking skills. *Mathematics and Computer Education, 32*(1), 37–43.

Owston, R. D. (1997). The World Wide Web: A technology to enhance teaching and learning? *Educational Researcher, 26*(2), 27–33.

Paulos, J. A. (1995). *A mathematician reads the newspaper.* New York: Basic Books.

# THE PRIMARY SOURCE SITES

**III**

## 1. ABSOLUTE VALUE OF A LINEAR FUNCTION

**URL: http://www.exploremath.com/activities/Activity_page.cfm? ActivityID=38**

**SUGGESTED LEVELS**: algebra (questions 1–3), advanced algebra (questions 1–8)

**SITE SUMMARY**: ExploreMath.com has an interactive linear function with graph. Using the function y = mx + b, you can adjust the values of m and b, and observe simultaneous changes in the graph. You can also create absolute value graphs, by examining $f(|x|)$, $|f(x)|$, and $|f(|x|)|$. You can modify the viewing window of the graph, view coordinates on the graph, and view a table that describe values of the function on any specified interval. You will need to download the Shockwave plugin because the activities were made with the tool Macromedia Director. You can see if you have the plugin, or download it, at (1a) http://www.exploremath.com/about/shockerhelp.cfm.

**TOPICS**: absolute value, function, reflection, translation, transformation, slope, even function, vertex, isosceles triangle, equilateral triangle

### DISCUSSION QUESTIONS AND ACTIVITIES

1. How does the absolute value relate to each of the function's reflective properties? Explain how each reflection corresponds to its line of reflection.

2. What factors affect the shape of the graph of $y = |f(|x|)|$? Explain why.

3. Without an absolute value sign, write the equations that determine the graph of $y = |f(x)|$ in terms of m and b. Explain how you determined this result.

4. Which function(s) will form an isosceles triangle with the x-axis? Which function(s) will form an equilateral triangle with the x-axis? Explain how you determined these results.

5. Under what circumstances will the intersection of the absolute value functions lie on f(x)? Explain why.

6. How are the slopes of the absolute value functions related? Explain why this is true.

7. Which of the absolute value graphs will always be even functions? Prove it.

8. How can you identify the location of the vertex of $|f(x)|$ from its equation? Explain.

## RELATED INTERNET SITE(S)

### Absolute Value of a Quadratic Function
(1b) http://www.exploremath.com/activities/Activity_page.cfm?ActivityID=37
   Investigate the changes in the graphs of $f(|x|)$, $|f(x)|$, and $|f(|x|)|$, when f(x) is a quadratic function in standard form.

# 2. AIRPORT PATTERN SIMULATOR

## URL: http://www.db.erau.edu/java/pattern/index.html

**SUGGESTED LEVELS**: prealgebra (questions 1–3), statistics (questions 1–3)

**SITE SUMMARY**: Embry-Riddle University hosts a Java applet that simulates airport traffic. The goal is to land as many planes as possible in the time given. If the planes are too close together, then they will not be able to land. When planes miss their landing, they will continue in a circling pattern and clutter air traffic. When you click on a plane, you remove it from the circling pattern, thus reducing the air traffic and increasing the distance between planes.

**TOPICS**: data collection, data analysis, simulation

## DISCUSSION QUESTIONS AND ACTIVITIES

1. Determine the criteria that will prevent a plane from landing. Use numeric values describing time and/or distance to justify your answer. Consider the number of planes in the air, distance between planes, and distance from landing as plausible factors.

2. When is the most appropriate moment to remove a plane from the circling pattern? How do you know?

3. Ask a partner to count the number of planes that reach the hangar in the time provided. Devise a method that produces the most efficient landing schedule—that is, how should you control the airplanes so that a maximum number of airplanes reach the hangar in the given time? Explain how you arrived at your solution.

### RELATED INTERNET SITE(S)

**Airplane Noise Simulator**
(2a) http://www.scican.net/~sos/jetNoise.html
(2b) http://www.caan.org/footprnt.html
  Examine how the noise from an airplane affects its surrounding area. Take note of changes in the observed loudness from the ground as you modify the plane's speed, direction, and climb.
See **(11ad) Traffic Simulation**

## 3. THE AMBIGUOUS CASE

### URL:http://home.netvigator.com/~wingkei9/javagsp/ambigu.html

  **SUGGESTED LEVELS**: geometry (questions 1–3), precalculus (questions 1–5)
  **SITE SUMMARY**: When studying the Law of Sines, it is possible to generate two solutions when solving for an angle. This diagram will help explain how this is possible. This applet is a construction that allows you to modify the length of two sides and an angle. Drag the X until you can form a triangle with vertices A, B, and C. Drag point C on the circle to close a gap with the ray extending from angle B.
  **TOPICS**: Law of Sines, triangle, SSA condition, congruent, ambiguous case, auxiliary line, triangle trigonometry

### DISCUSSION QUESTIONS AND ACTIVITIES

1. What is the largest number of triangles, with vertices A, B, and C, that can be created when AB is smaller than the radius of the circle? Explain why.

2. Under what conditions can you keep two side lengths fixed and an angle fixed (SSA) and produce two different triangles? Explain.

3. What type(s) of triangles will always be congruent under the SSA condition? Explain how you know.

4. Draw an auxilary line segment and prove the Law of Sines: the ratio of the sine of an angle to its opposite side is equal to the ratio of the sine of another angle to its opposite side.

5. What does this diagram tell you about using the Law of Sines to find an unknown angle in a triangle if you are given the SSA arrangement?

## RELATED INTERNET SITE(S)

**The Law of Sines**

(3a) http://www.ies.co.jp/math/java/trig/seigen/seigen.html

This applet is an interactive illustration of the Law of Sines. You will connect two triangles with equal opposite sides to form one triangle by matching vertices.

**The Law of Cosines**

(3b) http://www.ies.co.jp/math/java/trig/yogen1/yogen1.html

(3c) http://www.ies.co.jp/math/java/trig/yogen_auto/yogen_auto.html

These applets are interactive "proofs" of the Law of Cosines where you shear, translate, and move dissected pieces into different regions on the screen. The transformations are similar to the Pythagorean Theorem, but this time you have a leftover piece that you will need to explain.

# 4. AMTRAK RESERVATIONS AND MAPQUEST

## URL: http://reservations.amtrak.com
## http://www.mapquest.com

**SUGGESTED LEVELS**: algebra (questions 1–4)

**SITE SUMMARY**: Amtrak provides updated information about its train schedules. You can choose a destination and find out departure and ticket price information. Begin by clicking on "SCHEDULES & SAMPLE FARES." MapQuest will help you determine the driving distance between any two cities. Click on "Driving Directions." Assuming that the distance by automobile is approximately the distance by train, this information can help you determine the mean rate of the train, as well as formulate a conjecture about how tickets are priced.

**TOPICS**: data collection, data analysis, distance, rate, time, average, linear function

## DISCUSSION QUESTIONS AND ACTIVITIES

1. Get a variety of schedules for trains traveling between any two major U.S. cities. After you input the travel date and cities, you can view the price of a ticket by asking the computer to "show fares" on the following page. Form a mathematical relationship or function that describes the price of a ticket and the number of days until departure. Form a mathematical relationship or function that describes the price of a ticket and the day of the week of departure. Explain your solutions.

2. Use the arrival times from Amtrak and driving distance from Map-Quest to determine the average (mean) speed of the train. Assume the train travels at a constant rate. Is the speed of the train the same between all pairs of cities? Explain your analysis.

3. If a train does not have to stop, write a function that predicts the total time of a trip between two cities in terms of the distance between the two cities. Explain how you determined this result. If the train cannot take a direct route between two cities, write a function that predicts the total time of a trip between two cities in terms of the distance the train travels. Explain how you determined this result.

4. Form a mathematical relationship or function that describes the price of a direct route ticket and number of miles the train will travel. Discuss any additional variables that might affect your outcome. Explain your solution.

## RELATED INTERNET SITE(S)

**Map Blast**
(4a) http://www.mapblast.com/mblast/index.mb
Find the driving distance and estimated traveling time between any two cities in the United States.

**Yahoo! Travel**
(4b) http://travel.yahoo.com/
Find the cost of airline travel from cities around the world. Compare prices between airlines, time and day of departure, seating class, and the number of connections the plane makes.

**Greyhound**
(4c) http://www.greyhound.com/
Find fares for bus travel around the United States.

# 5. ANGLES IN PARALLEL LINES

## URL: http://www.saltire.com/applets/parallel/parallel.htm

**SUGGESTED LEVELS**: geometry (questions 1–6)

**SITE SUMMARY**: Examine the relationship between angles that are created with transversal and parallel lines. You can modify the slope of any of the lines and see resulting angle measures.

**TOPICS**: angles, parallel lines, transversal, parallelogram, angle sum

## DISCUSSION QUESTIONS AND ACTIVITIES

1. Which angles in the diagram will always be congruent? Explain how you know for each case.

2. Determine another relationship between noncongruent angles. State which pairs of angles hold this property. How do you know this is true?

3. What is the sum of all of the nonoverlapping angles in the diagram? How do you know?

4. In what situation will all of the angles in the diagram be congruent? Explain how you determined this.

5. What is the sum of the angles in a parallelogram? Explain how you can tell. What would you construct on the diagram to check your claim?

6. How could you modify the points to produce incorrect information on the screen? Explain how you determined this result.

## RELATED INTERNET SITE(S)

See **53. Floor Tiles**

**Sum of Angles in a Triangle**

(5a) http://home.a-city.de/walter.fendt/me/anglesum.htm

Drag around the vertices of a triangle and notice how each of the angles changes in relation to the angles formed by lines that determine the triangle.

See **70. Investigating Parallelograms**

**Problems of Angles and Parallel Lines**

(5b) http://www.ies.co.jp/math/java/geo/kakuapb/kakuapb.html

(5c) http://www.ies.co.jp/math/java/geo/kakucho/kakucho.html

These investigations examine the relationship between angles formed between two lines and a segmented transversal, or crook.

# 6.  AREA PROBABILITY

## URL: http://www.exploremath.com/activities/Activity_page.cfm? ActivityID=43

**SUGGESTED LEVELS**: geometry (questions 1–3), probability (questions 1–6), statistics (questions 1–6)

**SITE SUMMARY**: ExploreMath.com has an interactive dartboard that can be used to explore geometric probability. You can modify the radius of the shooting area and individual dimensions of the backboard rectangle. Once you set the desired dimensions of the throwing region, you can throw 100 or 1,000 darts at a time to estimate the ratio of the circular and rectangular regions. You will need to download the Shockwave plugin because the activities were made with the tool Macromedia Director. You can see if you have the plugin, or download it, at (1a) http://www.exploremath.com/about/shockerhelp.cfm.

**TOPICS**: probability, area of a circle, area of a rectangle, relative frequency, binomial distribution, data display, data collection, binomial probability, normal distribution, confidence interval, expected value, standard deviation, pi, linear function

## DISCUSSION QUESTIONS AND ACTIVITIES

1. What is the probability that a dart will land in a circle that is inscribed in a square? Explain how you determined this result. Will the radius of the circle affect the probability? Explain why or why not.

2. If you could move the sliders to any width or height for any given rectangle, what is the range of probabilities of throwing a dart inside the circle? Explain your reasoning.

3. How can this simulation estimate pi? Explain your reasoning.

4. Find pairs of widths and heights that would produce a rectangular region that is twice the area of the circle. Generate a function that describes the relationship between the widths and heights in these cases. Explain how you determined this result. How would your result change if the rectangular region had an area that was n times larger than the circle?

5. Your friend claims that she can throw a dart inside the circle with 80 percent accuracy. Your brother claims that he can throw a dart inside the circle with 85 percent accuracy. What are the chances that your friend will throw more darts in the circle than your brother? Assume

that both your brother and friend throw the same number of darts. Explain your analysis.

6. Suppose you throw 500 darts at the board. Predict and sketch a histogram that describes the frequency of occurrence vs. the number of hits inside the circle. Explain how you determined this result. How would your answer change if you changed the area of the circle, but not the area of the rectangle? Explain.

## RELATED INTERNET SITE(S)

See **87. Monte Carlo Estimation for Pi**

**Buffon Needle**

(6a) http://www.angelfire.com/wa/hurben/buff.html

(6b) http://www.shodor.org/interactivate/activities/buffon/index.html

(6c) http://www.mste.uiuc.edu/reese/buffon/bufjava.html

(6d) http://www.math.csusb.edu/faculty/stanton/m262/buffon/buffon.html

These simulations will estimate the value of pi by dropping a one-inch needle on a series of parallel lines that are spaced one inch apart. The goal is to compare the number of needles dropped to the number of times the needles cross one of the lines. A multiple of this ratio will estimate pi.

# 7. ASK JEEVES: WHAT IS THE DISTANCE?

## URL: http://www.ask.com

**SUGGESTED LEVELS**: prealgebra (questions 1 and 3), algebra (questions 1–3), precalculus (questions 4–6)

**SITE SUMMARY**: Ask Jeeves is a Web site where you can ask a question and then receive a list of possible locations on the Web to find the answer. Suppose you are taking an airplane trip and want to know how many miles will be credited to your mileage awards account. When you enter, "What is the distance between Atlanta and Chicago?", Ask Jeeves will give you a list of options that will lead you to a page that tells you the actual distance "as the crow flies." If you are driving, Ask Jeeves will provide a link to MapQuest that will tell you the actual driving distance between the two cities.

**TOPICS**: distance, percent, rate, time, arc length, radius, sine, cosine

## DISCUSSION QUESTIONS AND ACTIVITIES

1. Suppose a friend asks you, "How much farther would I expect to travel on a vacation if I traveled by car instead of by airplane?" As-

sume your friend doesn't know where she would like to travel. Instead she wants a rough percentage of the extra distance she would travel by car. Collect data from Ask Jeeves by starting your question with, "What is the distance between . . ."

2. Is the ratio of actual distance to driving distance always the same? How would your solution change to problem 1 if you were only travelling to rural locations at least thirty miles away from an interstate highway? Explain your mathematical procedures in your analysis.

3. Find the distance between two major U.S. cities. Click on the "driving directions" from MapQuest. What is the average speed you are expected to travel on interstate highways? Explain your analysis. Will this answer be the same between any two major U.S. cities? Explain why or why not.

4. Ask Jeeves, "Where can I find a map of the United States?" Use the longitudinal lines to find two cities that are almost exactly north and south of each other. Go back to Ask Jeeves and determine the actual distance between those two cities. Use the actual distance and the difference in latitudinal position between the two cities to calculate the radius of the Earth. Repeat the procedure for a couple more pairs of cities and compare your responses. Explain how you found the solution.

5. Repeat the procedures in problem 3, but examine cities that are almost exactly east and west of each other. Compare your result with problem 3.

6. The distance between two cities not on the same latitude or longitude can be determined by a combination of cosines and sines. Hypothesize a formula that relates the actual distance between two cities to their differences in latitudinal and longitudinal positions on the Earth. Test your hypothesis using several pairs of cities and explain your results.

## RELATED INTERNET SITE(S)

**Driving Directions**
(7a) http://www.mapquest.com
(7b) http://www.mapblast.com/mblast/index.mb
This site allows the user to find the driving distance and estimated traveling time between any two cities in the United States.

**How Far Is It?**
(7c) http://www.indo.com/distance/
This site provides the direct distance, as the crow flies, between cities around the world.

# 8. AUTO LOAN MONTHLY PAYMENT CALCULATOR

## URL: http://www.bankamerica.com/tools/auto_payment.html

**SUGGESTED LEVELS**: prealgebra (questions 1–2), advanced algebra (questions 1–5)

**SITE SUMMARY**: This calculator computes your monthly payment for an auto loan when you input the amount you would like to borrow, the interest rate, and the life of the loan.

**TOPICS**: exponents, interest, exponential functions

## DISCUSSION QUESTIONS AND ACTIVITIES

1. If you want to have a monthly payment of $500 and would like a loan of $20,000 with a 9.8 percent interest rate, then how long should your loan last? Explain your analysis.

2. Suppose the possible loan periods last from five to ten years and the possible interest rates range from 8.5 to 10.5 percent. Will you save more money in interest if you try to get a lower interest rate or a shorter loan period? Explain your analysis.

3. How often is the money compounded based on this calculator? Explain your analysis.

4. How would the monthly payment change if the principal were compounded continuously?

5. Suppose you have a ten-year loan of $20,000 with a 7.8 percent interest rate. If you paid an additional $100 in principal each month, how much earlier would you pay off the loan than if you did not pay the additional amount each month? Explain your analysis.

## RELATED INTERNET SITE(S)

See **42. Edmunds Used Car Prices**

See **12. Bank Interest Rates**

**Mortgage Rates**
(8a) http://www.mortgageloan.com/
(8b) http://www.interest.com/
Find the latest mortgage rates from different areas around the country. You can examine differences in rates according to their length and how they vary over time.

# 9. AVERAGE RATE OF CHANGE AND DERIVATIVES

**URL: http://www.ies.co.jp/math/java/calc/heihen/heihen.html**

**SUGGESTED LEVELS**: calculus (questions 1–7)

**SITE SUMMARY**: IES has created a Java applet which allows you to investigate the slope of secant lines formed by two points on the curve. You can modify the points on the curve and distance between the points to observe the limit effect in the slope of a secant line. The output will appear in a table, showing you an estimate of the derivative at a point as the distance between the secant points decreases.

**TOPICS**: slope, secant line, tangent line, limit, derivative, polynomial function, domain, average rate of change

## DISCUSSION QUESTIONS AND ACTIVITIES

1. The page states that the slope of the secant line is $(f(a+h) - f(a))/h$. How was this value determined?

2. What do you need to modify in order to transform the secant line into a tangent line? Will the secant line ever turn into a tangent line? Explain why.

3. How can you predict the limit as h approaches zero of the slope of the secant of $y = x^2$ at $x = a$? Give your answer in a formula in terms of a. Explain how you found the solution.

4. What effect does a constant have on the limit of a function? Explain.

5. How can you predict the limit as h approaches zero of the slope of the secant of $y = x^n$ at $x = a$, where n is any real number? Give your answer in a formula in terms of a and n. Explain how you found the solution.

6. Which of the functions, if any, will have a tangent line with an undefined slope for any value in its domain? Explain. Which of the functions, if any, will have a tangent line with a slope equal to zero for any value in its domain? Explain.

7. What does the sign of the slope of the tangent line describe about the function?

## RELATED INTERNET SITE(S)

See **40. Determine the Derivative of an Unknown Function**

**Derivative Puzzles**
(9a) http://www.univie.ac.at/future.media/moe/galerie/diff1/diff1.html

(9b) http://www.univie.ac.at/future.media/moe/tests/diff1/ablerkennen.html
    These activities test your understanding of the relationship between the graph of a function to the graphs of its first and second derivatives.

**Derivative Definition Java Applet**
(9d) http://www.csulb.edu/%7Ewziemer/TangentLine/TangentLine.html
    Enter the equation of a function at a point, and you will get the graph of the function, the tangent line, and values of the secant and tangent slopes. You can modify the value of the step size h, or delta x, in order to see how close the slope of the secant line approximates the slope of the tangent line as h approaches zero.

# 10. AVERAGE WEEKLY SALARIES

## URL: http://www.dol.gov/dol/wb/images/w&occ2.gif

   **SUGGESTED LEVELS**: prealgebra (questions 1–4), advanced algebra (questions 1–5)
   **SITE SUMMARY**: This data set compares the average salaries of men and women from 1983 to 1995.
   **TOPICS**: data analysis, modeling data, scatter plot, function, extrapolation

## DISCUSSION QUESTIONS AND ACTIVITIES

1. What occupation(s) could closely match these earnings levels? Explain your reasoning.

2. In what year will women's average salaries likely equal men's average salaries? What will be the expected average weekly salary during that year? Explain your analysis.

3. What do the real wages columns listed at the right side of the table represent? Use these values to predict the year when women's salaries will equal men's salaries. Explain your analysis. Compare your results with question 2.

4. What are some possible inferences that you can make about women's employment based on this data? What additional data would you need to validate these conclusions? Explain why.

5. Are this data proof that women are not earning enough money as compared to men? If so, explain why. If not, what additional information would you need to prove that men's salaries are currently significantly greater than women's salaries?

## RELATED INTERNET SITE(S)

**The Pay Gap by Occupation**
(10a) http://www.aflcio.org/women/a_z.htm
  This page by the AFL-CIO lists the average difference in pay between men and women for numerous occupations.

**Women's Jobs: 1964–1997**
(10b) http://www.dol.gov/dol/wb/public/jobs6496.htm
  These statistics show how women's salaries and employment equity have gradually increased over the past thirty-five years.

See **94. Nonfarm Payroll Statistics from the Current Employment Statistics**

# 11. BALL PARKS

## URL: http://www.ballparks.com/

  **SUGGESTED LEVELS**: prealgebra (questions 1–4), algebra (questions 5–6), advanced algebra (questions 5–7), statistics (questions 1–7)
  **SITE SUMMARY**: This site provides information about professional sports stadiums, including seating, attendance, the facility, and other facts. Learn about stadiums in soccer, basketball, baseball, football, and hockey. Click on the images to view the stadiums set up for the different sports. Once you are viewing a particular sport's page, use the navigation bar at the left of the screen to select different stadiums.
  **TOPICS**: data collection, data analysis, modeling data, function, linear function, line of best fit, slope, y-intercept, interpolation, percent

## DISCUSSION QUESTIONS AND ACTIVITIES

1. What sport typically has the greatest seating capacity? Explain your reasoning.

2. On average, would it be more difficult to get tickets to a basketball game or football game? Explain your analysis.

3. What sport obtains the greatest revenue on ticket sales for a season? Explain your analysis.

4. How many regular season home games are played by each sport? Explain your analysis.

5. Graph the cost to build a major league baseball stadium as a function of the year it was built. Find a line of best fit that models the data. What is the significance of the slope and y-intercept? Are newer stadiums typically more or less expensive to build than older stadiums,

considering the time and economy in which they were built? Explain your analysis.

6. Which baseball stadium was the cheapest to build considering the era in which it was built? Explain your analysis.

7. How does the mean price of a sporting ev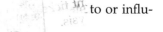 to or influence its total attendance? Explain your a

## RELATED INTERNET SITE(S)

**Ticketmaster.com**
(11a) http://www.ticketmaster.com/
   Find the prices for available tickets in a wide variety of sporting events.

**NFL Stadium and Ticket Information**
(11b) http://sportsillustrated.cnn.com/football/nfl/stadiums/gateway/
   This CNN Sports Illustrated site has seating and capacity information available for NFL teams.

# 12. BANK INTEREST RATES

## URL: http://www.pcm-ca.com/bankrate.htm

**SUGGESTED LEVELS**: prealgebra (questions 1, 2, and 4), algebra (questions 1 and 4), advanced algebra (questions 1–7)

**SITE SUMMARY**: This site lists a variety of bank CDs available depending on the minimum amount of investment and length of investment. You can compare rates with over ten different financial institutions.

**TOPICS**: interest, compound interest, exponential function, $e$, polynomial function

## DISCUSSION QUESTIONS AND ACTIVITIES

1. Suppose you just received an endowment of $25,000. You want to save the money for college, so you decide to acquire a bank CD. Which bank CD would you get? Explain why.

2. Design an advertisement that includes a deceiving data display or graph so that you can lure customers to go to a specific bank.

3. How would you set the Southern Pacific Bank's CD rates if they compounded interest annually? Monthly? Daily?

4. Suppose you save $1,000 this summer and place it into a one-year CD. You save another $1,000 next summer and place your previous sav-

ings from the CD and this summer's earnings into another one-year CD. You continue the pattern until you graduate from college. How much will you have in your account at that time? Explain your analysis.

5. A friend wants to buy a car but does not have enough money right now. She doesn't like to work, but has enough in her savings to cover half of the price of the car. How long will she have to wait to buy the car? Explain your analysis.

6. You receive a graduation gift of $3,000. You want to take a $1,200 vacation within thirty months, buy a $650 television set within a year, buy $550 in clothes within eighteen months, and still have $800 remaining to pay off a loan in three years. Devise a plan to use this money for all of these purposes. Explain your reasoning.

7. You and your friend decide that you would like to retire once you become millionaires. You decide to start putting $5,000 in a CD each year beginning this summer. Your friend starts working for a company, earns a higher salary, but waits twelve years to start investing. Therefore, in twelve years, your friend invests $15,000 each year in a CD at the beginning of every summer. Who will retire first? Explain your analysis.

## RELATED INTERNET SITE(S)

**Bankrate.com**
(12a) http://www.bankrate.com/brm/rate/dep_home.asp
This site gives data on the latest savings interest rates for CDs, checking, and money market accounts in banks across the country. You can also find information on auto loans, mortgages, home equity, and more.
See **(8a)** and **(8b) Mortgage Rates**

## 13. BART SCHEDULE ANIMATION

### URL: http://www-itg.lbl.gov/vbart/

**SUGGESTED LEVELS**: prealgebra (questions 1–6), algebra (questions 1–6)
**SITE SUMMARY**: This simulation of the BART train system in the San Francisco Bay area gives the user an idea of how fast, how often, and how timely the trains run. Click on "BART simulation" to begin. There are five different train routes in operation with numerous trains on each route. You can view the trains moving on a scale map in standard time or increased time by a scale of sixty (one second in the sim-

ulation equals one minute of real-time transportation). Change the speed of the trains by clicking on the radio buttons in the upper right hand corner of the screen. The time of the day is displayed on the screen and can be modified at the user's convenience. Enter a time of the day in the upper left hand corner using *a* for A.M. and *p* for P.M.

**TOPICS**: simulation, data collection, data analysis, rate, average, distance

## DISCUSSION QUESTIONS AND ACTIVITIES

1. Start the simulation. How fast do the trains cross the San Francisco Bay? Explain how you arrived at your answer. Do the trains travel at the same or different rates? Explain how you know.

2. What is the average time spent at a train stop? Explain the procedures and calculations that helped you arrive at this answer.

3. Which station is busiest? Use numerical evidence to support this claim. Why might this station have the most traffic?

4. Which line has the greatest number of trains at any given time? Is this always true? Explain why this may or may not be the case.

5. At what time(s) of day is the train system most active? Use numerical evidence to support this claim. Explain why this might be true.

6. Which intersection is busiest? Use numerical evidence to support this claim. Explain why this might be true.

## RELATED INTERNET SITE(S)

**Applet Metropolitan**
(13a) http://www.babel.fr/vaillant/metro/turbo/metro_angl.html
   Examine interactive train maps of Los Angeles; Lyon, France; and Paris, France. Input the departure and arrival information, and determine how long the trip will take.
See **119. Smartraveler**

# 14. BASEBALL MILLIONAIRES

**URLs: http://www.cnnsi.com/baseball/mlb/news/1999/04/07/ baseball_millionaire/ http://www.cnnsi.com/baseball/mlb/news/2000/04/05/ baseball_millionaires_ap/**

**SUGGESTED LEVELS**: prealgebra (questions 1, 2, and 4–7), algebra (questions 1–7), advanced algebra (questions 1–7), statistics (questions 1–7)

**SITE SUMMARY**: These data sets report the 1999 and 2000 salaries of the major league baseball players who earned at least one million dollars.

**TOPICS**: data collection, data analysis, data display, percent, modeling, linear function, exponential function, extrapolation

## DISCUSSION QUESTIONS AND ACTIVITIES

1. Which player had the largest raise over the year? Which player had the greatest percent increase in pay over the year? Explain how this is possible.

2. How does a person's salary relate to his position on the league leader board at (14a) http://www.cnnsi.com/baseball/mlb/ml/stats/index.html? Explain your analysis.

3. Generate a function that describes the salary change of a player over a year. Explain how you determined this result.

4. How does a player's salary change if he plays for a different team the next year? Explain your analysis.

5. Use the league leader board at (14a) http://www.cnnsi.com/baseball/mlb/ml/stats/index.html to analyze this investigation. Which player(s) earns too much money when comparing his (their) performance to the rest of the league? Which player(s) does not make enough money when comparing his (their) performance to the rest of the league? Explain your analysis.

6. Devise a mathematical analysis that will predict the salary of the highest paid player in the next couple of years. Explain your reasoning.

7. Generate a question that would use a graph to support your analysis. Answer the question and show your work.

## RELATED INTERNET SITE(S)

**Sports Statistics**
(14b) http://www.sportsline.com/
(14c) http://espn.go.com
These sites give you updated sporting news and statistics. You can find information on your favorite sports and players.

**Sports Statistics on the Web**
(14d) http://www.amstat.org/sections/sis/sports.html

This site is a list of links to data related to baseball, basketball, cycling, fencing, football, golf, horseracing, hockey, Olympics, soccer, tennis, volleyball, and weightlifting.

**Major League Baseball Statistics**

(14e) http://www.mlb.com/NASApp/mlb/mlb/stats/mlb_stats_entry.jsp

View a wide array of updated individual and player statistics from majorleaguebaseball.com.

# 15. BASEBALL TIME MACHINE

## URL: http://www.exploratorium.edu/baseball/timemachine.html

**SUGGESTED LEVELS**: prealgebra (questions 1–6)

**SITE SUMMARY**: Look at seven different baseball players throughout the history of baseball. The baseball time machine makes predictions about each player's performance if they played during different time periods.

**TOPICS**: data collection, data analysis, decimals, ratios, proportions

## DISCUSSION QUESTIONS AND ACTIVITIES

1. What statistics contribute to the batting average? How is it calculated?

2. In what time period would you expect to see the most home runs hit in a season? Why do you think the statistics support this claim? Explain how you determined this result.

3. During which time period(s) would Barry Bonds improve his hitting? Explain the criteria that you used to support your reasoning.

4. Who was a better baseball player, Dan Brouthers or Ted Williams? Explain how you arrived at your answer.

5. Is a player more likely to obtain a base on balls (BB) during a specific time period? Explain why or why not.

6. Suppose you hold a draft next year with all seven players, where each player is selected from best to worst. Rank the order in which you think they will be selected. Explain your criteria for selecting and how you determined the outcome of the draft.

7. Find the statistics on your favorite baseball player who is still playing at (15a) http://www.majorleaguebaseball.com/u/baseball/mlbcom/stats/playerstats.htm. You will need to click on the player's name to view his career stats. Determine what his career stats would have been if he had played from 1905 to 1928. Explain how you determined each result.

## RELATED INTERNET SITE(S)

See **(14e) Major League Baseball Statistics**
See **14. Baseball Millionaires**

# 16. BATH TIME WITH ARCHIMEDES

## URL: http://www.numeracyresources.co.uk/archi4.html

**SUGGESTED LEVELS**: prealgebra (questions 1, 2, 4, and 7), algebra (questions 1–7), advanced algebra (questions 4–6)

**SITE SUMMARY**: This simulation investigates the height of water in a bathtub in relation to time and water pressure out of the faucet. You can select the power of the tap, remove the plug from the drain, and place a person (Archimedes) in the tub. As the faucet runs, you are shown a real-time depth of the tub vs. time graph. You can also view a table of values that displays the depth of the tub for ten second intervals. You need the Flash plugin to view this site. If you cannot see the file appear on the screen, then you will need to download the free plugin from Macromedia at (16a) http://www.macromedia.com/shockwave/download/index.cgi?P1_Prod_Version=ShockwaveFlash. This file may take a couple of minutes to load onto your screen because it acts like a piece of software. Once the file is ready, you will be able to interact with the screen without any additional waiting time. Click on Refresh or Reload on your browser to restart the simulation.

**TOPICS**: rate, linear function, units, function, mass

## DISCUSSION QUESTIONS AND ACTIVITIES

1. How many ways can you create a straight line on the graph from 0 to 100 seconds? Explain your reasoning.
2. How fast does the tub drain? Explain your analysis.
3. Develop an equation that relates the power of the tap, the depth of the water, and time. Explain how you developed your solution.
4. Design a strategy that will fill the bathtub completely in exactly 100 seconds. Explain your method. Are there other solutions? Explain.
5. Generate a graph over time that would describe a situation where the faucet is running and then Archimedes sat in the tub with his whole body submerged under water. Explain each component of the graph.
6. What functions can you create with this graph? Explain each case.
7. What additional information would you need in order to calculate Archimedes' mass? Explain how you know.

## RELATED INTERNET SITE(S)

See **89. Moving Man**


# 17. THE BILLIARDS SIMULATION

## URL: http://serendip.brynmawr.edu/chaos/home.html

**SUGGESTED LEVELS**: geometry (questions 1, 2, 3, and 5), precalculus (questions 1–5)

**SITE SUMMARY**: This simulation illustrates how reflections can be used to determine the path of a ball on a billiards table. You can run the simulation with a regular polygon, circle, ellipse, or stadium, and determine which has regular motion and which demonstrates chaotic motion. You can monitor the speed and position of the ball when it is hit.

**TOPICS**: reflection, polygon, parallel, circle, ellipse, chaos


## DISCUSSION QUESTIONS AND ACTIVITIES

1. Generate a hypothesis about how a ball bounces from a side of a pool table in the shape of a polygon. How would this hypothesis change with a surface that is not flat?

2. In which pool table(s) is the trace of the reflections parallel? Continue the path of the ball until you can recognize a pattern. Explain why.

3. How is the trace of the reflections in a circle dependent on the initial x and y positions? Explain.

4. How do you determine the location of the foci of the ellipse? What does the trace of the reflections of the ellipse form? Is this true for any initial x and y position? Explain.

5. Change the ratio in the stadium table. Which ratios will repeat the reflection trace? Explain why.


## RELATED INTERNET SITE(S)

**Chaos Game**
(17a) http://math.bu.edu/DYSYS/applets/chaos-game.html
(17b) http://www.geom.umn.edu/java/LeapFractal/
    The goal of this game is to hit a target in Sierpinski's Triangle by strategically targeting vertices of a triangle. The game provides you the opportunity to think about the algorithm used to randomly generate points in Sierpinski's Triangle. This game is similar to chaos, except the points are purposefully selected with the intention of locating a specific region inside the triangle. You have the option

to choose a variety of difficulty levels and a variety of shapes for gaming environments.

See **57. The Game of Chaos**

**The Ant Hill**
(17c) http://polymer.bu.edu/java/java/anthill/Anthill.html
   This simulation represents ants tunneling through the soil by walking randomly. You have the option to control the number of ants walking, the survival rates, and the probabilities that an ant will walk in a certain direction. Observe how this last factor impacts how quickly a group of ants can develop a formation in a certain direction.

**Fire!**
(17d) http://www.shodor.org/interactivate/activities/fire1/index.html
(17e) http://www.shodor.org/interactivate/activities/fire2/index.html
   These forest fire simulations allow you to modify the direction of the wind and probabilities of a fire spreading.


# 18.  BINOMIAL DISTRIBUTION


**URLs: http://www.ruf.rice.edu/~lane/stat_sim/binom_demo.html**
      **http://www.ruf.rice.edu/%7Elane/stat_sim/binom_demo.html**
      **http://stat.wvu.edu/SRS/Modules/Binomial/binomial.html**


   **SUGGESTED LEVELS**: probability (questions 1–5)
   **SITE SUMMARY**: These similar Java applets display a histogram describing the probability outcomes of multiple coin tosses. The goal of this exercise is to observe patterns in the distributions as you modify the probability of success, p, and the sample size, N. You begin by looking at the case of a fair coin where the probability of successfully landing heads is 0.5. The coin is unfair if the probability is not equal to 0.5. In this case, you might think of this simulation as a different scenario with two complementary and independent events, such as the probability of rolling a six on a die and not rolling a six on a die.
   **TOPICS**: binomial distribution, probability


## DISCUSSION QUESTIONS AND ACTIVITIES

1. What happens to the distribution as the number of tosses, N, increases and the probability of success, p, remains the same? Explain how you determined this result.

2. What happens to the distribution as the number of tosses, N, remains the same and the probability of success, p, increases? Explain how you determined this result.

3. The outcome on the x-axis that occurs most frequently is the expected value, or mean. Determine how the number of tosses, N, and the probability of success, p, can be used to calculate the mean.

4. A binomial distribution can be generated using a polynomial in the form $(aH + bT)^N$, where N is the number of coin tosses. In terms of a, b, or N, what is the probability of success, p? For example, with a fair coin and p=0.5, the distribution can be represented by $(1H + 1T)^N$, or $(2H + 2T)^N$, or any case where a=b.

5. In a fair coin toss with N repetitions, you can get heads k times, where k is N, N – 1, N – 2, . . . , or 1. In terms of N, what is the probability of getting heads exactly k times? For example, if a fair coin is tossed three times, then the probability of getting heads 2 times is ⅜. Think about how the value of k in this case, 2, relates to the number of coin tosses, N, and the number of terms in the sample space.

## RELATED INTERNET SITE(S)

### Binomial Expansion—The Ball Drop
(18a) http://thinks.com/java/balldrop/normal.htm
   In this demonstration, balls are randomly dropped into a grid with eight rows of pins. As the balls hit a pin, they move either right or left until they hit another pin. After the eighth row they will fall into a pattern which will resemble a histogram illustrating the binomial theorem.

### Galton's Quincunx
(18b) http://www.stattuchino.com/berrie/dsl/Galton.html
   This applet is a simulation of Galton's Board, in which balls are dropped through a triangular array of nails until they fall into a resting location. The series of resting balls will form a histogram resembling a binomial distribution.

### The Normal Distribution
(18c): http://www-stat.stanford.edu/~naras/jsm/NormalDensity/NormalDensity.html
   Modify the mean and standard deviation of the normal distribution and observe how it changes size and shape.

# 19. BIRTHDAY PROBLEM

## URL: http://www.mste.uiuc.edu/reese/birthday/

**SUGGESTED LEVELS**: prealgebra (questions 1–2), probability (questions 1–4)

**SITE SUMMARY**: The Office for Mathematics, Science, and Technology Education (MSTE) has created a Java-based simulation of generating random birthdays. The goal of this problem is to determine the chances that two or more people in the same class would have the same birthday. The simulation will list random birthdays and tell you if any of the birthdays were repeated. You can also repeat the simulation with adjusted class sizes to determine any patterns with the relative frequencies.

**TOPICS**: simulation, data collection, sample space, permutations, probability distribution

## DISCUSSION QUESTIONS AND ACTIVITIES

1. Suppose your class has n people. What is the probability that someone else in the class will have the same birthday as you?

2. Suppose your class has twenty-five people. Run the simulation multiple times and estimate the probability that at least two people in the class will have the same birthday. Compare this result with question 1 and explain why there would be any similarities or differences.

3. How does class size relate to the probability that two or more people will share the same birthday? Graph and describe this probability distribution as a function.

4. Estimate the probability that three or more people in the same class of twenty-five students will have the same birthday. If you examine this problem with a class of n students, how would the probability distribution compare with the one you described in question 3?

## RELATED INTERNET SITE(S)

See **24. Cereal Box Problem Simulation**
See **(6a)–(6d) Buffon Needle**

# 20.  BODY MASS CALCULATOR

## URL: http://cc.ysu.edu/~doug/hwp.cgi

**SUGGESTED LEVELS**: prealgebra (questions 1–3), algebra (questions 1–5)

**SITE SUMMARY**: This calculator determines your height and weight proportion (HWP) once you input your height and weight.

**TOPICS**: ratio, proportion, equation, data collection, scatter plot, data analysis, linear function, line of best fit, slope, y-intercept

## DISCUSSION QUESTIONS AND ACTIVITIES

1. How is your body mass ratio determined? Write an equation and verify your hypothesis using multiple data points.

2. After you submit an entry, how does the computer determine your "ideal" weight range? Show how the computer came up with these numbers.

3. The HWP calculator indicates that the ratio can be used to represent most people's ideal weight. What types of people would the calculator not represent accurately? Explain.

4. Create a scatter plot that describes the height and mass of all of your classmates. Determine the equation of the line that best fits the data. What is the significance of the slope and y-intercept? Is the class, on average, at an ideal weight? Explain your reasoning. What do the points below the line represent?

5. Create a scatter plot that describes the height and mass of the football players from your favorite professional team. You can find the statistics at (20a) http://sports.espn.go.com/nfl/players. Determine the equation of the line that best fits the data. What is the significance of the slope and y-intercept? Is the class, on average, at an ideal weight? Explain your reasoning. What do the points above the line represent?

## 21. BRAKING AND STOPPING DISTANCES

### URL Address: http://www.scottsdalelaw.com/shepston/braking.html

**SUGGESTED LEVELS**: algebra (questions 1, 5, and 6), advanced algebra (questions 1–6)

**SITE SUMMARY**: This data set compares the relationship between the speed of a car and the estimated braking distance to stop the car. The information is provided for cars traveling between ten and ninety miles per hour, in five-mile-per-hour intervals.

**TOPICS**: speed, distance, time, units, square root function, quadratic function, interpolation, extrapolation, data analysis, modeling

## DISCUSSION QUESTIONS AND ACTIVITIES

1. Convert miles per hour into feet per second. Write an equation that relates the two variables. Based on this information, how many feet are there in a mile? Explain how you determined this result.

2. Which set of variables can be modeled using a square root function? Explain your solution.

3. Which set of variables can be modeled using a quadratic function (different from problem 2)? Explain your solution.

4. The speed limit on certain highways in Europe is over 100 miles per hour. How fast is a car traveling if its tire marks are 526 feet? Assume the tire mark appears on the road when the car begins to brake. Explain your solution.

5. In rush hour traffic, three cars are traveling eight feet behind one another. The first car, traveling at fifty-five miles per hour, slams on the brakes. The second car was traveling at fifty miles per hour, but took an extra second to react to the brake. The third car was traveling at fifty-five miles per hour, and only took 0.5 second to react to the first car's braking. Assuming that none of the cars swerved out of the way, did any of the cars hit each other? If so, which ones? Explain your solution.

6. Will the data represent the braking distances for any car? What factors will influence differences from the numbers reported in the table? In each case, explain why you think the numbers will be larger or smaller than those stated.

## 22. CAM'S JAVA WEB COUNTER APPLET: DYNAMIC COUNTER APPLET

### URL: http://www1.counter.bloke.com/

**SUGGESTED LEVELS**: prealgebra (questions 1, 2, 4, and 5), algebra (questions 1–5)

**SITE SUMMARY**: This page counts and displays the number of times it has been accessed under a title "This Page." It also counts and displays the number of times any page with the same counter is accessed under a title "Counts Served." These numbers can give you an idea about the rate and consistency of activity on the Web.

**TOPICS**: frequency, rate, data collection, data analysis, linear function, equation of a line, slope, y-intercept, extrapolation

### DISCUSSION QUESTIONS AND ACTIVITIES

1. Describe the rate of the frequency of each of the counters over time. Is this what you would expect? Explain why or why not.

2. Record each of the values on the counters and click reload or refresh

on your Web browser. How does the current counter reading affect your response to problem 1? Determine and describe a method that will help you keep the most accurate account of the number on the counter each minute.

3. Generate a function comparing the number on the "This Page" counter to the time in minutes. Explain the significance of each of the numbers in the equation. How do you think this function would compare with a function in terms of time over many hours or days? Explain your reasoning.

4. Predict how long it will take for the "This Page" counter to reach all zeros. Explain how you determined this result. Show any calculations that you used to determine the answer.

5. Predict how long it will take for the "Counts Served" counter to represent a number whose digits are all of the same. Predict how long it will take for this event to occur again. Explain how you determined these results. Show any calculations that you used to determine the answers.

### RELATED INTERNET SITE

See **32. CNET Download.com**

## 23. CARTESIAN COORDINATES

### URL: http://www.univie.ac.at/future.media/moe/galerie/zeich/zeich.html#koord

**SUGGESTED LEVELS**: prealgebra (questions 1, 2, 4, and 5), algebra (questions 1–5), geometry (questions 1–5)

**SITE SUMMARY**: This Java applet can be used to explore the coordinate plane. It demonstrates the coordinates of the cursor on the graph as you drag the mouse around. You can create line segments on the plane to show the existing relationship between corresponding coordinates on a line. You create a point by clicking on the screen, and a line segment by clicking and dragging on the screen. Click on the box titled "Coordinate system" to begin.

**TOPICS**: coordinates, graphing, line, ratio, horizontal line, vertical line, origin, lattice point

## DISCUSSION QUESTIONS AND ACTIVITIES

1. Click on the Auxiliary lines tool. The intersections of the lines are called lattice points. What relationship exists among all of the lattice points?

2. What relationship exists among all of the points on the x-axis? Create a horizontal line parallel to the x-axis. What relationship exists among all of the points on this horizontal line? Form a conjecture about the coordinates on horizontal lines. Repeat the exercise for the y-axis and vertical lines.

3. What type of triangle is formed with vertices (0,a), (b,0), and (−b,0), where a and b are any real numbers? Explain how you determined this answer.

4. Draw a segment that passes through the origin (0,0). Find the ratio of the y-coordinate to the x-coordinate for any point chosen on this line segment. Is this ratio always the same, or does it change? Explain why or why not.

5. Clear the screen. Draw a line segment that passes through at least two lattice points, but does not pass through the origin. Find the ratio of the y to the x coordinate for any point chosen on this line segment. Is this ratio always the same, or does it change? Explain why or why not.

## RELATED INTERNET SITE(S)

### General Coordinates Game
(23a) http://www.shodor.org/interactivate/activities/coords2/index.html
This applet at the Shodor Foundation will plot a random point on the coordinate plane. Input the coordinates based on a graph and obtain feedback.

### Maze Game
(23b) http://www.shodor.org/interactivate/activities/coords/index.html
In this game, you must navigate among the coordinate plane to make it safely to the finish. You start in the lower left-hand corner of the screen and have to navigate around mines in order to arrive at the finish in the upper right-hand portion of the screen. Each move you make depends on the coordinate you enter. Your player will take a direct path to the coordinate and will survive if it does not hit a mine along the way. A goal might be to make it to the finish in the least number of moves.

### Battleship
(23c) http://www.mathgym.com.au/htdocs/japplets/battle/battle.htm
Play this classic game on the coordinate plane. You are given a series of ships and your goal is to "bomb" your opponent's ships by guessing different coor-

dinate points. You will need to sign in to the math gym arcade and then select the battleship game to begin.

# 24.  CEREAL BOX PROBLEM SIMULATION

## URL: http://www.mste.uiuc.edu/users/reese/cereal/cereal.html

**SUGGESTED LEVELS**: prealgebra (questions 1–6), probability (questions 1–6), statistics (questions 1–7)

**SITE SUMMARY**: This simulated shopping trip allows you to collect electronic animal cards until you have completed a set. The Java applet will show you which cards and multiples of cards that you have acquired while gathering the set. You have the option to modify the numbers of cards in the set and log trials that contain statistical information related to repeated trials.

**TOPICS**: simulation, data collection, data analysis, histogram, expected value, confidence intervals, probability, probability distribution

## DISCUSSION QUESTIONS AND ACTIVITIES

1. What assumptions are made about collecting the animal cards in this situation? How could you test these assumptions? Try to test them and explain your results.

2. What is the range of number of possible cereal boxes that you would need to buy in order to collect all of the prizes? How does this range vary with the number of possible prizes? Explain.

3. How many cereal boxes do you need to buy in order to guarantee receiving duplicate animal cards? How does this number vary with the number of possible prizes? Explain.

4. Create a histogram that describes the frequency of trials needed to collect all three animal cards. How does the histogram change as you increase the number of trials? How would this histogram change if there were a different number of animal cards in the set?

5. How many boxes of cereal would you expect to buy if you want to collect a set of three animal cards? Explain the procedures that lead to your solution.

6. How many boxes of cereal would you expect to buy if you want to collect a set of n animal cards? Explain your solution.

7. How many boxes of cereal should you buy if you want to be 95 percent certain that you get all three prizes in a set of animal cards? Explain your solution.

## RELATED INTERNET SITE(S)

See **19. Birthday Problem**

See **87. Monte Carlo Estimation for Pi**

**Stock Exchange Game**
(24a) http://www.shodor.org/interactivate/activities/stock/index.html
This applet from the Shodor Foundation uses probability to predict payoff from the stock market. The user can assign probabilities to win and the expected payout in order to determine the expected value and total return from a stock.

# 25. CHANGING BORDER LINE

## URL: http://www.ies.co.jp/math/java/geo/tochia/tochia.html

**SUGGESTED LEVELS**: geometry (questions 1–5)
**SITE SUMMARY**: A rectangle is divided by a crooked boundary. Your task is to transform the boundary into one line segment without changing the area of two regions inside the rectangle.
**TOPICS**: area of a triangle, parallel lines, polygon

## DISCUSSION QUESTIONS AND ACTIVITIES

1. Click and drag the red point in the diagram for problem 1. Why do the areas not change?

2. How many ways can you solve problem 1? Explain all solutions.

3. Click and drag the red points in the diagram for problem 2. How are the gray lines formed? What theorem or postulate can support this construction?

4. How many ways can you solve problem 2? Explain how you know.

5. Is it possible to divide the region into three nonoverlapping polygons based on the construction? Explain. Is this possible with more than three nonoverlapping regions? Explain.

## RELATED INTERNET SITE(S)

**Quadrilaterals and Conservation of Area**
(25a) http://www.ies.co.jp/math/java/geo/quadri.html
These applets relate to nonroutine area problems that relate to transforming the shape of an object while preserving its area.

**Area of a Parallelogram**
(25b) http://www.math.csusb.edu/faculty/susan/area_par.gsp.html

Manipulate a figure to determine how the area of a parallelogram relates to the area of a rectangle.

**Area of a Triangle**
(25c) http://www.math.csusb.edu/faculty/susan/area_triangle2.gsp.html
(25d) http://www.math.csusb.edu/faculty/susan/area_triangle1.gsp.html
Use a Java environment to explore conjectures about the area of triangles.

See **112. Realtor.com Find a Home**

# 26. CIA MAP COLLECTION

## URL: http://www.lib.utexas.edu/Libs/PCL/Map_collection/cia99/

**SUGGESTED LEVELS**: prealgebra (questions 1–5), geometry (questions 1–6)

**SITE SUMMARY**: This database of maps from the CIA World Factbook is arranged alphabetically by countries around the world. Each map displays a legend, the country's capital, and major cities. You will need to print out some maps and use a ruler to make some measurements.

**TOPICS**: scale, proportion, area, area of irregular polygon, units, ratio

## DISCUSSION QUESTIONS AND ACTIVITIES

1. Based on the different legends, how many kilometers are in a mile? Explain how you determined this result.

2. If the distance represented on the legend was half as large, then how much larger should you make the paper in order to fit the entire country on the map? Explain how you determined this result.

3. What is the land area of the country in which you live? Explain how you determined this result.

4. Find a country with land area close to 500,000 square miles. Which country did you find? Verify your results. Do any of your classmates find a country with a closer approximation? If so, try to find another country with a closer approximation.

5. Suppose Ethiopia began a civil war and resolved its disputes by drawing a boundary through its capital, but made sure that each half of the country maintained the same amount of land. Create a possible boundary line and explain how each side will receive the same amount of land.

6. If you doubled the dimensions of the map, how many times more paper would you need? If you had only ten times as much paper to

make maps, then how many times longer can you make the dimensions? Explain your analyses.

## RELATED INTERNET SITE(S)

### Adjustable U.S. Maps
(26a) http://www.mapquest.com
(26b) http://www.mapblast.com/mblast/index.mb
  View scale maps from any location within the United States. You can zoom in and out from the street level to a view of the entire city.

### World Maps and Demographics
(26c) http://www.atlapedia.com/
(26d) http://www.graphicmaps.com/webimage/countrys/asia/ir.htm
  View scale maps from around the world. Various demographic information is available, such as population, capital, languages spoken, and currency.

See **49. Figure and Ratio of Area**

# 27. CIRCLE SOLVER

## URL: http://www.math.com/students/calculators/source/circle-solver.htm

**SUGGESTED LEVELS**: algebra (question 1), geometry (questions 1–3), advanced algebra (questions 1–3)

**SITE SUMMARY**: Input the area, diameter, or circumference of a circle, and the Java Script form will return the other two pieces of information. This could be used to collect data and generate an equation relating two of these variables, as well as to discover the number pi.

**TOPICS**: data collection, data analysis, function, linear, quadratic, area of a circle, circumference, diameter, circle, composite, equation, slope, y-intercept

## DISCUSSION QUESTIONS AND ACTIVITIES

1. Enter a number in the diameter box, and click on the circumference box. Start a table of values using the diameter of a circle as the independent variable and the circumference as the dependent variable. Record the data in the table and repeat the procedure until you have ten ordered pairs. Graph the data and find the equation of the line that passes through the data in the form $C = ?D + ?$. Describe the significance of the slope and y-intercept of the equation.

2. Enter a number in the diameter box and click on the area box. Start a table of values using the diameter of a circle as the independent

variable and the area as the dependent variable. Record the data in the table and repeat the procedure until you have ten ordered pairs. Graph the data and describe the pattern as linear or quadratic. Justify your answer. Find an equation relating the slope from problem 1, diameter of the circle, and area of the circle.

3. Use your answers to problems 1 and 2 to generate a function that relates the area of a circle to its circumference. Describe the steps and computations you make to derive an answer. Check your answer by inputting values into the Java Script form, and see if the corresponding numbers match the output from the function.

## RELATED INTERNET SITE(S)

**Approximating the Area of the Unit Circle with Regular Polygons**
(27a) http://math.furman.edu/dcs/java/circle.html
Examine what happens to the area of an inscribed regular polygon as the number of its sides increases. You have the option to increase the number of sides one at a time or ask the computer to create an inscribed regular polygon with up to 1,000 sides.

**The Pi Search Page**
(27b) http://www.angio.net/pi/piquery
Enter a string of numbers, such as your birth date, and the computer will locate it within the number pi. The computer will tell you how many decimal places are present before the string of numbers, as well as display fifty other numbers that surround it. This program can provide opportunities for looking at patterns within this transcendental number.

**Compute Pi with Java**
(27c) http://hockey.net/~wb0bwl/tom/java/pi4.htm
Input the number of digits of pi you would like to see. The Java applet can show up to several thousand digits at a time.

# 28. CIRCLE THEOREM 2

## URL: http://www.anglia.co.uk/education/mathsnet/dynamic/cindy/circle_theorem2.html

**SUGGESTED LEVELS**: geometry (questions 1–5)
**SITE SUMMARY**: Determine the relationship between an inscribed angle and central angle that intercept the same arc. You can drag vertices of angles and intersections on the circle in order to generalize an answer.
**TOPICS**: circle, central angle, inscribed angle, arc, semicircle

## DISCUSSION QUESTIONS AND ACTIVITIES

1. If an inscribed angle intercepts the same angle as the central angle of a circle, then derive an equation relating these two angles. Explain how you determined this result.

2. What is the measure of an angle inscribed in a semicircle? Explain how you manipulated the Java applet to determine this answer.

3. What flaws can you find in the Java applet? Explain how you know.

4. Drag point D and observe changes in its angle measure. Make an if-then conjecture that would describe this phenomenon.

5. What type of quadrilateral is formed when the sum of angles BAC and BDC is 180 degrees? Explain why this is true. What additional information would you like to measure to verify this conjecture?

## RELATED INTERNET SITE(S)

### Inscribed Angle and Central Angle
(28a) http://www.ies.co.jp/math/java/geo/enshup/enshup.html
This applet will help you determine the relationship between an inscribed angle and central angle in a circle.

### Inscribed Angle
(28b) http://www.ies.co.jp/math/java/geo/enshukaku/enshukaku.html
This applet demonstrates the relationship between two inscribed angles that intercept the same arc of a circle. You can also create a tangent-chord angle using the vertical angles of the inscribed angles.

# 29. CIRCLE ZAP

## URL: http://www.maths.uq.edu.au/~mrb/java/CircleZap/

**SUGGESTED LEVELS**: prealgebra (questions 1, 2, and 6), algebra (questions 1–6), statistics (questions 1–6)

**SITE SUMMARY**: This Java-based experiment will test your ability to use a mouse. As red or green dots appear on the screen, your goal is to click on them as fast as you can. After running the experiment, the computer will show you how far you had to move the mouse and how long it took you to click the mouse between trials. Begin by clicking Start Test and start clicking on the circles once you see them.

**TOPICS**: data collection, data analysis, line of best fit, linear function, slope, y-intercept

## DISCUSSION QUESTIONS AND ACTIVITIES

1. Is it easier to click on red dots or green dots? Use the data to support your answer. Explain your analysis.

2. Does the number of trials in the experiment affect your reaction time? Use the data to support your answer. Explain your analysis.

3. Generate a function that relates the distance your mouse travels and the time it takes to click the mouse. Explain your procedures and show your calculations. Explain the significance of each of the numbers in your equation in terms of reaction time and distance.

4. Repeat the experiment with the mouse in your other hand. What effect will changing hands have on your analysis and results in problems 1, 2, and 3?

5. Suppose you could run fifty trials in the experiment. Predict how long it would take to complete the experiment with each of your hands. Explain the methods and calculations that help you make this hypothesis.

6. Make up and answer another question that would use the simulation to create data and investigate the solution.

## RELATED INTERNET SITE(S)

**Reaction Time 2**
(29a) http://www.geocities.com/EnchantedForest/Cottage/5124/Games/react2.html
(29b) http://www.geocities.com/SouthBeach/Palms/9809/java/reaction.html
(29c) http://www.telusplanet.net/public/willisb/reaction.html
(29d) http://camptakajo.com/reaction.htm
   These Java script files will display a background color on the screen and test how long it takes you to react to the change in color.
See **123. Statistical Java**

# 30. CLASSIC FALLACIES

## URL: http://www.math.toronto.edu/mathnet/falseProofs/

**SUGGESTED LEVELS**: advanced algebra (questions 1–3), precalculus (questions 1–6)
**SITE SUMMARY**: This page contains a series of false arguments, such as a proof that 1 equals 2 and a proof that every person in Canada is

the same age. Your goal is to identify the incorrect logic or property applied in the argument that leads to the false conclusion.

**TOPICS**: proof, symbolic manipulation, logic, induction, complex numbers, *i*, imaginary numbers

## DISCUSSION QUESTIONS AND ACTIVITIES

1. What is the flaw in the proof using beginning algebra? Will the argument be true under any circumstances? Explain why.

2. What is the error in the proof using complex numbers? Why is this a flaw? What additional properties of real numbers are not true for complex numbers?

3. Devise a fallacy that shows 1 equals −1 with complex numbers.

4. Are all Canadians the same age? Explain what is wrong with the proof.

5. Devise an illogical statement that would require the process of induction in an attempted proof. Challenge a classmate with the statement to see if he or she can disprove your claim.

6. Can every natural number be unambiguously described in fourteen words or less? Find the fallacy in the logic and explain your reasoning.

## 31. THE CLIFF-HANGER

**URL: http://www.mste.uiuc.edu/activity/cliff/**

**SUGGESTED LEVELS**: prealgebra (question 1), probability (questions 1–5)

**SITE SUMMARY**: You are Homer Simpson standing at the edge of a cliff. Considering you never look where you are going, you might fall off the cliff because you have a 1/3 chance of walking forward, and a 2/3 chance of walking backward. From where you are standing, it takes one step forward to fall off the cliff and sixteen steps backward to reach safety. How often will you survive? This Java based simulation will help you get a sense of this probability.

**TOPICS**: simulation, probability, binomial probability, expected value

## DISCUSSION QUESTIONS AND ACTIVITIES

1. Run the simulation enough times to give you an indication on the chances for survival. Keep a tally of the total number of steps taken in each game, as well as if you survived. Based on the simulation,

how many steps does it normally take to escape from the cliff? How many steps does it normally take to fall off the cliff? Explain your answers.

2. Based on the simulation, what is the probability for Homer's survival? Determine the theoretical probability for Homer's survival. Explain your solutions.

3. What would you need to do in the simulation in order to produce results that would be closer to the theoretical probability? Explain why.

4. Suppose Homer had to take fewer steps back in order to survive. Predict the probability of survival with n steps back for survival. Explain your solution.

5. Suppose the probability of taking a step forward is $1/n$, where n is a positive integer. In terms of n, find the probability of Homer's survival if he needs to take sixteen steps back to survive.

## RELATED INTERNET SITE(S)

**Spinner**
(31a) http://www.shodor.org/interactivate/activities/spinner/index.html
(31b) http://www.mathresources.com/spinner.htm
These Java applets are spinners with at least three different regions. You can modify the number and size of each region before spinning. In addition, you can set how many times you would like the spinner to run in each trial. The screen's output will compare the experimental and theoretical probabilities in each of the regions.

**See (17c) The Ant Hill**

**Diffusion and Electric Field**
(31c) http://www.math.utah.edu/~carlson/teaching/java/prob/rp/Random Walk2.html
(31d) http://www.math.utah.edu/~carlson/teaching/java/prob/rp/Random Walk3.html
Examine the behavior of a particle when an electric field increases its probability to move in a certain direction.

# 32. CNET DOWNLOAD.COM

## URL: http://download.cnet.com/downloads/

**SUGGESTED LEVELS**: algebra (questions 1–6)
**SITE SUMMARY**: This menu of links leads to a series of shareware or trial versions that are accessible through the Internet. As you click

through the menus and stop at a specific piece of software, you are given a series of quick facts listed at the bottom of the screen. This investigation will examine the relationship between file size and approximate download time at a specific modem speed. You do not need to download anything in the data collection process.

TOPICS: data collection, data analysis, scatter plot, linear function, line of best fit, extrapolation, slope, y-intercept, proportion, rate

## DISCUSSION QUESTIONS AND ACTIVITIES

1. What is larger, a kilobyte or a megabyte? Explain how you can determine this from the data.

2. Begin a data set comparing file size and download time for file sizes greater than 500K. Create a scatter plot of the data and determine a line of best fit that will relate these two variables. Explain the significance of the slope and y-intercept in this function.

3. If you wanted to download a small file, the approximate download size is usually listed at less than one minute. Devise a plan that would provide download information for small files to the nearest five seconds. Explain your analysis.

4. If you had a modem speed of 28.8 kbps, how long would it take to download a 1 gigabyte hard drive? Explain your analysis.

5. The relationship between download time and modem speed for a 1 MB file can be found at (32a) http://www.russellherder.com/rh.download.html. How do these data compare with your analysis in question 1?

6. Many people now use modems with a speed of 56.6 kbps or faster. Devise a scheme that would convert the current approximate download times for a 28.8 kbps modem to a time for 56.6 kbps modem users. Explain your reasoning.

## RELATED INTERNET SITE(S)

See 22. Cam's Java Web Counter Applet: Dynamic Counter Applet

## 33. COMPLEX NUMBERS IN POLAR FORM

URL: http://www.exploremath.com/activities/Activity_page.cfm? ActivityID=41

SUGGESTED LEVELS: precalculus (questions 1–6)
SITE SUMMARY: ExploreMath.com has set up an interactive polar

coordinate plane with complex numbers. You can drag different points onto the coordinate system and view the relationship between their polar and complex forms. Click on the "show in z = a +bi form" box to view this relationship. You will need to download the Shockwave plugin because the activities were made with the tool Macromedia Director. You can see if you have the plugin, or download it, at (1a) http://www. exploremath.com/about/shockerhelp.cfm.

**TOPICS**: complex numbers, imaginary numbers, polar graphing, complex conjugates, *e*, pi, *i*

## DISCUSSION QUESTIONS AND ACTIVITIES

1. Which polar expression is equivalent to –1? How did you determine this result?

2. Where on the complex polar graph can you find only real numbers? Explain why this is true.

3. What is the relationship between a, b, and r? Why is this true?

4. How are complex conjugates related on the graph? Explain how you determined this result.

5. What is the relationship between any points that lie on the diagonal lines in the middle of each quadrant? Why is this true?

6. Devise a method that will convert polar form to rectangular form and vice versa.

## RELATED INTERNET SITE(S)

### Points in the Complex Plane
(33a) http://www.exploremath.com/activities/Activity_page.cfm?ActivityID= 25
Drag four points anywhere onto a complex plane and view its corresponding complex representation. You can also graph each of the complex conjugates.

### Polar Coordinates
(33b) http://www.univie.ac.at/future.media/moe/galerie/zeich/zeich.html# polar
This applet allows you to drag a point in the rectangular plane and then view the corresponding polar coordinates.

### A Complex Function Viewer
(33c) http://sunsite.ubc.ca/LivingMathematics/V001N01/UBCExamples/ ComplexViewer/complex.html
This applet allows you to visualize certain maps from the complex plane to itself. As you move to different points on the plane and click the mouse, you will see the image tansform to various locations on the screen.

### Complex Number Applets from IES
(33d) http://www.ies.co.jp/math/java/comp/index.html

This set of applets illustrates complex numbers graphically through definitions, transformations, functions, applications, and equations.

**Famous Curves Applet Index**
(33e) http://www-groups.dcs.st-and.ac.uk/~history/Java/index.html
This series of interactive polar functions provides opportunities to modify parameters and view changes in the curve.


# 34. COMPONENTS FOR R

## URL: http://www.ruf.rice.edu/~lane/stat_sim/comp_r/index.html

**SUGGESTED LEVELS**: statistics (questions 1–4)

**SITE SUMMARY**: Examine the components involved in computing a correlation coefficient and how it is affected as you modify the slope, standard deviation of x-values, and standard error from the regression line. This applet allows you to animate each of these factors, as well as view a display that illustrates the proportion of explained versus unexplained variance. Click on the Begin button to start.

**TOPICS**: correlation, slope, regression, standard error, standard deviation


## DISCUSSION QUESTIONS AND ACTIVITIES

1. Animate the standard error of estimate. How does this variable relate to Pearson's correlation coefficient, r ? Repeat this procedure for the standard deviation for x. Explain why these results are occurring.

2. How does the slope of the regression line relate to Pearson's correlation coefficient, r? Explain how you determined this result.

3. Use the variables on the screen to devise a formula that will compute Pearson's correlation coefficient, r. Explain how you determined this result. What are the largest and smallest possible values for r?

4. What factors affect the explained and unexplained variances? Explain how you determined this result.


## RELATED INTERNET SITE(S)

**Scatter, Correlation, and Regression**
(34a) http://www.stat.berkeley.edu/users/stark/Java/Correlation.htm
(34b) http://www.stat.berkeley.edu/~stark/Java/Correlation.htm
Observe changes in a scatter plot as you modify the correlation coefficient and number of data points. You can also view the regression line with the data, as well as a residual plot. Both sites contain the same Java applet.

**Putting Points**

(34c) http://www.stat.uiuc.edu/~stat100/java/guess/PPApplet.html

Enter a target correlation and number of points, and you will see a scatter plot with that corresponding correlation. You can instantly see changes in the graph as you modify the number of points and/or value of the correlation coefficient.

**Guessing Correlations**

(34d) http://www.stat.uiuc.edu/~stat100/java/guess//GCApplet.html

Play a matching game that asks you to compare a scatter plot with its correlation coefficient.

**Regression by Eye**

(34e) http://www.ruf.rice.edu/~lane/stat_sim/reg_by_eye/index.html

Predict the correlation coefficient from a scatter plot. You can draw in a regression line and view its corresponding mean square error.

**Correlation Calculator**

(34f) http://home.stat.ucla.edu/calculators/correlation.phtml

Enter a data set and view a scatter plot, along with its correlation.

# 35. CONIC SECTIONS AS THE LOCUS OF PERPENDICULAR BISECTORS

## URL: http://www.keypress.com/sketchpad/java_gsp/conics.html

**SUGGESTED LEVELS**: precalculus (questions 1–4)

**SITE SUMMARY**: Key Curriculum Press demonstrates the conic sections in their Java SketchPad gallery. This applet shows the locus of the perpendicular bisector of a segment with endpoints on the circle and not on the circle. As one endpoint is set in motion around the circle, the perpendicular bisectors will trace various conic sections, depending on the location of the other endpoint.

**TOPICS**: conic section, ellipse, hyperbola, perpendicular bisector

## DISCUSSION QUESTIONS AND ACTIVITIES

1. Click on "Show Bisector" and "Sweep Bisector" to visualize the construction of the locus of lines. Predict the conic sections formed with this locus as the focus is moved outside the circle, inside the circle, and on the circle's center. Explain your reasoning.

2. Stop the animation by clicking on "Sweep Bisector" again. Drag the focus and observe changes in the eccentricity. Describe how the eccentricity relates to the distance away from the center of the circle. Formulate a rule that describes the value of the eccentricity and the type of conic section.

3. Drag the focus inside the circle. On a sheet of paper, draw an auxiliary line segment connecting the point on the circle and the center of the circle. Draw another auxiliary line segment connecting the focus to the intersection of the perpendicular bisector and the first auxiliary segment. Use the triangles in your diagram to explain how this matches the definition of a certain conic section.

4. Drag the focus outside the circle. On a sheet of paper, draw an auxiliary line segment connecting the point on the circle and the center of the circle. Draw another auxiliary line segment connecting the focus to the intersection of the perpendicular bisector and the first auxiliary segment. Use the triangles in your diagram to explain how this matches the definition of a certain conic section.

## RELATED INTERNET SITE(S)

### Famous Curves Applet Index
(35a) http://www-history.mcs.st-andrews.ac.uk/history/Java/

Modify parameters in the equation of each conic section in parametric form. Observe patterns in the graph as you modify the equation.

### IES Miscellaneous Java Applets
(35b) http://www.ies.co.jp/math/java/misc/index.html

Explore reflective properties and alternate constructions of various conic sections.

### Projective Conics
(35c) http://www.anglia.co.uk/education/mathsnet/dynamic/cindy/locus_ellipse.html

(35d) http://www.anglia.co.uk/education/mathsnet/dynamic/cindy/parabola.html

Tangent lines are used to create the locus of different conics. You can modify the focus and directrix and observe changes in the conic immediately.

### Van Schooten's Conics
(35e) http://www15.addr.com/~dscher/vhyp.html

(35f) http://www15.addr.com/~dscher/schooten.html

(35g) http://www15.addr.com/~dscher/vellipse.html

These mechanical Java constructions of a hyperbola, parabola, and ellipse illustrate the ideas of seventeenth-century Dutch mathematician Frans van Schooten.

## 36. CONSUMER PRICE INDEXES

### URL: http://146.142.4.24/cgi-bin/surveymost?ap

**SUGGESTED LEVELS**: prealgebra (questions 1–7), algebra (questions 1–7), statistics (questions 1–7)

**SITE SUMMARY**: Search for prices on utilities, gasoline, and produce over the past twenty years. Data are listed by average price each month over a specified time interval.

**TOPICS**: data collection, data analysis, data display, percent, modeling, linear function, extrapolation

## DISCUSSION QUESTIONS AND ACTIVITIES

1. In what year(s) did car fuel become a bargain? Explain your analysis.

2. Use various types of produce to estimate the inflation rate over the last twenty years. Explain your analysis.

3. What is the cheapest month to buy tomatoes? Explain how you determined this result from the data. Explain why this might be true.

4. In which areas of the country would you expect the prices to be higher than those listed? In which areas of the country would you expect the prices to be lower than those listed? Explain why.

5. During which year would you most likely complain about rising prices? Explain how you determined this result.

6. Predict the price of 40 therms of natural gas when 500 kilowatt hours of electricity cost $52. In what year do you think this will happen? Explain your analyses.

7. Generate a question that would use a graph to support your analysis. Answer the question and show your work.

## RELATED INTERNET SITE(S)

**Inflation Conversion Factors for Dollars**
(36a) http://osu.orst.edu/dept/pol_sci/fac/sahr/sahr.htm
   Find numerous tables and graphs that describe the fluctuation in costs since the nineteenth century. Examine CPI indexes, government expenses, salaries, movie prices, and the wealth of people in the country.

# 37. COPY CAT

## URL: http://sunsite.ubc.ca/LivingMathematics/Packages/CopyCat/

**SUGGESTED LEVELS**: geometry (questions 1–5)
**SITE SUMMARY**: This game challenges students to match a geometric design on a grid. The goal is to rotate a cube until a piece of the

pattern appears and then either "stamp" or "bomb" a print on the grid. Make sure you read the rules before you play.

**TOPICS**: three-dimensional solids, surface area, rotations, reflections, translations, transformations

## DISCUSSION QUESTIONS AND ACTIVITIES

1. Try the hard cube. What is the difference in the prints when you make a "stamp" or a "bomb"? Use geometry terms in your response.
2. Try the hard cube. What is the smallest number of rotations needed to complete the design? The number of rotations you perform is located in the upper right-hand corner. Explain your findings.
3. Design on a piece of paper a pattern that can be created with the hard cube. Challenge a classmate to complete the pattern.
4. The three-dimensional object rotates along a runway of arrows. Depending on the object, the arrowed runways form different angles with each other. Is there a reason for angle differences, or is this just chance? Explain your reasoning.
5. What is the most complicated puzzle? Explain how you made this decision and compare your criteria with your classmates.

## RELATED INTERNET SITE(S)

**Soma Applet**
(37a) http://users.ids.net/~salberg/soma/Soma.html
A soma cube is a set of seven three-dimensional pieces that fit together to form a cube. Each of the pieces is a combination of three or four connected cubes in different shapes. There are numerous arrangements that will correctly solve this puzzle.

**Rubik's Cube**
(37b) http://www.rubiks.com/cubeonline.html
(37c) http://enchantedmind.com/puzzles/rubik/rubik.htm
This is an online interactive version of the famous cube puzzle.

## 38. DAVE'S SHORT TRIG COURSE

### URL: http://aleph0.clarku.edu/~djoyce/java/trig/

**SUGGESTED LEVELS**: advanced algebra (questions 1–6), precalculus (questions 1–6)
**SITE SUMMARY**: Examine the relationship between trigonometry functions on an interactive circle. The orange point on the circle can be

moved to change the size of the various segments. You can also learn about triangle trigonometry and trigonometric identities at this site. The applet can be viewed in a separate window if you click on it and type the letter u on your keyboard.

**TOPICS**: trigonometry, sine, cosine, tangent, cotangent, right triangle, unit circle, proportion, similarity, area of a triangle, area of a trapezoid

## DISCUSSION QUESTIONS AND ACTIVITIES

1. If the circle has a radius equal to 1, determine as many proportions as you can from the diagram. Explain how you found each case and why it is true.
2. When are any two of the functions equal to each other? Explain how this is possible.
3. If the circle has a radius equal to 1, determine the range of values for each function. Explain how you determined each result.
4. If the circle has a radius equal to 1, use right triangles to derive some true equations. Explain your analysis.
5. Construct a graph of each function using a domain from 0 to 90 degrees. Predict the graph of each function from 90 to 360 degrees. Explain your reasoning.
6. What are the acute angles in the right triangle when the triangle has the same area as the trapezoid (with bases labeled sin and tan)? Explain your reasoning.

## RELATED INTERNET SITE(S)

**IES Trigonometry**
(38a) http://www.ies.co.jp/math/java/trig/index.html
This page is a series of Java applets that illustrate constructions of various trigonometric functions and their transformations from a unit circle.

**Trigonometric Identities**
(38b) http://www.sisweb.com/math/trig/identities.htm
This reference list includes a variety of identities and relationships among triangles and functions. The UP link will send you to more tables of mathematical formulas.

# 39. DENSITY LAB

**URL: http://www.explorescience.com/activities/activity_page. cfm?activityID=29**

**SUGGESTED LEVELS**: prealgebra (questions 1–3), algebra (questions 1–5)

**SITE SUMMARY**: ExploreScience has created an activity that compares the density, mass, and volume of an object. Your goal is to measure the mass and volume of an object and then predict its density. An object is too dense for a liquid if it does not float and not dense enough if it does float. Realistically, it is difficult to find a liquid with the same density as an object, but you can use this information to estimate the density of an object. You need the Flash plugin to view this site. If the file does not appear on the screen, then you will need to download the free plugin from Macromedia at (16a) http://www.macromedia.com/shockwave/download/index.cgi?P1_Prod_Version=ShockwaveFlash.

**TOPICS**: data collection, data analysis, equation, ratio, density, units, volume, mass

## DISCUSSION QUESTIONS AND ACTIVITIES

1. Which object is most dense? Which object is least dense? How can you tell?

2. Do any of the objects have equal density? Explain why or why not.

3. Place each object in the liquid one at a time. Modify the density of the liquid until you can estimate the density of each of the objects. Measure the mass and volume of each object and record all of the data in a table. Predict an equation that relates density, mass, and volume. Explain how you determined and tested this hypothesis.

4. Suppose you have a larger green triangle with a mass of 18 grams that is made of the same material as the smaller green triangle. What would be the larger triangle's volume? Explain how you know.

5. Express density units in more than one way. Explain how you determined this result.

## RELATED INTERNET SITE(S)

**Floating Log**
(39a) http://www.explorescience.com/activities/Activity_page.cfm?ActivityID =30
Determine the mass, length, and radius of a cylindrical log that will keep it afloat in water. You can modify the density of the water to examine the relationship between mass, volume, and density. You need the Flash plugin to view this site. You can download it for free at (16a) http://www.macromedia.com/shockwave/download/index.cgi?P1_Prod_Version=ShockwaveFlash.

## 40. DETERMINE THE DERIVATIVE OF AN UNKNOWN FUNCTION

**URL: http://umastr1.math.umass.edu/~frankw/ccp/calculus/deriv/ derlimit/applet.htm**

**SUGGESTED LEVELS**: calculus (questions 1–4)

**SITE SUMMARY**: Collect data in order to determine the derivative of an unknown function. When you enter a number into the input box and run the experiment, you will receive the value of the derivative of the function at that point. This activity would be useful after an individual has been introduced to derivatives and their relationship to the graphs of functions.

**TOPICS**: increasing, relative minimum, relative maximum, derivative, function, inflection point, extrema

### DISCUSSION QUESTIONS AND ACTIVITIES

1. If the data describes the derivative f' (x) of a continuous function, then on what intervals is the function f(x) increasing? Explain how you used the data to determine this result.

2. For what values of x will the function f(x) have a relative minimum? Relative maximum? Explain how you used the data to determine this result.

3. For what values of x will the function f(x) have a point of inflection? Explain how you used the data to determine this result.

4. Determine an equation for f(x). Explain and show how you determined this result. Use this function to verify your answers to problems 1–3.

### RELATED INTERNET SITE(S)

**IES Calculus Java Applets**
(40a) http://www.ies.co.jp/math/java/calc/index.html
This series of Java applets includes explorations on limits, first and second derivatives, area, volume, and more.

See **(9a)** and **(9b) Derivative Puzzles**

See **(9c) Derivative Definition Java Applet**

**The MathServ Calculus Toolkit**
(40b) http://mss.math.vanderbilt.edu/~pscrooke/toolkit.html

This series of cgi scripts uses Mathematica to calculate limits, derivatives, antiderivatives, and more.

## 41. DISTANCE FORMULA

### URL: http://www.exploremath.com/activities/Activity_page.cfm? ActivityID=2

**SUGGESTED LEVELS**: prealgebra (questions 1 and 2), algebra (questions 1–3), and geometry (questions 1–6)

**SITE SUMMARY**: ExploreMath.com has an interactive coordinate plane. You can move coordinates on the screen by adjusting the sliders, and measure their distance using the mouse in the ruler mode. You will need to download the Shockwave plugin because the activities were made with the tool Macromedia Director. You can see if you have the plugin, or download it, at (1a) http://www.exploremath.com/about/shockerhelp.cfm.

**TOPICS**: distance, distance formula, Pythagorean Theorem, Pythagorean triples, circle

### DISCUSSION QUESTIONS AND ACTIVITIES

1. Let the grid lines on the graph represent roadways that you must stay on when traveling in Taxicab World. Godzilla has just attacked the origin and can run over any building. He moves two-thirds as fast as your taxi, but he can run through any building without slowing down. That means he does not need to follow taxicab rules. Your best friend is trapped eight blocks west, and six blocks south from the origin. What path will you take to try to save your friend? Will Godzilla have you and your friend for lunch? Explain.

2. Let the grid lines on the graph represent roadways that you must stay on when traveling in Taxicab World. On your trip, you will not turn around, and you will travel the same distance vertically as you will horizontally. Assuming a bird always flies in a straight path, how much farther in percentage will you have to travel on your destination? Explain your analysis.

3. Use $x_1$, $x_2$, $y_1$, $y_2$, and the distance between the two points (d) in the ruler mode to generate an equation that relates all of these variables. Explain how properties of the triangle relate to this equation.

4. Generate a graph of a set of points that are all the same distance from one particular point. Explain your findings.

5. What is the maximum number of segment lengths on this viewing

window of the graph that have an integer length, a nonzero slope, and endpoints on lattice points? Explain your reasoning. If you could expand the viewing window, identify some other lengths with these characteristics. Explain how you determined each answer.

6. What is the relationship between the length of the hypotenuse of a right triangle and the distance from the right angle vertex to the midpoint of the hypotenuse? Explain why this is true.

## RELATED INTERNET SITE(S)

See **7. Ask Jeeves: What Is the Distance?**

See **122. Squaring the Triangle**

## 42. EDMUNDS USED CAR PRICES

### URL: http://www.edmunds.com/used/

**SUGGESTED LEVELS**: advanced algebra (questions 1–5)

**SITE SUMMARY**: This site provides you with blue book prices for automobiles over the last ten years. Information about most of the popular models is available, including vehicle pricing, reviews, equipment, and adjusting for mileage. Trade-in and market values are available to get an idea of resale prices for used cars. These data are valuable for analyzing trends in a particular model over time, allowing you to extrapolate the price of a new car or an older car.

**TOPICS**: functions, exponential, extrapolation, data analysis, data collection, modeling

## DISCUSSION QUESTIONS AND ACTIVITIES

1. Find a make and model of an automobile that is currently available and has existed for at least five years. Go to the vehicle pricing for this automobile and determine the market value of the automobile each of these years. Create a scatter plot of market value vs. age of the automobile. What type of function would model the data based on the scatter plot and extrapolating beyond the data set? Explain your reasoning. Find the equation of this function. Explain how you determined this result.

2. Compare your function with a function from a different type of automobile. Explain the real world significance of each of the numbers in these functions.

3. Use your function from problem 1 to predict the price of a model from 1988. Explain how you determined your result.

4. Suppose you only have $1,200 to spend on an automobile and would like to purchase this model. Use your function from problem 1 to predict what year model you could afford. Explain your solution.

5. Compare the trade-in values to the market values for each of the years. What generalization can you make about these two numbers? How much profit would you expect a dealer to make from the time you trade in a car to the time it is resold?

## RELATED INTERNET SITE(S)

### Kelley Blue Book
(42a) http://www.kbb.com/kb/ki.dll/kw.kc.uy?kbb&;r&22&&
Analyze the pricing similarities and differences between Edmunds' and Kelley's ratings.

### Yahoo! Auto Classifieds
(42b) http://dir.yahoo.com/Business_and_Economy/Companies/Automotive/Classifieds/
This directory provides links to auto classifieds around the Web. Using a mathematical function from the used car data can help you determine if you are getting a good buy on a car for sale.

### Map Quest
(42c) http://www.mapquest.com

### Edmunds New Cars
(42d) http://www.edmunds.com/newcars/
Information from both sites can help you predict the fuel cost for a road trip. Use Map Quest to obtain driving directions and the distance between two cities in the United States. In the new car database at Edmunds, you can find EPA city and highway mileage estimates under the specifications and safety feature reports for each vehicle.

## 43. EFFECTS OF A, B, C, D ON THE GRAPH OF Y = A(SIN BX + C) + D

**URL: http://home.netvigator.com/~wingkei9/javagsp/asinbxcd.html**

SUGGESTED LEVELS: precalculus (questions 1–6)
SITE SUMMARY: This applet represents a graph of a sine function in the form y = a(sin bx + c) + d. You can modify the values of a, b, c, and d, and observe changes in the graph.

TOPICS: sinusoidal functions, amplitude, period, translation, transformation, graph, modeling, cosine, sine, domain, range

## DISCUSSION QUESTIONS AND ACTIVITIES

1. How do a, b, c, and d relate to the amplitude, period, phase shift, and vertical shift of a sine function?
2. This curve is also a cosine function. Determine the equation of the cosine function if the sine function is $y = a(\sin bx + c) + d$. Explain how you determined this result.
3. How could you change the graph into a straight line? Explain why this is true.
4. The screen shows a limited window of this function. In terms of a, b, c, and d, state the domain and range of the function. Explain your answer.
5. Derive an equation of a sine function that would represent the temperature of your hometown through one year. Explain your analysis.
6. Derive an equation of a sine function that would represent the height of a carnival Ferris wheel over time. Explain your analysis.

## RELATED INTERNET SITE(S)

**Play a Piano/Synthesizer/Oscilloscope**
(43a) http://www.frontiernet.net/~imaging/play_a_piano.html
   Play a piano and see an oscilloscope illustrating the sound waves in real time.

See **101. Pendulum**

See **95. Normal Daily Maximum Temperature, Deg F**

# 44. ELEVEN TIMES

## URL: http://www.learningkingdom.com/eleven/eleven.html

SUGGESTED LEVELS: prealgebra (questions 1 and 3), algebra (questions 1, 2, and 3)

SITE SUMMARY: The Learning Kingdom provides a Java-based game that teaches you how to multiply two-digit numbers by the number eleven. After showing some examples, the game provides opportunities for practice and efficiency. You have the option to set the difficulty level based on how long you think it will take to answer each of the questions.

**TOPICS**: multiplication, mental arithmetic, algebraic proof, symbolic reasoning

## DISCUSSION QUESTIONS AND ACTIVITIES

1. Try the game until you are successful at getting at least 80 percent of the problems correct. Devise a different strategy to get the correct answer and compare your method with a classmate. For example, one method would be to first multiply by ten and then add something else.

2. If you click on "Why It Works" at the bottom of the page, you will see an explanation to verify this number trick. Use an algebraic expression to prove that this number trick works.

3. Suppose eleven were multiplied by a three-digit number. Does the same rule apply? If so, explain why. If not, is there another "trick" that will help you compute this value in your head? Explain.

## RELATED INTERNET SITE(S)

**Blankety-Five Squared**
(44a) http://www.learningkingdom.com/five/five.html
A Java-based number trick game created by the Learning Kingdom that teaches you how to square two-digit numbers that end in five.

**BEATCALC: Beat the Calculator Archive**
(44b) http://forum.swarthmore.edu/k12/mathtips/beatcalc.html
Examine over 100 arithmetic shortcuts provided by the Math Forum, such as multiplying by mixed numbers, squaring special numbers, adding sequences of numbers, and more.

**Divisibility Rules**
(44c) http://forum.swarthmore.edu/k12/mathtips/division.tips.html
Learn shotcuts from Dr. Math on how to determine if large integers can be divided evenly by integers from 3 to 13. A Spanish translation is provided.

## 45. EUCLID'S ELEMENTS—BOOK 1

**URL: http://aleph0.clarku.edu/~djoyce/java/elements/book1/ book1.html**

**SUGGESTED LEVELS**: geometry (questions 1–6)
**SITE SUMMARY**: This site illustrates Euclid's books of elements as they were first written. You will find definitions, postulates, and propositions of fundamental principles in geometry, such as theories of triangles, parallels, and area. Most of the references in the text have

accompanying Java-based diagrams to help describe a mathematical phenomenon. All thirteen of Euclid's books of elements are available at this site for further investigation.

TOPICS: postulate, equilateral triangle, isosceles triangle, angle

## DISCUSSION QUESTIONS AND ACTIVITIES

1. Could Euclid have presented the postulates in Book 1 in a different order? Explain why or why not.

2. Is it possible to construct an equilateral triangle using a method different from the proof in proposition 1? Explain your reasoning.

3. How are the notation and vocabulary that describe geometric objects in Euclid's Elements similar to and different from the notation you use in your class? Give examples to help explain your analysis.

4. Suppose you did not have to rely solely on the definitions, postulates, common notions, and propositions in Euclid's first book. Identify alternate ways to justify proposition 5. Explain each solution.

5. What patterns do you notice that distinguish definitions, postulates, common notions, and propositions? Explain how you determined these results.

6. Which proposition seems unusual to you? Explain why. Change or reword the proposition so that it relates to your understanding of geometry. Verify that your proposition is true.

## RELATED INTERNET SITE(S)

**Euclid, Elements**
(45a) http://www.perseus.tufts.edu/cgi-bin/ptext?doc=Perseus:abo:tlg,1799,001
   The Perseus Project is in the process of producing an online version of the thirteen books of Euclid's Elements. You can also find historical information about Euclid, as well as mathematicians' commentary on his work.

**Oliver Byrne's Edition of Euclid**
(45b) http://www.math.ubc.ca/people/faculty/cass/Euclid/byrne.html
   Examine the first six books of Euclid's Elements through the translation and diagrams of Oliver Byrne. You can also view alternate translations by David Joyce and commentary by Heath.

## 46. EXPONENTIAL FUNCTIONS

### URL: http://www.exploremath.com/activities/Activity_page.cfm? ActivityID=4

SUGGESTED LEVELS: advanced algebra (questions 1–6)
SITE SUMMARY: ExploreMath.com has an interactive exponential

function with graph. Using the function $Y = Ma^{kx}$, you can adjust the values of M, a, and k, and observe simultaneous changes in the graph. You can modify the viewing window of the graph, view coordinates on the graph, and view a table that describes values of the function on any specified interval. You will need to download the Shockwave plugin because the activities were made with the tool Macromedia Director. You can see if you have the plugin, or download it, at (1a) http://www.exploremath.com/about/shockerhelp.cfm.

**TOPICS**: exponential function, y-intercept, graph, increasing, minimum, asymptote, horizontal line, modeling, decreasing, $e$

## DISCUSSION QUESTIONS AND ACTIVITIES

1. Which of the values M, a, or k, determines the y-intercept of the function? Why is this true?

2. What is the lowest possible value of an increasing exponential function in the form $Y = Ma^{kx}$? Explain how you determined this result.

3. For what values of M, a, and k does the graph turn into a horizontal line? Explain why this happens in each case.

4. Generate a real-world example that describes a situation with M>0, 0<a<1, k>1, and Y<1 for x>6.

5. Find an example of two exponential functions that have the same graph, but have different values of a and k. Explain how this is possible.

6. Determine a set of criteria relating to the values of M, a, and k that will generate a decreasing exponential function.

## RELATED INTERNET SITE(S)

**A Simple Logarithm Calculator**
(46a) http://www.math.utah.edu/~alfeld/math/Log.html
This device will solve $b^x = y$ when you input two of the variables. The applet can be used to compare exponential, logarithmic, and root functions.

See **132. Towers of Hanoi**

**Logarithms**
(46b) http://www.exploremath.com/activities/Activity_page.cfm?ActivityID=7
Graph $y = \log_a x$ and observe the relationship between the graph and the equation as you modify the value of a. You can view the line $y = x$ and the logarithmic functions corresponding to the exponential function on the same graph.

## 47. FACTOR TREE

### URL: http://www.mathresources.com/factor.htm

**SUGGESTED LEVELS**: prealgebra (questions 1–5)
**SITE SUMMARY**: The Math Probe has created an automated factor tree that will show you the prime factorization of any number between 1 and 500.
**TOPICS**: exponents, prime factorization, factor tree

### DISCUSSION QUESTIONS AND ACTIVITIES

1. What do the prime factorizations of perfect squares have in common? Is this true for all perfect squares? How about perfect cubes? Write a conjecture about the prime factorization of a number raised to the nth power. Explain your reasoning.

2. How can you use the factor tree to generate all of the factors of a number? Explain your reasoning.

3. Describe how the computer appears to create the factor tree. Is the computer's method for finding the prime factorization of a number the only method to create the factor tree? Explain why or why not.

4. What is the relationship between all of the numbers that have a factor tree four levels deep, including the original number?

5. Using the computer's method of factoring, are there any numbers that can generate a factor tree five levels deep? Explain why or why not.

### RELATED INTERNET SITE(S)

See **46. Exponential Functions**.

## 48. FIBONACCI SEQUENCE

### URL: http://home.netvigator.com/~wingkei9/fibon.html

**SUGGESTED LEVELS**: advanced algebra (questions 1–5)
**SITE SUMMARY**: This page will generate terms of Fibonacci's sequence (1, 1, 2, 3, 5, 8, 13, . . . ). Enter the number of terms you would like to see and click on Generate.
**TOPICS**: sequence, explicit, recursive, Fibonacci sequence, golden ratio, composite

## DISCUSSION QUESTIONS AND ACTIVITIES

1. What is the relationship between consecutive terms of the sequence? Can you generate a recursive equation to predict subsequent terms in the sequence? Can you generate an explicit equation to predict any term in the sequence? Explain why or why not.

2. Use combinations of multiples of the first eight terms to produce the tenth term. For example, twenty times the third term plus three times the fifth term is equal to the tenth term, because 20(2) + 3(5) = 55. Generate at least two other solutions. How many solutions can use the seventh term of the sequence? Explain your analysis.

3. Use combinations of multiples of the first eight terms to produce the sum of the first ten terms. How many solutions can use the seventh term of the sequence? Explain your analysis.

4. Find the ratio of consecutive terms of the sequence (for example, 1/1, 2/1, 3/2, 5/3, etc.). What happens to the sequence of ratios as the number of terms increases? Explain why. How would the results change if you started the sequence with a different value? Explain.

5. Generate another method that will predict a term or partial sum in the sequence. Explain your analysis.

## RELATED INTERNET SITE(S)

**Fibonacci Numbers and Nature**
(48a) http://www.ee.surrey.ac.uk/Personal/R.Knott/Fibonacci/fibnat.html
This page discusses applications, real-world phenomena, puzzles, patterns, and geometry associated with the Fibonacci numbers and golden section.

**Fibonacci's Elephant**
(48b) http://www.burleyms.demon.co.uk/numeracy/fibo.html
Input two numbers in the beginning of a Fibonacci-like sequence and view the next ten terms. You need the Flash plugin to view this site. You can download it for free at (16a) http://www.macromedia.com/shockwave/download/index.cgi?P1_Prod_Version=ShockwaveFlash.

## 49. FIGURE AND RATIO OF AREA

### URL: http://www.ies.co.jp/math/java/geo; shratioAB/ratioAB.html

**SUGGESTED LEVELS**: geometry (questions 1–4)
**SITE SUMMARY**: Examine the effects on the ratio of the areas of two objects as you change the ratios of the sides of the objects. You can compare ratios of rectangles and irregular objects by adjusting their length

and width. The screen will show you the simplified ratio of the lengths and heights between the two objects, as well as the ratio of their areas.

**TOPICS**: area of a rectangle, ratio, area of a square, similarity

### DISCUSSION QUESTIONS AND ACTIVITIES

1. Click on the arrows until both regions are squares. How does the ratio of their sides compare to the ratio of their areas? Is this always true? Explain.

2. Click on the arrows until both regions are rectangles, but not squares. Devise a method that will determine the ratio of the areas based on the ratio of the sides. Why is this true? Will this method work for every rectangle? Explain.

3. How do the ratios change when you modify a triangle, flower, or tree in the pull down menu? Explain why.

4. Two noncongruent figures have equal area. How do their dimensions relate? Explain.

### RELATED INTERNET SITE(S)

**Ratio**
(49a) http://www.ies.co.jp/math/java/geo/ratio/ratio.html
   This applet will help you investigate the relationship between the ratio of sides of two squares and the ratio of their areas.
See **67. Internet Pizza Server Ordering Area**

## 50. FINDING THE AREA UNDER A CURVE

### URL: http://www.math.utah.edu/~carlson/teaching/java/calculus/ApproxArea.html

**SUGGESTED LEVELS**: advanced algebra (questions 1–5), precalculus (questions 1–5), calculus (questions 1–5)

**SITE SUMMARY**: This applet will approximate the net area between the x-axis and a polynomial function up to three degrees on the interval $[-1,1]$. Four input boxes are given to represent the coefficients of the third degree polynomial. The default graph is $y = x^2$. When you begin, the input boxes should read 0, 1, 0, 0. That means $y = 0x^3 + 1x^2 + 0x + 0$, which simplifies to $y = x^2$. The Java applet uses rectangles to approximate the area with height determined by the location where the curve passes through the midpoint of the width of the rectangle. You can modify the number of rectangles used to get a sense of the limit as the number of rectangles increases without bound. The area of the rectangles is accurate, even though you may not see the graph if its range is beyond $[-1,1]$.

**TOPICS**: area of a rectangle, area under a curve, limit, Riemann sum, even function, odd function, linear function, quadratic function, integration

## DISCUSSION QUESTIONS AND ACTIVITIES

1. Is the area between $y = x^2$ and the x-axis more or less accurate when you increase the number of rectangles? Explain how you know. Is this true for all functions? Explain why or why not.
2. What is the net area of any odd function on the interval $[-1,1]$? Explain how you determined this result.
3. On the interval $[-1,1]$, how does the area between the x-axis and y $= x^n$ compare with $y = x^n + c$, where n is any degree of the polynomial (between 0 and 3) and c is the constant term of the polynomial?
4. Graph a line on the interval $[-1,1]$. Will changes in the slope or the y-intercept cause a change in the net area between the line and the y-axis? Explain why.
5. Generate a method that will help you predict the net area between an even quadratic function and the x-axis on the interval $[-1,1]$. Explain how you determined this result.

## RELATED INTERNET SITE(S)

**Minimum Value of Integral of Function**
(50a) http://www.ies.co.jp/math/java/calc/e-mininteg/e-mininteg.html
This exploration leads you through finding the minimum value of the area between two curves and the x-axis when secant and cosecant graphs intersect.
**Evaluating Integrals**
(50b) http://integrals.wolfram.com/
(50c) http://mss.math.vanderbilt.edu/cgi-bin/MSSAgent/~pscrooke/MSS/definiteintegral.def
These symbolic processors will determine an integral and calculate the value of a definite integral.
See **147–149. Xfunctions Xpresso**

# 51. FINDING THE LENGTH OF A CURVE

## URL: http://xanadu.math.utah.edu/java/ApproxLength.html

**SUGGESTED LEVELS**: precalculus (questions 1–4), calculus (questions 1–5)

**SITE SUMMARY**: Determine the length of an arc of a third-degree polynomial on the interval $[-1,1]$. The applet uses piecewise segments to approximate the length of a curve through a limit. You can modify the number of segments used to estimate the value of the arc length. The Reset button will put the applet in its starting position, $y=x^2$, and the Redraw button should be used to plot a new function.

**TOPICS**: length, integration, limit, segment, data collection, graphing, asymptote

## DISCUSSION QUESTIONS AND ACTIVITIES

1. Sketch a graph that describes the approximate length of a curve on the interval $[-1,1]$ as a function of n, the number of segments used to linearize the curve. Repeat this process for different functions. Explain any patterns you find in the graphs. What do you think the patterns represent? Why?

2. Use the segments to determine the length of $y = 2x^3 - 3x^2 + 1$ on the interval $[-1,1]$. Explain how you determined this result.

3. How many segments are needed in order to find a length within 1 percent of the actual value? Is this true for any third degree function? Explain your analysis and reasoning.

4. Find a function whose length approximation on $[-1,1]$ would always be exact. Explain how you would determine this exact length.

5. Let delta x represent the horizontal distance covered by each segment. Let delta y represent the vertical distance covered by each segment. What is the length of an arbitrary segment? Set up an integral to determine the length of the sum of infinitesimal segments of an arbitrary function on the interval $[-1,1]$. Rewrite this integral so that it includes the expression dy/dx. Use this expression to determine the length of $2x^3 - 3x^2 + 1$ on the interval $[-1,1]$. A symbolic integrating calculator can be found at (50b) http://integrals.wolfram.com/. Compare your results with question 2.

## RELATED INTERNET SITE(S)

See **147–149. Xfunctions Xpresso**

See **(50a) Minimum Value of Integral of Function**

**Problem of Area**

(51a) http://www.ies.co.jp/math/java/calc/probquad/probquad.html

This exploration searches for a general pattern between the area bounded by the curves $y = x^2 - 1$, $y = (x - 1)(x - a)$, and their common tangent line.

## 52. FIRST AND SECOND DERIVATIVE OF F(X) = A + BX + CX² + DX³

URL: http://www.univie.ac.at/future.media/moe/galerie/diff1/diff1.
html#zwabl

SUGGESTED LEVELS: calculus (questions 1–5)

SITE SUMMARY: This applet will graph a third degree polynomial, along with the graphs of its first and second derivatives. Students first learning this concept could modify the coefficients of the equation and identify patterns for differentiating polynomial functions.

TOPICS: function, graph, first derivative, second derivative, polynomial function, degree

### DISCUSSION QUESTIONS AND ACTIVITIES

1. Click on the red box titled, "Applet: First and second derivative." You should see a picture of three graphs in a new window, with four sliding boxes to the right side of the screen. If you click and drag each of those boxes, you will observe changes in the function and graphs of the derivatives. What type of function is the graph of the derivative, f'(x), and the second derivative, f''(x)? Describe the relationship between the degree of the function, the first derivative, and the second derivative.

2. Set the values a, b, and c equal to zero. Modify d to the highest integral value, 2, and determine the equations of the first and second derivatives based on the graphs. Use these results to start a table of values describing the function, derivative, and second derivative. Repeat the process by setting d = −1, 0, 1, and 2. Explain a shortcut that will help you find the derivative and second derivative functions given a third degree polynomial.

3. The second derivative is the same as the derivative of the first derivative. Will the shortcut pattern from problem two also work for second degree functions? Explain.

4. Generalize your rule for any polynomial function with degree n. Explain how you derived your answer.

5. Modify only the value of the constant, a, in f(x). Explain what happens to the graphs of f(x), f'(x), and f''(x), and why this might be happening.

### RELATED INTERNET SITE(S)

See (40a) IES Calculus Java Applets

See (9a) and (9b) Derivative Puzzles

See **(9c) Derivative Definition Java Applet**
See **(40b) The MathServ Calculus Toolkit**

# 53. FLOOR TILES

**URL: http://www.shodor.org/interactivate/activities/quadtess/index. html**

SUGGESTED LEVELS: geometry (questions 1–5)

SITE SUMMARY: The Shodor Foundation has created a Java applet that will tessellate quadrilaterals. You begin with a square tile and can modify the figure by choosing the Edit button, and then clicking and dragging one of its vertices. An information panel will give you the figures angle measures, vertex coordinates, area, and perimeter. You also have the option to change the colors of the tiles when they tessellate.

TOPICS: area of a rectangle, perimeter, quadrilateral, tessellation, translation, triangle, transformation

## DISCUSSION QUESTIONS AND ACTIVITIES

1. The Information button will tell you the area and perimeter of the first figure on the screen. What is the area and perimeter of the entire rectangular viewing area? Explain how you determined this result.

2. Tessellate a quadrilateral. What is the sum of the angles surrounding any vertex? Explain how you determined this result.

3. Do all quadrilaterals (both convex and nonconvex) tessellate? Explain why or why not.

4. Does every quadrilateral use the same transformation when tessellating? That is, will you use the same rotation, translation, or reflection guidelines when creating every tessellation? If so, explain why. If not, then explain how the transformations differ between different quadrilaterals.

5. You can collapse the quadrilateral into a triangle by dragging one of the vertices on top of one of the sides, and then adjusting the other vertex until you form a triangle. Do all triangles tessellate? Explain why or why not.

## RELATED INTERNET SITE(S)

**Patterns Program**
(53a) http://www.best.com/~ejad/java/patterns/patterns_j.shtml
This Java applet allows you to drag triangles, hexagons, trapezoids, and parallelograms onto a grid. You can use a variety of combinations to tessellate the plane.

**Catalog of Isohedral Tilings by Symmetric Polygonal Tiles**
(53b) http://forum.swarthmore.edu/dynamic/one-corona/
These Java Sketchpad files are dynamic illustrations of various tiling patterns, using triangles, quadrilaterals, pentagons, and hexagons.

**Tessellate**
(53c) http://www.shodor.org/interactivate/activities/tessellate/index.html
Tessellate a triangle, rectangle, or hexagon, using translations. You can modify the edges, vertices, and corners of the figures to help you create interesting designs that tessellate a plane.

**Interactive Tessellations**
(53d) http://home6.inet.tele.dk/bergmann/10galleri/idx10.htm
Explore over fifteen dynamic tessellations created using Java SketchPad. You can modify the shape and scale of each of the designs to better understand how a tessellation maintains its properties under a transformation.

**A Java Applet to Play with Penrose Tiles**
(53e) http://www.geocities.com/SiliconValley/Pines/1684/Penrose.html
Create tessellations using different kites or Penrose Tiles.

# 54. FOREST FIRE SIMULATION

## URL: http://dimacs.rutgers.edu/~biehl/fire.html

**SUGGESTED LEVELS**: probability (questions 1–5)
**SITE SUMMARY**: This simulation of a forest fire illustrates how the probability of fire spreading and the probability of wind changing direction have an effect on the magnitude of the fire. You can monitor the size of the fire by watching how it spreads, as well as monitor its magnitude in a reading called "fire size." You have the option to set the primary direction of the wind, modify probabilities that affect the fire, and set an obstacle to test if you can put out the fire. To begin, click on the green region, set the parameters, and click go. To restart the simulation, click on Clear Fire or Clear All.
**TOPICS**: chaos, probability, vector, iteration, area of a triangle, data collection, data analysis

## DISCUSSION QUESTIONS AND ACTIVITIES

1. Set the wind changes probability to zero. Modify the probability of the fire spreading and compare it to the fire size. Devise a mathematical method that will help you predict the fire size based on its probability of spreading. Explain how you found this solution.
2. Set the probability of fire spreading to zero. Modify the wind changes probability and compare it to the fire size. Devise a mathematical method that will help you predict the fire size based on the wind change probability. Explain how you found this solution.
3. As the fire size increases, so does the number of iterations. What do you think an iteration is? Devise a mathematical method that will help you predict the fire size based on the number of iterations.
4. Click and drag on the arrow that controls the direction of the wind. Generalize how the wind direction affects the spread of a forest fire. Explain how you determined this result.
5. In the draw mode, you have an option to select an obstacle and then draw it on the screen. Suppose you worked for the fire department and wanted to stop a forest fire. In order to do this, you need to predict how the fire will spread so that you can set a water obstacle to stop it from spreading. You do not want an obstacle too large because it may harm the ecosystem, and you do not want an obstacle too small because the fire may go around the obstacle and destroy more trees. Given the probabilities of the wind direction and of the fire spreading, create a general strategy that will help you place an appropriately sized obstacle in an appropriate location that will help prevent the fire from spreading.

## RELATED INTERNET SITE(S)

**Percolating Oil Simulation**
(54a) http://www.magpage.com/~youngej/oil.html
  This simulation represents the dispersion of an oil spill based on its probability of spreading.
See **(17c) The Ant Hill**
See **(17d)** and **(17e) Fire!**

# 55. 4TH DEGREE POLYNOMIAL

## URL: http://www.exploremath.com/activities/Activity_page.cfm? ActivityID=12

**SUGGESTED LEVELS**: advanced algebra (questions 1–6)
**SITE SUMMARY**: ExploreMath.com has an interactive quartic func-

tion with graph. Using the function $Y = ax^4 + bx^3 + cx^2 + dx + e$, you can adjust each of the coefficients and observe simultaneous changes in the graph. You can modify the viewing window of the graph, view co-ordinates on the graph, and view a table that describes values of the function on any specified interval. You will need to download the Shock-wave plugin because the activities were made with the tool Macromedia Director. You can see if you have the plugin, or download it, at (la) http://www.exploremath.com/about/shockerhelp.cfm.

**TOPICS**: x-intercept, polynomial function, degree, extrema, relative minimum, relative maximum, increasing, decreasing, symmetry, reflec-tion, rotation, graph

## DISCUSSION QUESTIONS AND ACTIVITIES

1. Make a conjecture about the largest number of x-intercepts for an nth degree function. Explain your analyses and results.

2. Make a conjecture about the largest number of relative extrema (min-ima and maxima) for an nth degree function. Explain your analyses and results.

3. Can you generate a fourth degree function that is strictly increasing or decreasing? Explain why or why not.

4. Which of the coefficients affect reflection symmetry over the y-axis? Explain why. Which of the coefficients affect rotation symmetry about the origin? Explain why.

5. Which coefficients affect the x-coordinate of relative or absolute ex-trema? Which coefficients do not affect the x-coordinate of relative or absolute extrema? Explain how you determined these results.

6. Describe the characteristics of a fourth degree polynomial with the least number of possible extrema. Explain any strategies that relate to the values of the coefficients.

## RELATED INTERNET SITE(S)

### See **65. Interactive Pascal's Triangle**
These applets generate different rows of Pascal's Triangle. You can use the coefficient of each of these rows to represent the expansion of a polynomial from the form $(x + y)^n$.

### See **52. First and Second Derivative of $f(x) = a + bx + cx^2 + dx^3$**

### **Polynomial of Third Order**
(55a) http://www.univie.ac.at/future.media/moe/galerie/fun1/fun1.html#pol3
Modify any of the coefficients of a cubic polynomial and view changes in the

graph. You can also isolate individual coordinates on the graph and in the co-ordinate plane.

# 56. GALO EXAMPLE (IQ TESTS)

**URL: http://ebook.stat.ucla.edu/gifi/examples/galo/galo.html**

**SUGGESTED LEVELS**: statistics (questions 1–5)

**SITE SUMMARY**: This data set of over 1,000 boys and girls from a 1959 study represents the relationship between IQ score, sex, teacher's advice, and father's profession. Teachers' recommendations for contin-ued education are also provided in the data set.

**TOPICS**: data analysis, data display, normal distribution, outliers

## DISCUSSION QUESTIONS AND ACTIVITIES

1. How many people were in the study? How did you determine this information?

2. Which of the students appear to be unusually smart? Explain how you determined this result.

3. Generate a histogram that describes the IQ of the students. Devise a scale that would classify students as gifted, accelerated, average, be-low average, and at risk. Explain your criteria and how you deter-mined these values. Based on your classification scheme, which students do you feel had poor recommendations? Explain your rea-soning.

4. Was the teacher more likely to give advice based on IQ or father's occupation? Explain your analysis.

5. Did one sex perform significantly better on the IQ test? Explain your analysis.

## RELATED INTERNET SITE(S)

**Brain Size Data**

(56a) http://web.calstatela.edu/faculty/ssapra/datafile/brainsiz.htm

This data set compares brain size to IQ by including people's height, weight, MRI count, and performance on IQ tests.

See **(18c) The Normal Distribution**

See **(18a) Binomial Expansion—The Ball Drop**

See **(18b) Galton's Quincunx**

## 57. THE GAME OF CHAOS

### URL: http://www.mgw.dinet.de/physik/ChaosSpiel/ChaosEnglish. html

**SUGGESTED LEVELS**: geometry (questions 1–4), probability (questions 1–3)

**SITE SUMMARY**: This Java-based game uses chaos theory to generate the Sierpinski's Triangle. Play begins with a point placed inside a triangle, and the user simulates a die toss. Depending on the result of the toss, a new point will be constructed halfway between the original point and one of the triangle's vertices. The process continues until the points start forming a pattern. This exploration can be used to discuss chaos, fractals, probability, and similarity.

**TOPICS**: chaos, fractals, similarity, area of triangle, Sierpinski's Triangle, probability

## DISCUSSION QUESTIONS AND ACTIVITIES

1. Play the game where you have plenty of time. This feature will roll the die one by one. Roll the die several times by clicking on the screen. Describe how the points are being placed on the screen.

2. Go back to the initial page and play the game where you have little time (this means you will be running 100 trials for each click). Click on the screen until you have a total of 2,000 rolls. Describe the pattern you see. Start a new game, but start at a point far away from the starting point in your other game. Describe any similarities and differences in the results.

3. Why is the random distribution of points creating this image? Does it matter where you start in the triangle? What happens if you start on the triangle?

4. How are the triangles related? How do the areas of the triangles relate? If the area of the whole triangle is one, what is the area of the shaded region? Explain your computations.

## RELATED INTERNET SITE(S)

### Sierpinski's Triangle Using Pascal Coloring
(57a) http://www.cs.washington.edu/homes/jbaer/classes/blaise/blaise.html
This Java applet will illustrate patterns in Pascal's Triangle when examining the divisors in each of its terms. You can modify the divisor and then view a picture describing those terms that can or cannot be evenly divided by that di-

visor. Common divisors will appear black in the triangle, pointing out each of the medial triangles in the creation of Sierpinski's Triangle.

See **(17a)** and **(17b) Chaos Game**

**Iterations of Sierpinski's Triangle**
(57b) http://www.shodor.org/interactivate/activities/gasket/
(57c) http://math.rice.edu/~lanius/fractals/sierjava.html

These applets show you multiple stages of Sierpinski's Triangle by creating medial triangles. Instead of randomly plotting points, the triangles are generated by connecting the midpoints of each of the sides of the triangles. You can view up to eight iterations of similar triangles.

**Random Walk Applets**
(57d) http://reylab.bidmc.harvard.edu/DynaDx/abc/Random_walk/def.html

Examine patterns when an ant walks in random directions in one and two dimensions. This simulation models tossing a coin $n$ times. The investigation explores the frequency of steps needed to complete a full cycle, as well as the mean square distance the ant walks away from the starting position.

## 58. GENDER RELATED DEVELOPMENT INDEX

### URL: http://www.dartmouth.edu/~chance/teaching_aids/data/98gdi.htm

**SUGGESTED LEVELS**: prealgebra (questions 1, 2, 3, 4, and 6), algebra (questions 1–7), statistics (questions 1–7)

**SITE SUMMARY**: This data set reports the life expectancy, literacy rate, and shared family income for males and females in various countries around the world. The countries are divided by their perceived human development in 1995.

**TOPICS**: data collection, data analysis, data display, box and whisker plot, average, median, mean, linear equation, modeling, slope, y-intercept, center of gravity

### DISCUSSION QUESTIONS AND ACTIVITIES

1. Create three box and whisker plots comparing the expected life span of people in high, medium, and low human development countries. What can you conclude from these graphs? Explain why there might be differences between the graphs.

2. In general, which sex is expected to live longer? By how much? Explain your analysis.

3. What do the red numbers represent on the page? Explain how you determined this result.

4. Which countries have an unusual proportion of females who contribute to their shared family income? Explain why this might be true. Explain how you determined this result.

5. Find an equation relating the literacy rates of males and females in different countries. What do the slope and y-intercept represent in this solution? How do the red numbers on the page relate to the equation? Explain your analysis.

6. What factors not listed on the page influence these data? Explain.

7. Devise an analysis of a topic of your choosing by grouping countries by region. Explain how the results compare or differ from an analysis with individual countries.

## RELATED INTERNET SITE(S)

See **78. The Longevity Game**

# 59. GLOBAL TEMPERATURE DATA

## URL: http://www.cru.uea.ac.uk/ftpdata/tavegl.dat

**SUGGESTED LEVELS**: advanced algebra (questions 1 and 3), statistics (questions 1–5)

**SITE SUMMARY**: This data set illustrates the presence of global warming by presenting the average monthly temperature and percent distribution of that temperature around the world from 1856 to 1998. Each column represents a month from January to December; the first row of a year represents the average temperature around the world during each month of the year, while the second row of a year represents the percentage of the globe that attained the listed temperature each month.

**TOPICS**: data collection, data analysis, modeling data, scatter plot, function, outlier, extrapolation, hypothesis testing

## DISCUSSION QUESTIONS AND ACTIVITIES

1. Graph the average temperature in a year vs. the year since 1856. What type of function best models these data? Predict the average temperature around the world in the year 2100. Explain your analysis.

2. Which year(s) had unusually warm weather? Which year(s) had unusually cold weather? Explain your reasoning.

3. Graph the percentage of the world obtaining the average temperature in January vs. the year since 1856. What type of function best models these data? What percentage of the world should attain the average temperature in January in the year 2100? Explain your analysis. Would this percentage change for different months? Explain.

4. Which month of the year has mostly similar temperatures around the world? Explain how you determined this answer.

5. Are the modern temperatures evidence for global warming, or are these higher temperatures occurring due to random chance? Explain how you know.

## RELATED INTERNET SITE(S)

See **95. Normal Daily Maximum Temperature, Deg F**

**National Climatic Data Center CLIMVIS Time Series Data**
(59a) http://www.ncdc.noaa.gov/onlineprod/drought/xmgr.html
   This historical graph database illustrates time series data about local and global temperature, precipitation, temperature, drought, and contour plots.

**Hourly U.S. Weather Statistics**
(59b) http://www.ems.psu.edu/wx/usstats/uswxstats.html
   Obtain data each hour and graphs displaying twenty-four-hour patterns in national cloud cover, precipitation, temperature, wind, air pressure, heat index, and more.

## 60. GUESS THE NUMBER

**URL: http://www.geocities.com/EnchantedForest/Cottage/5124/Games/guess.html**

   **SUGGESTED LEVELS**: prealgebra (questions 1, 2, and 4), probability (questions 1–4)
   **SITE SUMMARY**: The goal of this game is to guess a number inclusively between one and ten within three chances of guessing. After each guess, the computer will tell you to guess higher or lower.
   **TOPICS**: simulation, data collection, data analysis, expected value, probability, conditional probability

## DISCUSSION QUESTIONS AND ACTIVITIES

1. Can you design a strategy that will enable you to win every time? Explain why or why not.

2. What is the best strategy to take so you can increase your chances in winning? Explain why.

3. Are your chances of winning most affected by your first guess or second guess? Explain why.

4. Suppose you are in charge of a fundraiser at a carnival. Your goal will be to earn $1,000 after 500 people play this game. How much should you charge each contestant to play the game, and how much will each winner receive? Explain your analyses.

## RELATED INTERNET SITE(S)

See **88. Monty Hall, Three Doors**

**Bop the Mole**
(60a) http://www.geocities.com/EnchantedForest/Cottage/5124/Games/mole.html

Click on as many moles as you can in the given time period. If you "bop" a mole, then you receive a point. If you miss, you lose a point.

See **(29a)–(29d) Reaction Time 2**

# 61. HOBBES' INTERNET TIMELINE

## URL: http://www.zakon.org/robert/internet/timeline/

**SUGGESTED LEVELS**: algebra (question 6), advanced algebra (questions 1–6)

**SITE SUMMARY**: This timeline describes the evolution of the Internet since the 1950s. Significant years of development are listed with annotations of historic events. Internet growth data describe the number of hosts, networks, and domains online since 1969. World Wide Web growth data illustrate the number of sites online since 1993.

**TOPICS**: data analysis, modeling data, exponential function, rate, extrapolation, line of best fit, linear function, slope, y-intercept

## DISCUSSION QUESTIONS AND ACTIVITIES

1. What rate describes the growth of Internet hosts since 1969? Explain your analysis.

2. Predict the current number of Internet hosts. Explain how you determined this result.

3. Predict the number of networks and domains before July 1989. Explain your analysis. Why is this information missing from the table?

4. The more accurate survey mechanism for measuring the number of Internet hosts was developed in 1998. Based on the new data, revise the number of hosts before 1995 and create a new Internet growth table. Explain your analysis.

5. The population of the United States and the world can be found at the U.S. Census Bureau, 139. http://wwww.census.gov. Will the number of Web sites ever exceed the population of the United States? If so, when? Explain your analysis. What assumptions are made in your analysis? Repeat this investigation using the world population.

6. Plot the number of Web sites as a function of Internet hosts. What does the slope and y-intercept describe in the line of best fit? What information can you predict using this line? Explain.

## RELATED INTERNET SITE(S)

**Internet Growth**
(61a) http://www.isc.org/ds/
(61b) http://www.mids.org/growth/internet/
(61c) http://forum.swarthmore.edu/articles/epadel/loghostssld004.gif
These data and graphs describe the number of domain hosts and their popularity on the Internet over time.

**Internet Access and Use, and Online Service Usage**
(61d) http://www.census.gov/statab/freq/99s0923.txt
This data set from the Statistical Abstract of the United States describes the availability and use of the Internet among U.S. adults from 1997 to 1999. Percent distribution data is categorized in terms of age, sex, census region, household size, marital status, educational attainment, employment, and income.

**Irresponsible Internet Statistics Generator**
(61e) http://www.anamorph.com/docs/stats/stats.html
This site predicts the number of Web sites and number of people on the Internet at specific moments from 1993 to 2003.

## 62. HOW DOES WHERE YOU LIVE SHAPE WHO YOU ARE?

### URL:http://survey2000.nationalgeographic.com/index.html

**SUGGESTED LEVELS**: prealgebra (questions 1–6)
**SITE SUMMARY**: National Geographic and Northwestern University developed a worldwide survey over the Web with over 8,000 partici-

pants. The survey results on the Web site include data describing, mobility, social world, food, music, literature, community, and kids.

**TOPICS**: data analysis, data display, mean, median, mode

## DISCUSSION QUESTIONS AND ACTIVITIES

1. Using the demographics category, find a data value written in bold
   face. Why is it written in bold? Explain how that number was calculated.

2. In the food category, which foods appear to be significantly more
   recognized in specific cultures? Provide a mathematical analysis to
   support your reasoning. Do you think these results accurately represent the world population? Explain why or why not.

3. Using the kids category, create a graph that best describes where the
   kids live around the world. Explain why you chose this specific type
   of graph instead of any other.

4. In the kids category, which measure of center is represented in each
   of the data sets: the mean, median, or mode? Calculate the other two
   measures of center and determine which of these would be the most
   accurate representation of this question. Explain your reasoning.

5. Using the kids category, click on the tab describing Activities/Inter-
   ests. Based on the data, what type of activities and interests do kids
   enjoy? Which activities do kids gain or lose interest in as they get
   older? Explain your answers.

6. Using the kids category, click on the tab describing Social world.
   Based on the data, how do boys' and girls' social interests differ?
   Explain your answer(s).

## RELATED INTERNET SITE(S)

**Student Surveys**
(62a) http://www.highland.madison.k12.il.us/jbasden/data/default.html
(62b)  http://gbs.glenbrook.k12.il.us/Academics/gbsmat/Internet%20Projects/
EGtemp/Pages/project.html
(62c) http://www.kff.org/content/1999/1535/
   These nationwide and worldwide surveys collected data about students' features, interests, and activities. You can search their databases to view the results.

See **139. U.S. Census Bureau**

**CIA World Fact Book at www.geographic.org**
(62d) http://www.theodora.com/wfb/abc_world_fact_book.html
   Provides data describing geography, people, government, economy, transportation, and defense for all of the countries around the world.

# 63. HYPERBOLA

## URL: http://www.exploremath.com/activities/Activity_page.cfm? ActivityID=5

SUGGESTED LEVELS: precalculus (questions 1–5)

SITE SUMMARY: ExploreMath.com has a dynamic hyperbola where you can adjust each of the coefficients of the equation in standard form and observe simultaneous changes in the graph. You can modify the viewing window of the graph, modify the center and length of the axes, view coordinates on the graph, and view a table that describe values of the function on any specified interval. Moreover, you can ask to see the asymptotes and view the string property associated with the definition of a hyperbola. You will need to download the Shockwave plugin because the activities were made with the tool Macromedia Director. You can see if you have the plugin, or download it, at (1a) http:// www.exploremath.com/about/shockerhelp.cfm.

TOPICS: conic sections, hyperbola, degenerate conic, limit, Pythagorean Theorem, asymptotes

## DISCUSSION QUESTIONS AND ACTIVITIES

1. Click on the "Show string property" box, and drag the mouse to different parts of the graph. The red points are the foci of the graph. Based on the values associated with the string property, how would you define a hyperbola using this information? How does your answer change if you modify the values of a, b, h, or k in the equation?

2. What happens graphically as you take the limit as a approaches 0? What about as b approaches 0? Why does this happen? Make a conjecture about these limits if they approached infinity instead of 0.

3. What do the values a, b, c, h, and k represent on the graph? Will the orange, red, and green points always have the same order? Explain why or why not.

4. What is the relationship between a, b, and c? Why is this true?

5. How do you determine the equation of the asymptotes of the hyperbola from the values in the equation? How does your answer change if you modify the values of h and k?

## RELATED INTERNET SITE(S)

See 35. Conic Sections as the Locus of Perpendicular Bisectors

## 64. THE INTERACTIVE MATH PUZZLE ARCHIVES

**URL: http://www.microtec.net/academy/mathpuzzle/interactive/index.html**

**SUGGESTED LEVELS**: advanced algebra (questions 1–7)

**SITE SUMMARY**: These puzzles provide the first set of numbers or letters in a sequence, and you need to complete the next few terms. Submit your answer and it will be checked.

**TOPICS**: sequence, recursive, explicit, golden ratio, ratio, function

### DISCUSSION QUESTIONS AND ACTIVITIES

1. What famous mathematician would solve puzzle #2 most quickly? Explain why. Continue generating terms of the sequence. What happens to the sequence describing the ratio of consecutive terms (e.g., $5/3, 8/5, 13/8 \ldots$) as you increase the number of terms? How would this result change if you started with a different number?

2. Solve puzzle #8 using two methods: a recursive *and* an explicit pattern. Explain both solutions.

3. Generate an explicit function to represent the sequence in puzzle #9. Explain your solution.

4. What function is represented in puzzle #18? What is significant about the ratio of consecutive terms? Why is this true?

5. What function is represented in puzzle #26? Is it possible to generate values of the sequence *before* the first term, 1? What is the greatest possible term of the sequence? Explain.

6. Solve as many other puzzles as you can and explain their solutions.

7. Generate your own sequence of five numbers and challenge a classmate to find the next three numbers.

### RELATED INTERNET SITE(S)

See **132. Towers of Hanoi**

**Online Encyclopedia of Integer Sequences**
(64a) http://www.research.att.com/~njas/sequences/index.html
Find references, names, and terms of sequences in a searchable database with over 50,000 sequences at AT&T.

# 65. INTERACTIVE PASCAL'S TRIANGLE

**URL: http://forum.swarthmore.edu/~ken/pascal.cgi**

**SUGGESTED LEVELS**: prealgebra (questions 1–3), advanced algebra (questions 1–5), precalculus (questions 1–5), probability (questions 1–4)

**SITE SUMMARY**: These sites allow you to generate Pascal's Triangle one row at a time. You input the number of rows you would like to see, and the screen will show all of these rows. These sites would be a good introduction to Pascal's Triangle, emphasizing patterns and mathematical connections. The related Internet sites following the questions are recommended extension activities for Pascal's Triangle.

**TOPICS**: Pascal's Triangle, series, combinations, binomial theorem, polynomial expansion, exponents, probability

## DISCUSSION QUESTIONS AND ACTIVITIES

1. Generate five rows of Pascal's Triangle. Identify as many numerical patterns as you can find.

2. Predict the sixth row of Pascal's Triangle. How can you generate consecutive rows if you are given the previous row?

3. How does the sum of the numbers in a row relate to its row number? In other words, the sum of row n will equal what?

4. How can you predict any number in any row of Pascal's Triangle with combinations, $_nC_r$?

5. How do the numbers of row n relate to the coefficients of the expansion of the polynomial $(x+y)^n$?

## RELATED INTERNET SITE(S)

**Calculating Chance (Pascal's Triangle)**
(65a) http://www.gsat.edu.au/educate/cp/mathweb/pascal/pascal.htm
Drop random balls into an isosceles triangle and observe patterns in where they land. The simulation is an effort to compare Pascal's Triangle with tree diagrams using two events that have equal probability.

**Discovering Patterns**
(65b) http://forum.swarthmore.edu/workshops/usi/pascal/mo.pascal.html
The Math Forum has created an interactive pattern recognition of Pascal's Triangle using Java Script. It illustrates the locations of natural numbers, triangular numbers, tetrahedral numbers, and Fibonacci numbers in Pascal's Triangle.

**Coloring Multiples and Remainders in Pascal's Triangle**
(65c) http://www.shodor.org/interactivate/activities/pascal1/index.html

(65d) http://scan.shodor.org/interactivate_dev/activities/pascal2/index.html
(65e) http://www.ies.co.jp/math/java/misc/PascalTriangle/PascalTriangle.html
(65f) http://jwilson.coe.uga.edu/EMT668/EMT668.Student.Folders/
BrombacherAarnout/spreadsheets/SpreadsheetsnPascal.html

These activities allow the user to investigate number patterns in Pascal's Triangle created by placement of multiples and remainders. You modify the multiple or remainder and notice changes in the coloring scheme in the triangle. Each color signifies a different multiple or remainder.

## 66. INTERNET ACCESS AND USE, AND ONLINE SERVICE USAGE

### URL: http://www.census.gov/statab/freq/99s0923.txt

**SUGGESTED LEVELS**: prealgebra (questions 1–3), statistics (questions 1–6)

**SITE SUMMARY**: This data set from the Statistical Abstract of the United States describes the availability and use of the Internet among U.S. adults from 1997 to 1999. Percent distribution data is categorized in terms of age, sex, census region, household size, marital status, educational attainment, employment, and income.

**TOPICS**: data analysis, percent, extrapolation

### DISCUSSION QUESTIONS AND ACTIVITIES

1. Do you think that Internet access at work has influenced access at home? Explain why or why not. Use data to support your answer.
2. Which of the results seem surprising? Explain why.
3. Is there a specific group of people who have access to but do not often use the Internet? Explain how you know.
4. What additional data and/or statistics would you need in order to determine whether marital status related to Internet use?
5. If the survey was administered this year, predict the number of people who would say they used the Internet at home during thirty days of this year.
6. Suppose you are an Internet Service Provider (ISP). Create an advertisement targeted at the group of people who use the Internet less often than other groups. Explain how you determined this target audience.

### RELATED INTERNET SITE(S)

See **(61a)**, **(61b)**, and **(61c) Internet Growth**
See **(61e) Irresponsible Internet Statistics Generator**

## 67. INTERNET PIZZA SERVER ORDERING AREA

**URL: http://www.ecst.csuchico.edu/~pizza/pizzaweb.html**

**SUGGESTED LEVELS**: algebra (question 1), geometry (questions 1 and 2)

**SITE SUMMARY**: The Internet Pizza Server will build free electronic graphical pizzas, allowing you to vary the pizza's size and toppings. When you visit the ordering area, you have the option to choose a wide array of standard, as well as atypical, pizza toppings. For instance, your pizza can be filled with basketballs, kittens, or Legos! After ordering a pizza, you view a graphical display along with its cost. You really do not buy the pizza, but the price gives you an excellent opportunity to compare the cost of a pizza to its size and the number of toppings it has. This data can be valuable when discussing functions and proportional reasoning.

**TOPICS**: domain, function, area of a circle, linear, quadratic, proportional reasoning, data collection, data analysis, equation

### DISCUSSION QUESTIONS AND ACTIVITIES

1. Order only medium pizzas with varied toppings and record the cost in the table below.

| # toppings | cost |
|------------|------|
| 0          |      |
| 1          |      |
| 2          |      |
| 3          |      |
| 4          |      |
| 5          |      |

Derive a function that will relate the cost of a pizza to the number of toppings it has. What does each number in the function represent?

Explain your solution. Does this function have any limitations within its domain? That is, can you apply this rule for any number of toppings? Explain.

2. Order only cheese pizzas with varied size and record the radius and cost in the table below.

| size | radius (cm) | cost |
|------|-------------|------|
| small |  |  |
| medium |  |  |
| large |  |  |
| family |  |  |

What additional factor do you need to consider before determining which pizza is the best buy? Explain which pizza would be the most economical purchase and provide mathematical justification to support your answer.

## RELATED INTERNET SITE(S)

**Mr. Pizza Man**
(67a) http://www.mrpizzaman.com/pizza/index.html
   Obtain prices for gourmet pizzas with multiple toppings. Click on the "first timer's" box to find additional information about the pizzas and how they are priced.

**Godfather's Pizza**
(67b) http://www.godfathers.com/comp_menu.htm
   Obtain sizes and coupons for their pizza store. Your challenge is to determine an appropriate price for their pizzas. You can also analyze nutritional facts for different pizzas.

**Create Your Own Pizzas at Pizza Hut**
(67c) http://www.panola.com/biz/pizzahut/create.htm
   An array of pricing information can help you predict the sizes and best deals for their pizza.

## 68. INTUITIVELY UNDERSTANDING THE INTEGRAL

### URL: http://www.univie.ac.at/future.media/moe/galerie/int/int.html #intuitiv

**SUGGESTED LEVELS**: calculus (questions 1–7)

**SITE SUMMARY**: This applet compares the graph of a function to the graph of its integral. Click on the red function and drag it. As you modify the red function, its integral function in blue will simultaneously change into a new form.

**TOPICS**: definite integral, derivative, increasing, decreasing, x-intercept

### DISCUSSION QUESTIONS AND ACTIVITIES

1. How can you determine when a function will have a definite integral equal to zero? Provide two explanations using both of the graphs.
2. What does the x-intercept on the graph of a function (red) represent on the graph on the integral (blue)? Explain why this is true.
3. What is true about a function if its integral function is always increasing? What is true about a function if its integral function is always decreasing? Explain why this is true.
4. Devise a graph of a function that is the same as its integral function. Explain how this is possible.
5. How can you tell when the integral function has an inflection point?
6. Create a graph of a function that can have six definite integrals equal to zero. Explain how each case has a definite integral equal to zero. Is it possible to create a graph of a function that can have five definite integrals equal to zero? Explain why or why not.
7. If the blue graph represents a function, what would the red graph represent? Explain how you know.

### RELATED INTERNET SITE(S)

See **50. Finding the Area Under a Curve**

See **(50a) Minimum Value of Integral of Function**

See **147–149. Xfunctions Xpresso**

## 69. INVERSE SQUARE LAW

**URL: http://jersey.uoregon.edu/vlab/InverseSquare/index.html**

**SUGGESTED LEVELS**: advanced algebra (questions 1–4), precalculus (questions 1–4)

**SITE SUMMARY**: These applets illustrate the relationship between the flux and the distance of a source from a star. You collect data by moving the cursor to a position away from the star and clicking the mouse button. You will see a point appear on a graph for every data point you collect. You can repeat the experiment for stars with varying luminosity.

**TOPICS**: data analysis, data collection, inverse square function, limit

### DISCUSSION QUESTIONS AND ACTIVITIES

1. What does the term "inverse square" represent in this situation?

2. Generate a function that describes the flux from a given distance and a given luminosity. Test the function using multiple luminosity graphs. Explain your analysis. What is the value of the flux as the distance from the star approaches zero? Explain why.

3. Will all of the data points lie on the estimated curve? Explain why or why not.

4. What function would describe the flux with respect to the distance away from a star with $8 \times 10^6$ lumens? Explain your analysis.

### RELATED INTERNET SITE(S)

See **116. Simulated Ocean Dive**

## 70. INVESTIGATING PARALLELOGRAMS

**URL: http://forum.swarthmore.edu/~annie/gsp.handouts/pgram/**

**SUGGESTED LEVELS**: geometry (questions 1–5)

**SITE SUMMARY**: This applet of a parallelogram allows you to drag the vertices and view changes in the measures of its angles and lengths.

**TOPICS**: parallelogram, diagonal, bisect, quadrilateral properties, perpendicular

## DISCUSSION QUESTIONS AND ACTIVITIES

1. Create at least three questions about the figure that you could ask someone else in order to determine specific properties of the parallelograms. Write solutions to those questions, including an explanation of what you would expect someone to observe on the screen.

2. Susan claims that the diagonals of a parallelogram bisect each other. If her reasoning is sound, how did she figure that out? If her reasoning doesn't make sense, what information would you need to know in order for her to make that claim?

3. Can your figure turn into a square at some point? Explain how you can tell. How about a rectangle? A rhombus? A kite? A trapezoid? Explain each case.

4. Is it possible to turn the figure into a triangle? Explain why or why not.

5. What figure(s) do you form when the diagonals are perpendicular? Explain how you determined this result.

## RELATED INTERNET SITE(S)

**Identifying Polygons**
(70a) http://mathforum.com/~annie/gsp.handouts/quiz/
   Dynamically monitor the changes in the lengths and angle measures of a parallelogram and an isosceles triangle as you modify its vertices.
**Name This Quadrilateral**
(70b)    http://forum.swarthmore.edu/geopow/solutions/solution.ehtml?puzzle =19
   This problem uses Java to help you visualize a quadrilateral that has one pair of opposite sides congruent, the other pair not congruent, and a pair of opposite angles that are supplementary.
See **(25b) Area of a Parallelogram**
See **(25c)** and **(25d) Area of Triangle**
**Sum of Angles in a Triangle**
(70c) http://home.a-city.de/walter.fendt/me/anglesum.htm
   Drag around the vertices of a triangle and notice how each of the angles change in relation to the angles formed by lines that determine the triangle.

# 71. A JUGGLING PATTERN ANIMATOR

## URL: http://www.juggling.org/programs/java/nichols/

**SUGGESTED LEVELS**: prealgebra (questions 1, 4, and 5), algebra (questions 1–5), advanced algebra (questions 1–5), precalculus (questions 1–6)

**SITE SUMMARY**: This applet simulates juggling multiple balls. You can adjust the height, speed, startup position, and number of balls in the pattern. You will need a ruler and stop watch to collect data.

**TOPICS**: data collection, data analysis, position, time, speed, modeling, linear function, quadratic function, sinusoidal function

## DISCUSSION QUESTIONS AND ACTIVITIES

1. How does the height of the ball (gravity) affect the time to travel from one hand to another? Explain how you determined this result.

2. Generate an equation that relates the numeric value of the speed to the time it takes a ball to travel between hands. Explain the significance of the coefficients in the equation.

3. Generate an equation that relates the height of the ball (cm) to the gravity equivalent. Explain the significance of the coefficients in the equation.

4. How does the number of balls affect the juggling pattern? Explain how the pattern of the balls relates to the number of balls in the pattern. Explain how the pattern relates to the value in the startup position.

5. Which startup and pattern combinations require you to hold two balls at the same time? Explain how you determined this result.

6. Derive a sinusoidal function that relates the horizontal position of any given ball after t seconds. Explain your analysis.

## RELATED INTERNET SITE(S)

**How to Juggle**
(71a) http://www.acm.uiuc.edu/webmonkeys/juggling
  This site demonstrates an animated introduction to juggling. Step by step procedures are shown as the process gets more challenging with more balls.

## 72. LEAST SQUARES REGRESSION APPLET

## URL: http://www.keypress.com/sketchpad/java_gsp/squares.html

**SUGGESTED LEVELS**: statistics (questions 1–4)
**SITE SUMMARY**: The goal in this applet is to understand how the least squares regression line of best fit is created to model a set of data. The user can move up to six data points around the screen, and then modify the slope and y-intercept of a regression line to determine its best

fit. The applet illustrates the sums of the squares of the deviations by showing the relative areas of squares created as the regression line is modified.

**TOPICS**: least squares regression line, line of best fit, equation of line, slope, y-intercept, area of a square, deviation, error, outlier

## DISCUSSION QUESTIONS AND ACTIVITIES

1. Why are squares used to represent the amount of error between the data and the regression line? When you modify the slope and y-intercept, can you find a regression line that produces the least amount of error? Most amount of error? Explain.

2. Modify the data points, the slope, and/or the y-intercept so that the total area of the squares is equal to zero. Determine the relationship between the data and the line in this situation. If you do not move the data, is it possible to create another line of best fit that will produce a total area of the squares equal to zero? Explain why or why not.

3. The least squares regression line has a slope and y-intercept that will produce the least amount of error between a data set and a line. If you have data points that lie on two parallel paths, where would you place the least squares regression line? Explain.

4. An outlier is a data point far above or far below the regression line. Create a least squares regression line with the data on the screen and then drag one of the points far away from the line. Modify the slope and y-intercept of the regression line until you have a minimum error. How does the least squares regression line change when you introduce an outlier? Explain why these changes occur.

## RELATED INTERNET SITE(S)

**Linear Regression Applet**
(72a) http://www.mste.uiuc.edu/activity/regression/
Plot points on a graph and observe changes in error when you modify the slope of the regression line. You can predict the location of the least squares regression line, and then check your answer with the computer's response.

**The Least Squares Line**
(72b) http://www.ies.co.jp/math/java/misc/least_sq/least_sq.html
Plot points on a graph and determine the regression line by modifying the slope and y-intercept. You can view the changes in the equation and the sum of the squared deviations as you modify the slope and y-intercept.

**Simple Regression**
(72c) http://www.hofstra.edu/~matscw/newgraph/regressionframes.html

Enter a data set and receive a linear or quadratic regression function and the predicted y-values for each of your data points.

**Linear Regression**

(72d) http://chemmac1.usc.edu/bruno/java/linreg.html

(72e) http://suzy.unl.edu/bruno/java/linreg.html

Enter data points and the Java applet will give you the equation of the least squares regression line and graph the data and regression line. Both URLs have the same applet.

# 73. THE LIMACON

## URL: http://www15.addr.com/~dscher/limacon.html

**SUGGESTED LEVELS**: precalculus (questions 1–4)

**SITE SUMMARY**: Daniel Scher has used JavaSketchPad to demonstrate a construction of a limacon using a circle, a line tangent to the circle, a floating point, and a line perpendicular to the tangent and passing through the point. The Java applet allows you to drag the construction and trace a locus at the intersection of the two perpendicular lines, as well as modify the floating point to see multiple constructions of a limacon. Click Refresh or Reload on your browser to start over.

**TOPICS**: limacon, polar graphing, cardioid, circle, cosine

## DISCUSSION QUESTIONS AND ACTIVITIES

1. How does the location of the external point, P, relate to the shape of the limacon? Explain all possible cases.

2. Devise a rule that will predict the location where the limacon intersects the circle in the construction. Explain how you determined this result. Why do you think this might be true?

3. Why does this construction produce this shape?

4. The equation of a limacon in polar form is $y = b + 2acosx$. Determine how each of these parts is related to the construction. In other words, what do y, b, and 2acosx represent on the graph?

## RELATED INTERNET SITE(S)

**Limacon of Pascal**

(73a) http://www-groups.cs.st-and.ac.uk/history/Java/Limacon.html

(73b) http://www-history.mcs.st-andrews.ac.uk/~history/Java/Limacon.html

(73c) http://www-groups.mcs.st-and.ac.uk/~history/Java/Limacon.html

This Java applet allows you to modify the parameters of the equation of a limacon in polar form, y = b + 2acosx. Each time you change the value of a or b, you instantly see modifications on the graph. Each of these URLs contains the same Java applet.

**Limacon (GSP)**
(73d) http://www.mathlove.or.kr/GSP/limacon.htm
This dynamic limacon was created with Java SketchPad. The construction is based on two tangent circles where you trace a locus of a point on a circle by dragging the center of that circle around another circle.

# 74. LINEAR EQUATIONS

## URL: http://randy.bower.com/graph/index.html

**SUGGESTED LEVELS**: algebra (questions 1–6)
**SITE SUMMARY**: Graph any linear function of the form ax + by = c. You can graph many lines on the same coordinate plane in order to generate patterns and discover relationships that relate to properties of lines. Each line is graphed with a different color with corresponding equation.
**TOPICS**: linear function, linear equation, graph, origin, parallel, perpendicular, slope, reflection, vertical line, x-intercept, y-intercept

## DISCUSSION QUESTIONS AND ACTIVITIES

1. How can you tell when a line of the form ax + by = c passes through the origin? Explain.

2. How can you tell when two lines with different coefficients of the form ax + by = c are the same exact line? Explain.

3. How can you tell when two lines of the form ax + by = c are parallel? Perpendicular? Explain.

4. What is the slope of a line of the form ax + by = c? Explain how you determined this result.

5. How can you tell when two lines of the form ax + by = c are reflections over a vertical line? Explain.

6. What happens to the intercepts when you reverse the order of a and b? What happens to the slope in this situation? Explain how you determined these results.

## RELATED INTERNET SITE(S)

**Line Graphing Applet**
(74a) http://216.247.77.187/algebra/lines/graph_applet.html

This applet illustrates the relationship between the slope, y-intercept, equation, and graph of a line. You have the option to translate and rotate the graph, and see changes in the values of the slope and y-intercept. The applet will also state the corresponding ordered pair where your mouse pointer is located in the Cartesian plane.

See **118. Slope**
Modify two points on a coordinate plane and observe changes in the slope and equation of a line in a Java applet.

**Interactive Algebra (select graphing)**
(74b) http://www.accessone.com/~bbunge/Algebra/Algebra.html
These Java applets test your understanding of associating the graph of a line with its equation.

**Function Graphers**
(74c) http://www.frontiernet.net/~imaging/graph_my_equation.html
(74d)    http://www.ycef.com/VGame/math/graph_plotters/tFunction/index.html
(74e) http://www.shodor.org/interactivate/activities/sketcher/index.html
(74f) http://www.ugrad.cs.jhu.edu/~russell/classes/grapher/
(74g) http://www.garrink.com/java/graph/
(74h) http://www.info.ucl.ac.be/people/chp/java/function/index.html
(74i) http://members.tripod.com/~gvogl/graph/graph.htm
(74j) http://www.javathings.com/graphapplet.asp
These Java applets will graph a function to a specified window.

## 75. LINEAR FUNCTION MACHINE

### URL: http://www.shodor.org/interactivate/activities/lfm/index.html

**SUGGESTED LEVELS**: algebra (questions 1–4)
**SITE SUMMARY**: This Java Script function machine from the Shodor Foundation challenges you to guess the equation of a linear function based on data values that are input and output from the machine. You start by entering a value into the X = box, click Enter, and then see a value show up in the Y = box. You can repeat this process or guess the equation that is running the function machine by clicking on Check Formula.
**TOPICS**: function, equation of a line

## DISCUSSION QUESTIONS AND ACTIVITIES

1. Start the game by typing a value into X= and click Enter. Is this information sufficient to be sure of the answer? Explain why or why not.

2. Play the game until you find a correct equation. How can you use your formula to predict what the function machine will give in the Y= box after you enter any value in the X= box? Justify your reasoning with calculations. How will you know if your method works?

3. Enter and record a variety of x-values, and make sure you repeat some of your entries. Will you ever get a different y-value for the same x-value entered? Explain why or why not. Is this possible for any function? Explain why or why not. Draw a picture or graph to support your reasoning.

4. Will you ever get the same y-value when different x-values are entered? Explain why or why not. Is this possible for any function? Explain why or why not. Draw a picture or graph to support your reasoning.

## RELATED INTERNET SITE(S)

See **(74a) Line Graphing Applet**

**Graphing a Line (y = mx + b)**
(75a) http://www.accessone.com/~bbunge/Algebra/Algebra3–3.html
  Given an equation of a line, your goal is to successfully graph the line by identifying the y-intercept and another point on the line. The computer will guide you through the process and give you feedback.

**Function Machines**
(75b) http://www.shodor.org/interactivate/activities/plfm/index.html
(75c) http://www.shodor.org/interactivate/activities/fm/index.html
  These Shodor Foundation games are simpler versions of the Linear Function Machine, where either the y-intercept is set to zero or the slope is strictly positive.

**IES Linear Function Machine**
(75d) http://www.ies.co.jp/math/java/geo/linf/linf.html
(75e) http://www.ies.co.jp/math/java/geo/linfg/linfg.html
  These Java applets show how a function takes input values, processes them, and then reveals an output value. In the second applet, you need to use a linear representation to determine the output values from the machine.

## 76. LOCUS OF CRITICAL POINTS

**URL: http://jwilson.coe.uga.edu/EMT668/EMAT6680.F99/Glazer/essays/locus/criticalpoint.html**

  **SUGGESTED LEVELS**: advanced algebra (questions 1–2), precalculus (questions 1–4), calculus (questions 1–6)
  **SITE SUMMARY**: This series of explorations examines the patterns

established between critical points (inflection points and relative extrema) of a function when one of its coefficients is modified and the others are kept constant. There are four interactive diagrams that describe polynomial functions and two that relate to asymptotic functions. Use the navigation bar at the left to look at the applets. The first applet may be slow to load, but the remaining applets should appear quickly.

**TOPICS**: completing the square, relative minimum, relative maximum, extrema, inflection point, derivative, function, proof, asymptote, limit, quadratic function, cubic function

## DISCUSSION QUESTIONS AND ACTIVITIES

1. In terms of a, b, and c, what are the coordinates of the vertex of a parabola? Explain how you determined this result.

2. Modify the leading coefficient, a, of the quadratic function. What type of function or relation does the vertex trace? How do you know? Find the equation of this function or relation. Repeat these questions for modifying b and c in the function.

3. In the investigation with one vertical and one slant asymptote, what are the equations of the asymptotes? Explain how you determined this result.

4. What type of coefficient in a function produces a vertical translation? Explain why. Indicate all cases.

5. Modify the leading coefficient, a, of the cubic function that will trace its inflection points. What type of function or relation do the inflection points trace? How do you know? Find the equation of this function or relation. Repeat these questions for modifying b, c, and d in the function. Explain your analysis.

6. Modify the constant, a, of the function with two vertical and one horizontal asymptotes. What type of function or relation does the relative extremum trace? How do you know? Find the equation of this function or relation. Repeat these questions for modifying b, c, and d in the function. Explain your analysis.

## RELATED INTERNET SITE(S)

See **111. Quadratics: Polynomial Form**

**Derivative Puzzles**
(76a) http://www.univie.ac.at/future.media/moe/galerie/diff1/diff1.html
(76b) http://www.univie.ac.at/future.media/moe/tests/diff1/ablerkennen.html
These activities test your understanding of the relationship between the graph of a function to the graphs of its first and second derivatives.

## 77. LOG HOME FLOORPLANS

### URL: http://www.homebuyerpubs.com/foorplans/floorplans.htm

**SUGGESTED LEVELS**: algebra (questions 5–6), geometry (questions 1–4)

**SITE SUMMARY**: This set of floorplans gives detailed information about the dimensions of many log homes. Some of the homes list pricing information.

**TOPICS**: data collection, data analysis, modeling data, area, function, percent, extrapolation, interpolation

### DISCUSSION QUESTIONS AND ACTIVITIES

1. Suppose you are hired by a company to design log homes. What percentage of the floorplan would you reserve for the bedrooms? Explain your analysis.
2. Design a trapezoidal-shaped kitchen in a house with 1,200 square feet in its floorplan. Explain why you used these dimensions.
3. Find a floorplan that lists some, but not all, of its dimensions. Determine the missing dimensions. Explain how you found your measurements.
4. A buyer would like a one-story 2,100-square-foot floorplan in the shape of a concave irregular hexagon. Design a possible floorplan and verify that the house will be constructed according to the buyers' specifications.
5. Predict the cost of one of the homes that does not have an available price. Explain your analysis.
6. Predict the cost of a house with 4,000 square feet. Explain your analysis.

### RELATED INTERNET SITE(S)

See **112. Realtor.com Find a Home**
See **(112d) Home Prices**

## 78. THE LONGEVITY GAME

### URL: http://www.northwesternmutual.com/games/longevity/

**SUGGESTED LEVELS**: prealgebra (questions 1–5), algebra (question 6)

**SITE SUMMARY**: Input characteristics about yourself and your lifestyle and find your estimated life expectancy. Characteristics such as fitness, diet, alcohol, smoking, heredity, and blood pressure are taken into consideration. Your life expectancy is continuously updated in the upper left portion of the screen as you answer each question.

**TOPICS**: data collection, data analysis, function, range

## DISCUSSION QUESTIONS AND ACTIVITIES

1. How much longer are females expected to live than males? Is this true for every circumstance? Explain your reasoning.

2. Which factor produces the greatest risk to your life? Explain how you know. Which factor is least influential on your life expectancy? Explain how you know.

3. According to the game, what is the range in possible life expectancies? Explain how you know. Is it possible to live longer or shorter than your expectancy? If not, explain why. If yes, explain how.

4. A long lost cousin finds out that his life expectancy is sixty-five years old. Create a profile that describes some possible characteristics about him and his lifestyle. Design a plan that will help him add fifteen years to his life.

5. What part of the survey seems to inaccurately affect life expectancy? Explain why, and justify your response.

6. Complete the survey. Go back and increase your age by five years, press tab, and record the new age and life expectancy (it may be the same). Repeat the process until you reach 100 years old. What type of function best represents this data? Explain your reasoning. Change some characteristics about yourself and repeat the analysis with the new data. Compare and contrast your results with the first graph.

## RELATED INTERNET SITE(S)

**Target Heart Rate Calculator**
(78a) http://www.stevenscreek.com/goodies/hr.shtml
  Examine the relationship between the efficiency of your maximum heart rate when compared with your age and activity level.

See **120. Smoking and Cancer**

See **62. How Does Where You Live Shape Who You Are?**

See **(62a), (62b),** and **(62c) Student Surveys**

## 79. MAJOR LEAGUE BASEBALL LEAGUE LEADERS

URL: http://www.mlb.com/NASApp/mlb/mlb/stats_historical/
mlb_stats_historical_entry.jsp

**SUGGESTED LEVELS**: prealgebra (questions 1–6), statistics (questions 1–6)

**SITE SUMMARY**: The official major league baseball site provides updated data on the all-time and single season leaders throughout the history of the sport. Statistics are available for a large number of categories including hitting, games played, pitching, and base running. Awards, honors, and historical information are also available through this page.

**TOPICS**: data collection, data analysis, modeling, extrapolation

### DISCUSSION QUESTIONS AND ACTIVITIES

1. What categories would you look at to determine the best pitcher of all time? Explain why you chose these categories. Design a set of criteria that will help you combine these categories in order to determine the best pitcher of all time. Who is the best pitcher of all time according to your criteria? Explain your results.

2. When calculating the number of innings pitched, what number base is represented by the digit to the right of the decimal place? What number base is represented by the digits to the left of the decimal place? Explain why there may or may not be any differences in these results.

3. If a player is on the games played leader list, then what other all-time leader list would he most likely be on? Explain how you determined this result.

4. Devise a function that will predict the number of career hits a player would have based on his number of at-bats. Explain how you determined this function and the baseball significance of each of the numbers in the function.

5. Baseball has been around for over a century, but many of the best records occur in a small time frame. Look at the single season leaders in different categories. Explain why some categories would have better performances in the first half of the twentieth century, and vice versa.

6. Assuming that most superstar baseball players will retire by the age of forty-two, which active player is most likely to break the all time home run record? Explain how you determined this result. In what

year will that record most likely take place? Explain how you determined this result.

## RELATED INTERNET SITE(S)

See **146. World-Wide Track & Field Statistics On-Line**

See **(14b)** and **(14c) Sports Statistics**

# 80. MATH SURVEY PROJECT

**URL: http://gbs.glenbrook.k12.il.us/Academics/gbsmat/
Internet%20Projects/EGtemp/Pages/project.html**

**SUGGESTED LEVELS**: prealgebra (questions 1–4), statistics (questions 1–4)

**SITE SUMMARY**: This survey project asked students from a middle school and high school to answer questions about themselves, their interests, and their culture. Data from over 150 student responses can be searched and categorized in terms of survey question, school, and student's sex.

**TOPICS**: data collection, data analysis, outliers, statistical significance, correlation

## DISCUSSION QUESTIONS AND ACTIVITIES

1. Go over the survey and pick a question that interests you. Search the database, and determine if there are any significant differences in the responses according to school and/or sex. Explain your analysis.

2. Which data points seem unreasonable? Explain how you determined this result. Why do you think the student(s) gave an unreasonable answer?

3. Does the number of hours of television watched relate to the number of books read? Does your age or sex make a difference in the results? Explain your analysis for each individual group of students, as well as for the whole data set.

4. Find two questions that you think might have strongly related results. For example, maybe students who sleep more usually tend to eat breakfast less often. This relationship may or may not be true. Choose two data sets and analyze the data to see if they are strongly related. The order of the data from students on the screen is identical for every

student; for example, the eighth person to answer the survey will have the eighth data point in each of the data sets. Explain your analysis.

## RELATED INTERNET SITE(S)

See **139. U.S. Census Bureau**

See **(62d) CIA World Fact Book at www.geographic.org**

See **62. How Does Where You Live Shape Who You Are?**

# 81. MATHEMATICAL QUOTATION SERVER

## URL: http://math.furman.edu/~mwoodard/mqs/mquot.shtml

**SUGGESTED LEVELS**: math history (questions 1–7)

**SITE SUMMARY**: This site has over eighty-three pages of historical quotations related to all facets of mathematics.

**TOPICS**: math history

## DISCUSSION QUESTIONS AND ACTIVITIES

1. Give a real-world example of Paul Valery's quote. Can you find a counterexample to this claim? How might the time period of Valery's life have influenced his judgment?

2. What type of lifestyle do you think Paul Erdos had? Can you make this argument for another profession, or do you think the nature of the individual influences this quote? Explain your analysis.

3. How did Gauss view the world? How does he make connections between mathematical reasoning and society? Do you agree with these perspectives? Explain.

4. Identify a cynical quotation. What are some possible causes for this type of comment?

5. Find an inspirational quote from Albert Einstein. Explain what he meant by his remarks.

6. Find a quote that interests you. Explain why this interests you.

7. Devise your own quote about mathematics. Explain why you feel this way.

## RELATED INTERNET SITE(S)

**The MacTutor History of Mathematics Archive**
(81a) http://www-groups.dcs.st-and.ac.uk/~history/

This database has a series of history topics, biographies of mathematicians, famous curves, and more.

**History of Mathematics Home Page**
(81b) http://aleph0.clarku.edu/~djoyce/mathhist/mathhist.html
This page contains historical documents, such as references to Euclid's Elements and Hilbert's address about twenty-three important problems.

**Biographies of Women Mathematicians**
(81c) http://www.agnesscott.edu/lriddle/women/women.htm
This database gives credit to the mathematical accomplishments of women in the history of mathematics.

# 82. MAXIMIZE AREA

## URL: http://www.exploremath.com/activities/Activity_page.cfm? ActivityID=42

**SUGGESTED LEVELS**: algebra (questions 1 and 2), geometry (question 4), advanced algebra (questions 1–6), calculus (questions 1–6)

**SITE SUMMARY**: ExploreMath.com has an interactive rectangle with a corresponding area vs. base graph. A point on the area vs. base graph will simultaneously update each time you move a part of the rectangle. You can modify individual dimensions of a rectangle or produce a scale change by modifying the perimeter. You can modify the viewing window of the graph, view a trace of the path of a coordinate, view critical coordinates on the graph, and view a table that describes values of the function on any specified interval. You will need to download the Shockwave plugin because the activities were made with the tool Macromedia Director. You can see if you have the plugin, or download it, at (1a) http://www.exploremath.com/about/shockerhelp.cfm.

**TOPICS**: linear function, quadratic function, graph, area of rectangle, perimeter, optimization, maximum, hyperbola, regular polygon

## DISCUSSION QUESTIONS AND ACTIVITIES

1. Modify each of the variables using the sliders. What type of function is generated on the graph in each situation? Explain your analysis.

2. What is the best graphing window for the perimeters available on the slider? Explain how you determined this result.

3. Based on a fixed perimeter, what type of function would be represented when comparing the base and height? Explain how you know.

4. How would the graph change if you were looking at the area of a different quadrilateral? The area of a regular polygon?

5. Click on Show/Hide curve. How does the perimeter affect the equation of the graph? Prove this conjecture algebraically.

6. What perimeter values will produce a maximum area that is an integer? Explain your analysis.

## RELATED INTERNET SITE(S)

See **83. Maximizing the Area of a Field with Fixed Diameter**
See **110. Quadratic Equations 2**
See **111. Quadratics: Polynomial Form**

# 83. MAXIMIZING THE AREA OF A FIELD WITH FIXED DIAMETER

**URL: http://home.netvigator.com/~wingkei9/javagsp/maxarea. html**

**SUGGESTED LEVELS**: algebra (questions 1–3), advanced algebra (questions 1–5), calculus (questions 1–5)
**SITE SUMMARY**: You are given an interactive rectangle with fixed perimeter equal to eight units. You can modify the length of the sides by dragging X on the screen. You will see the graph of a locus of points that represent the area of the rectangular region as a function of its side length. Your task is to determine the dimensions of a rectangle that will produce a rectangle with maximum area. Click on the refresh or reload button on your browser to clear the locus of points.
**TOPICS**: quadratic function, graph, area of rectangle, perimeter, optimization, maximum, x-intercepts

## DISCUSSION QUESTIONS AND ACTIVITIES

1. What type of function is generated by the locus of points? Explain how you know.

2. How are the x-intercepts from the graph represented in the rectangle?

3. What is the maximum area of the rectangle? Verify this result using as many algebraic methods as you can think of.

4. Suppose you are going to repeat this investigation with a different fixed perimeter. How can you predict the maximum area of the rectangle with any perimeter? Explain your analysis.

5. Suppose the rectangular region represented an area for a horse pen. If you have a fixed amount of fencing, how does the shape of the

region with maximum area change if you use a barn as one side of the fence, and the fencing to cover the other three sides? Explain your analysis.

## RELATED INTERNET SITE(S)

See **82. Maximize Area**

See **(100a) Exploring Parabolas (Java SketchPad)**

See **110. Quadratic Equations 2**

See **106. Projectile Motion Applet**

# 84. MEASUREMENT CONVERTER

## URL: http://www.convert-me.com/en/

**SUGGESTED LEVELS**: algebra (questions 1–5), advanced algebra (questions 1–5)

**SITE SUMMARY**: This site will convert various forms of measurement, such as weight, capacity and volume, length, area, speed, pressure, temperature, circular measure, and time. The conversions are performed through a Java Script form that will show equivalent representations of a measurement in a different array of units. Enter in one value and the computer will respond with the remaining equivalent measurements.

**TOPICS**: proportions, linear functions, composite functions, data collection, data analysis, units, slope, y-intercept, equation of a line

## DISCUSSION QUESTIONS AND ACTIVITIES

1. Click on the link for converting speed measurements. Enter a value in the kilometers-per-hour box and click on the miles-per-hour box to notice the equivalent measurement. Create a data table with these two variables, and find at least five more kilometers-per-hour measurements that correspond with miles-per-hour measurements. Use the data table to write a function that relates kilometers-per-hour to miles per hour. State the real-world significance of the slope and y-intercept of this function.

2. Could you create equivalent proportions with the data in problem 1? Explain why or why not.

3. Return to the starting page, and click on the link for converting temperature measurements. Enter a value in the degrees Kelvin box and click on the degrees Fahrenheit box to notice the equivalent measure-

ment. Create a data table with these two variables, and find at least five more degrees Kelvin measurements that correspond with degrees Fahrenheit measurements. Use the data table to write a function that relates degrees Kelvin to degrees Fahrenheit. State the real-world significance of the slope and y-intercept of this function.

4. Could you create equivalent proportions with the data in problem 3? Explain why or why not.

5. Generate data from the temperature measurement page and create a function relating degrees Celsius to degrees Kelvin. Without using the data, explain how you could use this function with the function in problem 3 to create a new function relating degrees Celsius to degrees Fahrenheit.

### RELATED INTERNET SITE(S)

See **138. The Universal Currency Converters**

**Base Converters**
(84a) http://www.geocities.com/Heartland/Village/3757/Eric/basecnvrtr.html
(84b)http://www.objectsfusion.com/javascripts/scripts/script112.html
(84c)http://www.fiu.edu/~alacam01/base.htm
(84d)http://hubcap.clemson.edu/~nglover/convert.html
(84e)http://www-scf.usc.edu/~zkyaw/converter.html
(84f)http://cosmo.marymount.edu/~edf75971/convert.html
   These converters will show you alternate versions of the same number in different bases.

## 85. MEASURING TREE HEIGHT

### URL: http://cgee.hamline.edu/Fall/height.html

**SUGGESTED LEVELS**: geometry (question 7), precalculus (questions 1–6)
**SITE SUMMARY**: Examine different methods that will calculate the height of a tree. You are given diagrams and a text description for each case.
**TOPICS**: trigonometry, angles, right triangle, tetrahedron, Law of Cosines, Law of Sines, similarity, proportion, unit conversion

## DISCUSSION QUESTIONS AND ACTIVITIES

1. Does method one work? Does it matter what type of object you are holding? Draw a three-dimensional diagram and use trigonometry to prove or disprove this case.

2. Will method two always work? Does the distance from the tree or the height of the tree matter? What type of triangle is assumed in the diagram? Explain your reasoning.

3. Suppose you attached a protractor to the clinometer in method 3 and you did not know your own height. If you knew how far you were standing from the tree, then how would you determine the height of the tree? Explain your reasoning.

4. What assumption(s) is made about trees in all of these methods?

5. Is it possible to measure the height of the tree using only angle measurements? Explain why or why not.

6. How would you find the height of a mountain? Explain your procedures, and devise a general formula that can compute the height with one input.

7. Devise a method to find the height of a tree that would use similarity. Explain your procedures and why the method will work.

## RELATED INTERNET SITE(S)

See **(3a) The Law of Sines**

See **(3b)** and **(3c) The Law of Cosines**

## 86. MIDPOINTS OF ANY QUADRILATERAL

**URL: http://home.netvigator.com/~wingkei9/javagsp/midpt.html**

**SUGGESTED LEVELS**: geometry (questions 1–5)

**SITE SUMMARY**: The goal of this page is to explore the relationship between a quadrilateral and the medial quadrilateral, the quadrilateral formed by connecting midpoints from its consecutive sides. You are given a dynamic quadrilateral, trapezium, parallelogram, rhombus, rectangle, and a square to manipulate.

**TOPICS**: medial quadrilateral, midpoint, nonconvex, concave, area of a quadrilateral, area of a triangle, symmetry, quadrilateral, trapezium, trapezoid, parallelogram, rhombus, rectangle, square

## DISCUSSION QUESTIONS AND ACTIVITIES

1. What medial quadrilateral is formed in every diagram? Explain how you know. What would you measure on the diagram to verify this claim? Why?

2. How does the medial quadrilateral change if the figure is nonconvex? Explain how this is possible.

3. Which figure(s) will create a more specific medial quadrilateral? Explain how you know.

4. How does the area of the quadrilateral relate to the area of the medial quadrilateral? Explain why. How would this answer be different from a medial triangle formed by connecting consecutive midpoints of any triangle? Explain.

5. In the last diagram titled "further question," find a way to join A and D'. Once the points are overlapping, you can drag them together. Why does this happen? Drag the joined point until the figure is a triangle. How many ways is this possible? How does the area of the figure inside the triangle relate to the area of the triangle? Explain how you know.

## RELATED INTERNET SITE(S)

**Quadrilaterals and Conservation of Area**
(86a) http://www.ies.co.jp/math/java/geo/quadri.html
These applets relate to nonroutine area problems about transforming the shape of an object while preserving its area.

See **(25b) Area of a Parallelogram**

**Midpoint Theorem**
(86b) http://home.netvigator.com/~wingkei9/javagsp/mid-thm.html
Explore the relationship between the base of a triangle and the segment formed by connecting the midpoints of the remaining two sides.

## 87. MONTE CARLO ESTIMATION FOR PI

**URL: http://polymer.bu.edu/java/java/montepi/montepiapplet.html**

**SUGGESTED LEVELS**: geometry (questions 1–2), probability (questions 1–4), statistics (questions 1–4)
**SITE SUMMARY**: A Monte Carlo simulation allows you to place random points in a region to help determine its area by examining the ratio

of times the points land inside the region to the total number of points. This Java applet is designed to allow the user to throw darts (place points on the screen) 1, 100, 1,000, or 10,000 at a time. This feature can provide opportunities for investigations about pi, asymptotic behavior, binomial distributions, and the central limit theorem.

**TOPICS**: simulation, area of a square, area of a circle, binomial distribution, pi, histogram, mean, standard deviation, Monte Carlo probability

## DISCUSSION QUESTIONS AND ACTIVITIES

1. Start throwing darts at the target. How is the computer using the number of darts in the circle and the number of darts in the square values to estimate pi? Provide mathematical calculations and justification to support your reasoning.

2. How does the number of darts thrown compare to the actual estimation of pi? How many more darts do you need to throw in order to increase your precision of pi by one decimal place? Describe any patterns you detect and show any calculations used to support your reasoning.

3. Reset the simulation. Throw 100 darts and record the number of darts in the circle. Reset the simulation. Throw another 100 darts and record the number of darts in the circle. Repeat this process at least 100 times. Create a histogram describing the frequency of each outcome (or range of outcomes). Describe the shape of the distribution. What is the average of the data set? What do you think that average should be? Explain.

4. Compare your average of the data set from question 3 with those of the rest of your class members. Create a histogram describing the frequency of the averages. Describe the shape of this distribution and compare it with the distribution in problem 3. How do the mean and standard deviation of the distribution of means (problem 4) relate to the mean and standard deviation of each individual data set (problem 4)?

## RELATED INTERNET SITE(S)

**Alternate Monte Carlo Simulations for Estimating Pi**
(87a) http://rene.ma.utexas.edu/users/tyilk/PiProj/PiCalc.htm
(87b) http://www.mste.uiuc.edu/activity/estpi/
(87c) http://www.daimi.aau.dk/~u951581/pi/MonteCarlo/pi.MonteCarlo.html

See **(6a)–(6b) Buffon Needle**
See **(31a)** and **(31b) Spinner**

# 88. MONTY HALL, THREE DOORS

**URL: http://www.shodor.org/interactivate/activities/monty3/index. html**

    **SUGGESTED LEVELS**: prealgebra (questions 1–3), probability (questions 1–3)

    **SITE SUMMARY**: The Shodor Foundation has created a Java applet to simulate the Monty Hall problem from the television show *Let's Make a Deal*. There is a pig concealed behind two of the three doors, and a new car behind the third door. First you select the door behind which you think you will find the car, and the program reveals a pig behind a different door. With two doors remaining, you have the option to stick with initial choice, or change your mind and switch to the other door.

    **TOPICS**: simulation, data collection, sample space, probability

## DISCUSSION QUESTIONS AND ACTIVITIES

1. When you are confronted with sticking or switching doors, will one method produce better results? Run the simulation until you have a strong case to support your hypothesis. Explain your procedures and your results.

2. What is the probability that you will get the car if you stick with the same door? How about switching to a different door? Explain how you determined this result.

3. What if you began the experiment with more doors? Assume you would have the option to stick or switch until only two doors remain. How would this affect the probability of staying or switching? Generalize the probabilities using n doors. You can run a simulation of this question at (88a) http://www.shodor.org/interactivate/activities/monty/index.html.

## RELATED INTERNET SITE(S)

**Monty Hall Simulations**
(88b) http://www.stat.sc.edu/~west/javahtml/LetsMakeaDeal.html
(88c) http://www.intergalact.com/threedoor/threedoor.cgi
(88d) http://mgw.dinet.de/physik/Quiz/Ziegenproblem/Win_A_Car/win_a_car.html

(88e) http://www.cut-the-knot.com/hall.html
(88f) http://www.stat.uiuc.edu/~stat100/java/Monty.html
(88g) http://cs.franklin.edu/~olsone/monty.html
    Java, Java Script, and CGI simulations and explanations behind the Monty Hall problem.

### Debate Over the Monty Hall Problem

(88h) http://www.wiskit.com/marilyn.gameshow.html
    This site provides the background of the problem as it was posed to Marilyn vos Savant of *Parade* magazine. It includes a debate over the correct solution, including alternative explanations.

## 89. MOVING MAN

### URL: http://www.mste.uiuc.edu/murphy/MovingMan/MovingMan.html

**SUGGESTED LEVELS**: algebra (question 1), advanced algebra (questions 1, 2, and 4), precalculus (questions 1, 2, and 4), calculus (questions 1–4)

**SITE SUMMARY**: This Java applet illustrates one-dimensional motion and a real-time distance vs. time graph as a person walks from home to school. The user can drag the walker from home to school and notice changes in the graph. The user also has the option to view velocity vs. time and acceleration vs. time graphs in real time or following an experiment. To begin, click the Restart button and click, hold, and drag the walker on the screen from home to school. Notice the changes on the graph as you change the walker's speed and direction. If necessary, pause the experiment by releasing the mouse button, and repeat the experiment by clicking on the Restart button. This applet would be useful for understanding an application of rate of change in algebra, advanced algebra, or calculus.

**TOPICS**: functions, linear, quadratic, step, sinusoidal, average rate of change, position, velocity, acceleration, graphing, slope, arithmetic mean, harmonic mean

### DISCUSSION QUESTIONS AND ACTIVITIES

1. How does the slope of the distance vs. time graph relate to the direction the walker is moving? What does the slope of the velocity vs. time graph describe?

2. How is the walker moving if the position vs. time graph is a linear function? Quadratic function? Step function? Sinusoidal function?

3. Explain how you could use two of the graphs to determine the average (mean) velocity of the walker as he travels from home to school. Use both graphs to calculate the average (mean) velocity. Repeat the experiment to confirm your hypothesis.

4. Is the arithmetic mean rate of the walker the same or different from the harmonic mean rate of the walker? Explain.

## RELATED INTERNET SITE(S)

**One-D Motion (Displacement, Velocity, Acceleration)**
(89a) http://www.phy.ntnu.edu.tw/java/xva/xva.html
   This Java applet demonstrates simultaneous position, velocity, and acceleration vs. time graphs.

**Motion with Constant Acceleration**
(89b) http://webphysics.ph.msstate.edu/jc/library/2–6/index.html
   This Java applet examines the changes in the position vs. time graph when you touch the brake in a car. You can adjust velocity of the car, friction of the road, and reaction time as a traffic light changes.

**Velocity and Displacement**
(89c) http://www.openteach.com/physics/applets/velDispl.html
   This Java applet allows you to modify the direction and speed of a car by adjusting the displacement vs. time graph.

**Kinematic Graphing**
(89d) http://www.glenbrook.k12.il.us/gbssci/phys/shwave/graph.html
   Try to match a piecewise velocity time graph in this Shockwave simulation by setting the appropriate initial velocity and acceleration during three different time intervals. You will need to download the Shockwave plugin because the activities were made with the tool Macromedia Director. You can see if you have the plugin, or download it, at (1a) http://www.exploremath.com/about/shockerhelp.cfm.

# 90. MYSTERIOUS MIND READER

**URLs: http://bonus.lycos.com/lycos/card/MysteriousMindReader. html**
   **http://www.sandlotscience.com/Games/_Reader.htm**

   **SUGGESTED LEVELS**: prealgebra (questions 1, 2, and 4), algebra (questions 1–4)
   **SITE SUMMARY**: This game identifies a mystery number that you pick in your head. Your goal is to figure out how the computer is reading your mind or using mathematics to trick you! Both URLs have the same game.

**TOPICS**: order of operations, composite function, algebraic expression, symbolic reasoning

## DISCUSSION QUESTIONS AND ACTIVITIES

1. Click on the Mysterious Mind Reader link (if necessary). Follow the directions on the page. Play the game several times. Is the computer accurate all of the time? Explain.

2. In the Mysterious Mind Reader Game, at what step will everyone have the same number? Explain how you determined this.

3. If the final answer is x, use algebra to show how the Mysterious Mind Reader game works.

4. Generate your own game with at least four steps that will always produce the same answer. Explain why you will always end up with the same answer. Try it with a few classmates.

## RELATED INTERNET SITE(S)

**Pick a Number**
(90a) http://www.geocities.com/~mathskills/picknmbr.htm
   Pick a number, follow several arithmetic steps, and the computer will tell you your answer.

**Pick a Number Between 0–2100**
(90b) http://www.route21.com/kac/pick.html
   Try and guess a number between zero and 2100. Each time you guess, the computer decreases the range based on your previous answer. For example, if you guess 300 and are incorrect, then the computer will ask you to guess between 0 and 300 or 300 and 2100, depending on the answer.

**Puzzling Number Games**
(90c) http://www.niehs.nih.gov/kids/brnumber.htm
   These number games have you input answers after following a series of arithmetic steps. Even though you may use different numbers along the process, most often the game will predict your final answer.


# 91. NATIONAL EARTHQUAKE INFORMATION CENTER

## URL: http://wwwneic.cr.usgs.gov/neis/eqlists/eqstats.html

**SUGGESTED LEVELS**: geometry (question 6), advanced algebra (questions 1–3), precalculus (questions 1–3), statistics (questions 4–6), probability (question 7)
**SITE SUMMARY**: These U.S. and worldwide statistics tables describe

the frequency of earthquakes and their magnitude throughout the twentieth century and give more specific data through the 1990s. The number of estimated deaths is listed below the total number of earthquakes for a specific year.

**TOPICS**: data collection, data analysis, modeling data, extrapolation, logarithm, exponential function, expected value, proportion, percent, probability, surface area, sphere

## DISCUSSION QUESTIONS AND ACTIVITIES

1. What type of function models the average number of earthquakes compared to their magnitude? Explain how you determined this result. Why might this be true?

2. Use the data in table four to graph magnitude change vs. ground motion change. What type of function models this data? Explain how you determined this result. Why might this be true?

3. Create a function that would determine the relative size of two earthquakes based on the difference of their measured magnitudes. Explain and verify your findings.

4. In a random earthquake in a random location on the globe, what would you expect the magnitude reading to be on the Richter scale? Explain your analysis.

5. Which category, if any, contributes the most to the number of deaths resulting from earthquakes? Explain how you determined this result.

6. If you were in an earthquake, would you rather be standing in the United States or in another random location around the world? Geographic information about the United States can be found at (91a) http://www.odci.gov/cia/publications/factbook/us.html#geo. Information about the earth can be found at (91b) http://www.seds.org/nineplanets/nineplanets/data1.html. Explain the statistical and/or mathematical procedures used to determine this result.

7. What is the likelihood that there will be a great earthquake two years in a row? Explain your analysis.

## RELATED INTERNET SITE(S)

**U.S. Geological Survey**
(91c) http://www.usgs.gov/
    This site includes numerous data sets about current and historical geological phenomenon.
See **(46a) A Simple Logarithm Calculator**
See **(46b) Logarithms**

## 92. NATIONAL PERINATAL STATISTICS

**URL: http://www.modimes.org/HealthLibrary2/InfantHealthStatistics/ stats.htm**

SUGGESTED LEVELS: prealgebra (questions 1–5), algebra (question 4), statistics (questions 1–5)

SITE SUMMARY: The March of Dimes has posted a series of statistics about prenatal care, birth defects, infant mortality, live births, and more.

TOPICS: percent, scatter plot, line of best fit, slope, y-intercept, expected value, extrapolation

### DISCUSSION QUESTIONS AND ACTIVITIES

1. On an average day in the United States, what percentage of births are from teen mothers? How many teenage moms have children with birth defects? Explain your reasoning.

2. In the substance use by pregnancy status, what types of drugs are pregnant mothers most likely to give up? Explain your reasoning.

3. Which type of condition category (in bold) contributes to the greatest financial hardship? Explain your analysis.

4. In the economic costs of birth defects data, plot a scatter plot and line of best fit describing total cost vs. incidence rate. What is the significance of the slope and y-intercept of the line?

5. Inflation rate data can be found at (92a) http://neatideas.com/info/ inflation.htm. Design a new table that would be an accurate update of the economic costs of birth defects data. Explain your analyses.

### RELATED INTERNET SITE(S)

**Infant and Fetal Mortality Rates**
(92b) http://www.cdc.gov/nchs/datawh/statab/pubd/hus97t23.htm
This data set compares death rates among fetal and newborn children among different races since 1950.

**Infant Mortality Rates**
(92c) http://www.sfrpc.com/region/vitalc07.htm
This chart describes infant mortality rates in the state of Florida from 1980 to 1985.

**Latin America and the Caribbean Data**
(92d) http://www.qesdb.cdie.org/lac/index.htm
View information on infant mortality rates, fertility rates, and children's health from these countries.

# 93. NFL.COM STATISTICS

**URL: http://www.nfl.com/stats/**

**SUGGESTED LEVELS**: prealgebra (questions 1–2), algebra (questions 1–6), advanced algebra (questions 1–6)

**SITE SUMMARY**: This site includes a searchable database and team outlines of NFL statistics. You can search categories such as rushing, sacks, and quarterback rating by the entire league or by each division. You also have the option to view statistics though each week of the year, by the end of the regular season, or throughout the playoffs.

**TOPICS**: data collection, data analysis, linear function, scatter plot, line of best fit, slope, extrapolation, line graph

## DISCUSSION QUESTIONS AND ACTIVITIES

1. Based on the statistics, who would you vote as the MVP (most valuable player) of the AFC? NFC? The entire NFL? Explain your reasoning.

2. Suppose salaries were based strictly on performance; quarterbacks were paid twice as much as wide receivers, on average; and the highest salary for a wide receiver could be two million dollars per year. Based on these criteria, predict next year's salary of the quarterback and wide receivers from your favorite team. Explain your reasoning.

3. Create a scatter plot comparing the yards a quarterback obtains with his number of attempts. Use a line of best fit to predict the average yards per completion among passing leaders. Explain your findings. How do the results change if you do this analysis for a different week of the year?

4. Create a scatter plot comparing the yards a running back receives with the number of attempts (carries). Use a line of best fit to predict the average yards per attempt among rushing leaders. Explain your findings. How do the results change if you do this analysis for a different week of the year?

5. Choose one of the top three NFL leaders in a particular category (rushing, passing, kicking, etc.) by the end of the regular season (week 17) or by the most current week. Collect and plot data on the player's statistical performance in that category throughout every week of the entire season. What does a horizontal line represent on a line graph with this data set? How does the slope of the line graph relate to the player's performance each week?

6. Choose one of the top three NFL leaders in a particular category (rushing, passing, kicking, etc.) by the end of the regular season (week 17) or by the most current week. Collect and plot data on the player's statistical performance in that category throughout every week of the entire season. What does the slope of the line of best fit represent on this graph? Explain. Predict the player's statistic if there were twenty weeks in a season. Explain your reasoning.

## RELATED INTERNET SITE(S)

**NFL Statistics**
(93a) http://espn.go.com/nfl/statistics/index.html
(93b) http://cbs.sportsline.com/u/football/nfl/stats.html
   Find NFL current statistics by teams, players, or performance leaders in both conferences.

# 94. NONFARM PAYROLL STATISTICS FROM THE CURRENT EMPLOYMENT STATISTICS

## URL: http://146.142.4.24/cgi-bin/surveymost?ee

**SUGGESTED LEVELS**: prealgebra (questions 1, 2, 3, 5, and 6), algebra (questions 1–6), statistics (questions 1–6)

**SITE SUMMARY**: Search for average wages and hours worked for various national employment sectors over the last fifty years. The user has the option to view multiple data files at once and can choose to see data over a short or long period of time.

**TOPICS**: data collection, data analysis, data display, percentage, modeling, linear function, extrapolation, exponential function

## DISCUSSION QUESTIONS AND ACTIVITIES

1. How much do seasonally adjusted data differ from nonseasonally adjusted data? Explain your analysis. Why is this difference important?

2. Which type of employment pays the highest salary? Explain how you determined this information. Predict how much a worker in this field will be earning two years from now. Show your work.

3. In which decade have people spent the most time at work? Explain your analysis.

4. What type of function best models the growth in salaries over the last fifty years? Explain your analysis.

5. What types of workers are not represented in the data sets? Explain your reasoning.

6. Generate a question that would use a graph in the solution. Answer the question and show your work.

## RELATED INTERNET SITE(S)

See **10. Average Weekly Salaries**

## 95. NORMAL DAILY MAXIMUM TEMPERATURE, DEG F

**URLs: http://nimbo.wrh.noaa.gov/Reno/max.htm
http://www.nws.mbay.net/maxtemp.html**

**SUGGESTED LEVELS**: precalculus (questions 1–4)

**SITE SUMMARY**: These locations provide the average maximal temperature throughout a year in over 250 U.S. cities. Twelve monthly averages and an annual average are displayed in a table to represent average monthly temperatures from 1961 to 1990. Both URLs listed above contain the same data set. A sine or cosine curve can be generated to model the data's behavior throughout the year. Real-world significance can be drawn from each of the variables in the equation's standard form. Moreover, modeling a variety of cities can illustrate that temperature patterns are similar in each city throughout the country.

**TOPICS**: data analysis, sinusoidal functions, interpolation, translations, transformations, modeling

## DISCUSSION QUESTIONS AND ACTIVITIES

1. Choose a city that reaches temperatures below 65 degrees and above 85 degrees sometime throughout the year. Generate a function in the form $y = A\cos[B(x - C)] + D$ that models the data, where x represents the number of the month and y represents the temperature. Graph the function and modify any of the parameters A, B, C, or D until you feel you have a curve that best represents the data. Explain how you found each of these values.

2. In terms of the physical temperature, what do the values A, B, C, and D represent? In other words, state a real-world significance to each of these values.

3. Assume that a city has ideal temperature when the temperature is between 65 and 85 degrees for some portion(s) of the year. Use the

function to predict the time(s) of the year when your city (from problem 1) is most pleasant.

4. Suppose you wanted to move away from a city when the temperature was no longer ideal. Once you leave, you want to find another city with ideal temperatures during the same time of the year. Generate a series of sinusoidal functions and predict the time(s) of the year and cities you would visit so that you could live in the United States in ideal temperatures all year round. The only restriction you have is that you may not choose a city that already has temperatures between 65 and 85 degrees all year round (e.g., San Diego).

## RELATED INTERNET SITE(S)

See **(59a) National Climatic Data Center CLIMVIS Time Series Data**
See **(59b) Hourly U.S. Weather Statistics**
See **125. Sun or Moon Rise/Set Table for One Year**

## 96. NUMBER OF PRISONERS UNDER SENTENCE OF DEATH

### URL: http://www.ojp.usdoj.gov/bjs/glance/drrace.txt

**SUGGESTED LEVELS**: advanced algebra (questions 1–4), statistics (questions 4–6)
**SITE SUMMARY**: This data set from the Bureau of Justice Statistics describes the number of people on death row classified by race from 1968 to 1998.
**TOPICS**: data analysis, modeling data, scatter plot, function, extrapolation, outlier

## DISCUSSION QUESTIONS AND ACTIVITIES

1. What type of function best represents the growth of the number of people on death row over time? Explain your reasoning.
2. Predict the number of people on death row by the end of this year. Explain how you determined this result.
3. Suppose a group of "death row" jails will need to be built when 5,000 people are sentenced to death. If you were in charge of the building planning, when would you suggest the completion of these jails? Explain your analysis.
4. Based on the data, do you think the number of blacks on death row

will exceed the number of whites on death role in the future? Explain why or why not. What additional data would help support or verify your claim? Explain why this would help.

5. In what year(s) were there an unusual number of executions? Explain the criteria and computations that you used to determine this result. Why do you think there were an unusual amount of executions in that year?

6. Is this data proof that whites are sentenced to death more often than blacks? If so, explain why. If not, what additional information would you need to prove that this is true? Explain.

## RELATED INTERNET SITE(S)

**Men and Women Receiving the Death Penalty**
(96a) http://hepg.awl.com/weiss/e_iprojects/c12/c12dat03.htm
    This data set provides the number of men and women receiving the death penalty from 1973 to 1995.

**Key Crime and Justice Facts**
(96b) http://www.ojp.usdoj.gov/bjs/glance.htm
    These statistics describe trends in crimes, federal investigations and prosecutions, state convictions, corrections, and expenditures.

**Public Attitudes towards Crime and Criminal Justice**
(96c) http://www.albany.edu/sourcebook/1995/toc_2.html
    This extensive database of poll results represents public attitudes towards crime, police, the judicial system, safety, violence, abortion, drug use, gun control, and more.

# 97. OFF THE WALL MATH

**URL: http://www2.dgsys.com/~rdc/rdcpub/Off_wall/DRT.html**

**SUGGESTED LEVELS**: prealgebra (questions 1–4), algebra (questions 1–6)

**SITE SUMMARY**: Investigate a situation that compares distance, rate, and time. You have three different places to visit, and you are given how long it will take to get to and from each place. You have control over the distance between the objects, the path you take between the three places, and your average speed. Click and drag an object if you want to change the speed of transportation and the position of the landmarks.

**TOPICS**: distance, rate, time, average speed, slope, linear function, rhombus, y-intercept, Pythagorean Theorem

## DISCUSSION QUESTIONS AND ACTIVITIES

1. What is the shortest period of time for the entire trip based on the initial positions of the landmarks? Explain how you determined this result.

2. If the organizer's manufacturing plant is sixty-three miles from the hideout, how fast do you have to drive in order to get there in exactly one hour? Explain how you determined this result.

3. You are driving at thirty miles an hour for the entire trip. How far apart are the landmarks if it takes exactly two hours for each trip? Explain how you determined this result. In this situation, what type of geometric shape is formed on the map? Explain how you know.

4. An equation relating distance, rate, and time is listed on the page. Is this equation correct? How do you know? Use the data on the screen to support your answer.

5. Set the speedometer to any speed. Drag the landmarks to a different position on the screen. Create a graph that describes the total distance traveled over the course of the trip. Label each landmark on your graph. What is the significance of the slope and y-intercept on your graph? Explain how you know.

6. Reload the page to make sure that the landmarks are in their original position. Suppose there were roads that connected all of the landmarks so that the map had diagonals connecting the diner to the organizer's manufacturing plant and the ski shop to the hideout. Assuming that you travel at the same rate throughout the trip, what is the shortest possible route that you can take so that you visit the three locations and return back to the hideout? Explain your analysis.

### RELATED INTERNET SITE(S)

See **89. Moving Man**

See **4. Amtrak Reservations and MapQuest**

## 98. OXYGEN CONCENTRATIONS IN WATER AND SEAWATER

**URL: http://www.fishlinkcentral.com/calculators/oxygencon.htm**

**SUGGESTED LEVELS**: prealgebra (questions 1–4), advanced algebra (questions 5–6)

**SITE SUMMARY**: This calculator determines the amount of oxygen present in water depending on its salinity and temperature. You can adjust these two variables and calculate the new oxygen levels present.

**TOPICS**: data collection, data analysis, scatter plot, function, extrapolation, proportion

## DISCUSSION QUESTIONS AND ACTIVITIES

1. Do saltwater fish need more or less oxygen than freshwater fish to survive? Explain your reasoning.
2. Suppose a certain fish at an aquarium needed five ml/l of oxygen to survive. What type of water would you put in the tank in order for it to survive? How would your answer change if the fish lived in the Caribbean? Explain your reasoning.
3. How do you convert among the three different oxygen concentration units? Verify your hypothesis with calculations.
4. Why are the temperature and salinity levels restricted to lie between certain numbers?
5. What type of function describes the relationship between the salinity, water temperature, and oxygen concentration? Explain how you determined this result.
6. What type of function describes the relationship between the salinity of the water and the oxygen concentration? Explain how you determined this result.

## 99. PACKING EGGS

**URL: http://schoolsite.edex.net.uk/323/spreadsheet/html/packing_eggs.htm**

**SUGGESTED LEVELS**: prealgebra (questions 1–2), statistics (questions 1–6)

**SITE SUMMARY**: Your goal in this activity is to pack as many "eggs" as possible into a bin within a given time period. You pack eggs by clicking checkboxes until your time runs out. Your time is up when you are not able to check any more boxes.

**TOPICS**: data collection, data analysis, normal distributions, mean, median, mode, central limit theorem, hypothesis testing

## DISCUSSION QUESTIONS AND ACTIVITIES

1. Pack eggs for ten trials. Compare the mean, median, and mode of your data set with those of your classmates. Are they the same?

Should they be the same? Will they ever be the same? Explain your findings.

2. Is there a certain packing strategy that is better than others? Pack eggs for as many trials needed to produce results that will help justify your answer.

3. Pack eggs for ten trials. Plot all of the class data using dot plots or histograms. Examine the relationship between the class mean, median, and mode. What assumptions could be made about packing eggs if the distribution were normal?

4. Pack eggs for ten trials. Compare your data with the data of your classmates. Is there enough evidence to suggest that your strategy for packing eggs is unusually better than your classmates' strategies? Explain.

5. Pack eggs for ten trials. Plot the means of the class data using dot plots or histograms. Examine the relationship between the mean and standard deviation of this data set compared to the mean and standard deviation of all of the data. Are they the same? Should they be the same? Will they ever be the same? Explain your findings.

6. Pack eggs with your right hand for five trials and with your left hand for five trials. Keep the data recorded separately. Compare your data with the data of your classmates. Is there enough evidence to suggest that you pack eggs better with one hand than the other? Explain your analysis.

### RELATED INTERNET SITE(S)

See **(60a) Bop the Mole**

See **(29a)–(29d) Reaction Time 2**

## 100. PARABOLA DEFINED BY THREE POINTS

**URL: http://www.openteach.com/mathematics/applets/parabola. html**

**SUGGESTED LEVELS**: advanced algebra (questions 1–5), precalculus (questions 1–5)

**SITE SUMMARY**: This Java applet displays the graph of a quadratic equation determined by three points. As you move any of the three points, the graph and equation will adjust to a new quadratic function.

**TOPICS**: graphing, parabola, matrices, system of equations, symmetry, quadratic functions, coefficients, properties of quadratic functions, collinearity, position, equation

## DISCUSSION QUESTIONS AND ACTIVITIES

1. What happens to the graph when the leading coefficient changes sign?
2. What happens to the equation when the graph is symmetric with the y-axis?
3. What happens to the leading coefficient when the three points are collinear?
4. If the x-coordinate represents time in seconds and the y-coordinate represents height in meters, state an appropriate location for the three points if you want the graph to represent the position of a falling object over time. Justify your answer.
5. Use the three points to write and solve a system of equations that verifies the equation of the function. Using this information, generalize the solution in terms of unknown coordinates $(x_0, y_0)$, $(x_1, y_1)$, and $(x_2, y_2)$.

## RELATED INTERNET SITE(S)

**Exploring Parabolas (Java SketchPad)**
(100a) http://www.mste.uiuc.edu/dildine/sketches/parabola.htm
   This Java applet will show a step-by-step geometric construction of a parabola using its definition.

**Solving Quadratic Equations**
(100b) http://www.engr.iupui.edu/~selvakum/quad.html
(100c) http://members.tripod.com/~kselva/quad.html
   These Java Script forms will give you the solution to a quadratic equation in the form $ax^2 + bx + c = 0$, given each of the coefficients in the equation. The solution(s) will be given in exact and approximate form, including imaginary components.

See **110. Quadratic Equations 2**

See **111. Quadratics: Polynomial Form**

# 101. PENDULUM

### URL: http://home.a-city.de/walter.fendt/physengl/pendulum.htm

**SUGGESTED LEVELS**: precalculus (questions 1–3), calculus (questions 3–4)

**SITE SUMMARY**: This applet is a simulation of a pendulum. As the pendulum moves, you can view a position vs. time, velocity vs. time, or acceleration vs. time graph. The screen will also display the oscillation period of the pendulum and the maximum value of the graph. You have the option to pause the pendulum so you can make specific observations or collect data. When you click on the Reset button, you can adjust the length, mass, and amplitude of the pendulum to detect variables that affect the pendulum's motion. Both of the URLs contain the same applet.

**TOPICS**: sinusoidal function, data collection, data analysis, square root function, position, velocity, acceleration, derivative, maximum, minimum, optimization, modeling

## DISCUSSION QUESTIONS AND ACTIVITIES

1. Generalize the pendulum's physical location and movement when its position (elongation), velocity, and acceleration are each equal to zero on the graph. Generalize the pendulum's physical location and movement when its position (elongation), velocity, and acceleration reach a minimum or maximum on the graph.

2. Which of the length, mass, and amplitude of the pendulum affect its period, or one full swing? Collect data that will help you predict a function that compares some of these variables.

3. Derive an equation relating the position (elongation) of the pendulum over t seconds. Explain the pendulum's physical representation of each of the values in your equation. Explain how you derived this equation.

4. Use the position function in problem 3 and generate the equations relating the velocity and acceleration of the pendulum over t seconds. Explain the methods you use to confirm the accuracy of your work.

## RELATED INTERNET SITE(S)

### Spring Pendulum
(101a) http://home.a-city.de/walter.fendt/physengl/springpendulum.htm
   This Java applet is a simulation of a pendulum at the end of an oscillating spring. As the pendulum moves, you can view a position vs. time, velocity vs. time, or acceleration vs. time graph. You have the option to pause the pendulum so you can make specific observations or collect data. When you click on the Reset button, you can adjust the spring constant, mass, and amplitude of the pendulum to detect variables that affect the pendulum's motion.

### Simple Harmonic Pendulum
(101b) http://www.ozemail.com.au/~dcrombie/java/Pendulum.htm
(101c) http://wigner.byu.edu/pendulum/Pendulum.htm

(101d) http://www.control.co.kr/java1/pendulum/Pendulum.html
This Java applet simulates the motion of a pendulum. You click and drag on the pendulum to set a desired length, and then release it.

See **(43a) Play a Piano / Synthesizer / Oscilloscope**

# 102. POLLUTION RANKINGS

## URL: http://www.scorecard.org/ranking/

**SUGGESTED LEVELS**: prealgebra (questions 1–3), algebra (questions 4–5), advanced algebra (questions 4–5), statistics (questions 1–5)

**SITE SUMMARY**: Locate environmental pollution data through the environmental defense's database. You can view rankings by state, county, zip code, or facility. After the search, you can narrow results by looking at specific classifications of data.

**TOPICS**: data collection, data analysis, modeling data, linear function, line of best fit, slope, correlation

## DISCUSSION QUESTIONS AND ACTIVITIES

1. Which geographic locations in the country, if any, produce the lowest amounts of hazardous air pollutants? Explain your analysis.

2. Near what type(s) of facilities would you *not* want to live? Explain why. Use the data to support your answer.

3. Which livestock produces the greatest risk to the environment? Is your response true for all parts of the country? Explain.

4. Graph the amount of air pollution from carbon monoxide emissions vs. the population of each state. State population data can be found at (102a) http://www.census.gov/population/estimates/state/st-99-3.txt. Find an equation of a line that will best fit the data. Interpret the slope of the line. Which states have unusually high carbon monoxide emissions pollution? Explain how you know. What actions can be taken by the government to reduce the amount of this type of pollution?

5. The cancer risk score from toxic chemicals is most strongly related to what type of pollution? Explain your analysis.

## RELATED INTERNET SITE(S)

**United States Environmental Protection Agency**
(102b) http://www.epa.gov/

View data and information on pollution, cleanup, waste, air, water, ecosystems, economics, and more.

**Yearly Consumption of Cigarettes**
(102c) http://www.cdc.gov/tobacco/research_data/economics/consump1.htm
(102d) http://www.graceland.edu/~jsjones/cs101/datafiles/cigarettes.txt
This data set provides the total number of cigarettes produced and consumed per capita each year throughout most of the twentieth century.

**Daily Ultraviolet Index**
(102e) http://sedac.ciesin.org/ozone/maps/2000_ept_uvi.shtml
View the ultraviolet (UV) index throughout the year in various locations around the world by viewing daily sensor maps.

# 103. POSTAGE RATE CALCULATORS

**URLs: http://postcalc.usps.gov/**
**http://wwwapps.ups.com/servlet/QCCServlet**
**http://www.federalexpress.com/us/rates/**

**SUGGESTED LEVELS:** prealgebra (questions 1–3), advanced algebra (questions 1–6)

**SITE SUMMARY:** The United States Postal Service (USPS), United Parcel Service (UPS), and Federal Express (FedEx) all have rate calculators that will tell you the shipping price based on the size and weight of a package. If you need to find a zip code, go to (153b) http://zip.langenberg.com/.

**TOPICS:** data collection, data analysis, modeling, step function, domain, greatest integer property

## DISCUSSION QUESTIONS AND ACTIVITIES

1. Suppose you want to send a five-pound birthday gift to my friend who lives in Chicago. Which company should you use to send the package? Explain why. Justify your reasoning with mathematical calculations. Will your answer to this question depend on where you live, or will this postal company always provide the best deal for a five-pound package? Explain how you determined this result.

2. Under what circumstances is it best to use the post office (USPS)? Explain how you determined this result. Justify your reasoning with mathematical calculations. Repeat this process with the other companies, UPS and FedEx.

3. View the domestic rate chart for the USPS at (103a) http://www.usps.gov/consumer/domestic.htm. How would you determine the cost of

a package if its weight were a fraction or irrational number? Why does the single-piece table stop at thirteen ounces and tell you to look at the Priority Mail table?

4. Use the USPS rate chart at (103a) http://www.usps.gov/consumer/ domestic.htm. Generate a graph describing the price of a small object (that can fit in a standard envelope) compared to its weight using a realistic domain. You can send heavy metals in the mail if you want.

5. Use the USPS rate chart at (103a) http://www.usps.gov/consumer/ domestic.htm. Why do you think there are restrictions to the size and weight of postcards and Priority Mail packages? Justify your answers.

6. Collect data from the UPS rate calculator and generate a function that compares the price of a package being sent to your favorite U.S. city (outside of your own) compared to its weight. Describe the significance of each of the numbers in the equation. Compare and contrast your results with those of your classmates and hypothesize how UPS determines its rates.

### RELATED INTERNET SITE(S)

See **153. Zip Find Central**

**Houston Lighting and Power Calculator**
(103b) http://www.energydotsys.com/lgscalc.htm
   Try to determine how seven different variables affect the savings in a Houston area electric bill when they use the Large General Service.

**Telephone Rate Calculator**
(103c) http://www.geocities.com/WallStreet/5395/ratecalc.html
   View predicted monthly long distance telephone fees with different companies based on the number of minutes and calls you make each month.

## 104. POWERS OF TEN

### URL: http://www.wordwizz.com/10exp0.htm

**SUGGESTED LEVELS**: prealgebra (questions 2–5), algebra (questions 1–5)

**SITE SUMMARY**: Zoom in and away from a human being on Earth by factors of ten. This microscope allows you to view an item as small as a proton, or the expansive amount of space that scientists are familiar with. You can zoom by factors of 10, 100, or 1,000. You will see a new picture each time you zoom.

**TOPICS**: exponent, scale, units, speed, time, distance

## DISCUSSION QUESTIONS AND ACTIVITIES

1. How does the area of the region covered change each time you increase the zoom factor by +1? How does the area of the region covered change each time you increase the zoom factor by +n, where n is any integer? Explain.

2. How many times larger is the view of metropolitan Chicago compared to the view of a lymphocyte? What region is the same magnification above metropolitan Chicago? What other pair of pictures illustrates this magnification? How many other pairs of pictures illustrate this change in magnification? Explain how you know.

3. How would the view in space be different from the view of Chicago at 109 meters away if you started from a different city? Explain.

4. How would the views be different if the units were in yards? How would the views be different if the units were in inches?

5. The speed of light is $3 \times 10^8$ meters per second. Describe a journey of a light particle, including time, starting from the outer limits of our galaxy headed to a proton inside our bodies.

## RELATED INTERNET SITE(S)

**Map Quest**
(104a) http://www.mapquest.com
   View scale maps from any location within the United States. You can zoom in and out from the street level to a view of the entire city.

See **132. Towers of Hanoi**

See **139. U.S. Census Bureau**

## 105. PREDICTING OLD FAITHFUL

**URL: http://www.jason.org/expeditions/jason8/yellowstone/oldfait1.html**

   **SUGGESTED LEVELS**: algebra (questions 1–5), advanced algebra (questions 1–5), statistics (questions 3–5)
   **SITE SUMMARY**: The JASON project has collected data that compare the length of an eruption in Yellowstone's famous geyser and the time until a new eruption.
   **TOPICS**: linear function, scatter plot, line of best fit, slope, y-intercept, extrapolation, interpolation, domain, range

## DISCUSSION QUESTIONS AND ACTIVITIES

1. Suppose an eruption lasts 135 seconds at 2:00 P.M. At what time would you expect the next eruption? Explain your reasoning.

2. What are a reasonable domain and range for the data set? Explain how you determined these figures.

3. Make a scatter plot with the data and determine a line that best represents the data. Find an equation of the line and describe the significance of the slope and y-intercept.

4. Suppose it's 3:00 P.M. and the park closes at 5:00 P.M. You just missed the last eruption at 2:45 P.M. and heard that it lasted 7.5 minutes. Should you stick around the park and wait for the next eruption? Explain why or why not.

5. Examine the recorded observations at (105a) http://www.jason.org/expeditions/jason8/yellowstone/oldfait2.html. Based on these results, how much leeway would you provide (in seconds) with your predicted line so that you accurately account for at least 95 percent of the outcomes? Explain your analysis.

## RELATED INTERNET SITE(S)

**Time Trouble for Geyser: It's No Longer Old Faithful**
(105b) http://www.dartmouth.edu/~chance/chance_news/recent_news/chance_news_5.03.html#Time trouble
   This 1996 *New York Times* article addresses whether or not the geyser can still be predictable.

**Geysers: A Big Splash at Yellowstone**
(105c) http://www.wyoming.com/~yellowstonejournal/YellowstoneGeysers.html
   This 1994 article from the *Yellowstone Journal* provides historical information and data about geysers in the park.

# 106. PROJECTILE MOTION APPLET

## URL: http://www.phys.virginia.edu/classes/109N/more_stuff/Applets/ProjectileMotion/jarapplet.html

**SUGGESTED LEVELS**: precalculus (questions 1–7), calculus (questions 4–7)

**SITE SUMMARY**: This applet is a simulation of a ball thrown in a two dimensional plane. You set parameters such as velocity, angle, and mass, and then watch a projectile of the ball as it is displayed on a height vs. distance graph. You have the option to leave a trail of the path of the ball, as well as include air resistance in the simulation. After the ball has landed, the screen will display the maximum horizontal and vertical distances, end velocity, and time that the ball was in the air. Click on the Reload or Refresh button on your browser to clear the graph.

**TOPICS**: quadratic function, projectile motion, sine, cosine, optimization, maximum, derivative

## DISCUSSION QUESTIONS AND ACTIVITIES

1. What is the relationship between the starting and ending velocity of the ball? Is this always true during the flight path of a ball? Explain.

2. How much will air resistance affect the horizontal and vertical distance the ball travels? Predict the direction of the wind. Explain how you determined this solution.

3. Which of the factors of velocity, angle, and mass affect the path of the ball? Explain how you determined this result.

4. The equation $h(t) = v_0 t - 4.9t^2$ describes the one-dimensional vertical height of a ball (in meters) t seconds after it is thrown from the ground. In two dimensions, derive a general equation that will predict the vertical distance the ball travels based on the time the ball is in the air and the variables you mentioned in problem 3. At what angle should you throw the ball for maximum height? Explain how you determined this result.

5. Derive a general equation that will predict the horizontal distance the ball travels based on the time the ball is in the air and the variables you mentioned in problem 3. At what angle should you throw the ball for maximum horizontal distance (range)? Explain how you determined this result.

6. Derive a general equation that predicts the vertical distance the ball travels based on the horizontal distance the ball travels and the variables you mentioned in problem 3. Show your work.

7. In a baseball game, the batter has just hit the ball to right field for a single. The runner from second base is trying to score, so the outfielder has to decide whether he should throw straight to home, or throw to the cutoff man at second base. If the ball is thrown to the cutoff man, he will then throw the ball to home plate. Assuming the outfielder and second baseman have good throwing accuracy, which option should he choose? Explain your analysis and verify your results with the simulation.

**RELATED INTERNET SITE(S)**

See **100. Parabola Defined by Three Points**

## 107. PROJECTIONS OF THE VOTING AGE POPULATION FOR STATES

**URL: http://www.census.gov/population/www/socdemo/voting/tabs00.html**

**SUGGESTED LEVELS**: prealgebra (questions 1, 2, and 4), advanced algebra (questions 3 and 6), statistics (questions 1–6)

**SITE SUMMARY**: This data set from the U.S. Census Bureau describes demographics of the estimated and actual voting population since 1930. Demographic categories include age, sex, race, and location.

**TOPICS**: data analysis, modeling, exponential function, extrapolation, outlier, hypothesis testing, central limit theorem

### DISCUSSION QUESTIONS AND ACTIVITIES

1. In Table 1, if the presidential candidate wants to improve his Hispanic vote, to what age group and part of the country should he pay closer attention? Explain why. Use the data to support your answer.

2. In Table 2, what presidential election resulted in an usual percentage of people in favor of or against voting for the president? Explain your criteria for selection and your analysis.

3. In Table 2, predict the population of the voting age in the next election. Explain how you determined this result.

4. In Table 3, which parts of the country appeared to favor Bill Clinton? Explain how you determined this result. Use the data to support your answer.

5. In Table 3, was there a significant decrease in Clinton's popularity during the 1996 election? Explain why or why not. Use the data to support your answer.

6. In Table 4, assume that the growth rate of races will remain constant. Predict the year when the sum of the voting minority populations will be greater than the voting white population. Explain how you determined this result.

## RELATED INTERNET SITE(S)

See **141. U.S. Senate Votes on Clinton Removal**

**Information About Candidates, Parties, and Other Committees**
(107a) http://www.fec.gov/finance/finmenu.htm
These data sets describe financial information used to fund different campaigns during the 1996 and 2000 elections.

**Politics.com**
(107b) http://www.politics.com/
Examine statistics about election results, campaign finance, and viewer polls.

**2000 Election Data from CNN**
(107c) http://www.cnn.com/ELECTION/2000/results
View national, state, and county data for the 2000 presidential and congressional elections.

## 108. PROOFS OF THE PYTHAGOREAN THEOREM

**URL: http://www.math.csusb.edu/courses/m129/pyth_proof.html**

**SUGGESTED LEVELS**: geometry (questions 1–5)
**SITE SUMMARY**: Examine interactive geometric constructions that prove the Pythagorean Theorem. Use translations and rotations to reveal why the theorem is true.
**TOPICS**: translation, rotation, Pythagorean Theorem, proof, symbolic manipulation, similarity, area, right triangle

### DISCUSSION QUESTIONS AND ACTIVITIES

1. In the cut-and-paste proof, where are sides a, b, and c located on the diagram? Redraw the diagram on a sheet of paper, label all of the points, and label the sides that represent a, b, and c. Is it possible to label the sides a, b, and c in any other way? Explain why or why not.

2. In the cut-and-paste proof, how do you know that the areas of the blue and green squares represent $a^2$ and $b^2$?

3. In the cut-and-paste proof, move the three triangles into locations that would illustrate the Pythagorean Theorem. Explain how this translation shows that $a^2 + b^2 = c^2$.

4. Use an algebraic proof to show that the movements of triangles in the cut-and-paste diagram maintain the same area.

5. In Leonardo Da Vinci's proof, click on the Hide Original button to slice the figure in half along its diagonal. When you click on the Reflect figure button, how does the figure reflect? What other type of

transformation is associated with this type of reflection? Rotate the triangles using the circle and explain how these transformations illustrate the Pythagorean Theorem.

## RELATED INTERNET SITE(S)

**IES Manipula Math with Java**
(108a) http://www.ies.co.jp/math/java/geo/pythagoras.html
These Java applets explore the Pythagorean Theorem eight additional ways.

**Pythagoras' Theorem**
(108b) http://java.sun.com/applets/archive/beta/Pythagoras/
These Java-based, animated demonstrations of the Pythagorean Theorem use dissections, shears, translations, and similarity. The animations allow students to generate commentary and conjectures about each of the diagrams.

**Cut-the-Knot**
(108c) http://www.cut-the-knot.com/pythagoras/index.html
View twenty-nine proofs of the Pythagorean Theorem with additional references to texts and Internet sites.

# 109. PYTHAGOREAN THEOREM FROM IES

## URL: http://www.ies.co.jp/math/java/geo/pytha2/pytha2.html

**SUGGESTED LEVELS**: geometry (questions 1–3)
**SITE SUMMARY**: This Java applet explores the Pythagorean Theorem through a dissection method. Given a right triangle, squares are constructed on each of the sides of the triangle. You are asked to make two cuts in the middle-sized square and then rearrange the smaller pieces to fit in the larger square. This demonstration can be performed by dissecting the middle-sized square in multiple locations, and thus verifies many cases of the Pythagorean Theorem.
**TOPICS**: area of a square, Pythagorean Theorem, right triangle

## DISCUSSION QUESTIONS AND ACTIVITIES

1. The top of the page reads the formula $a^2 = b^2 + c^2$. In the United States, however, the Pythagorean Theorem is represented by $a^2 + b^2 = c^2$ in most textbooks. Which formula is correct? Explain.

2. Why are $a^2$, $b^2$, and $c^2$ written inside the squares? What do they represent?

3. Follow the directions next to the Java applet and drag the five pieces in the larger square without any overlapping. Explain how this tran-

sition from the smaller squares to the larger squares verifies the Pythagorean Theorem.

## RELATED INTERNET SITE(S)

See **108. Proofs of the Pythagorean Theorem**

# 110. QUADRATIC EQUATIONS 2

**URL: http://www.univie.ac.at/future.media/moe/galerie/gleich/
gleich.html#quadr2**

**SUGGESTED LEVELS**: algebra (questions 1, 2, and 5), advanced algebra (questions 1–5)

**SITE SUMMARY**: This applet illustrates solutions to equations in the
form $x^2 + px + b = 0$ by completing the square and substituting into a
formula. A graph of the corresponding quadratic function highlighting
each of the roots is next to the algebraic solution. You can dynamically
adjust the coefficients and watch changes in the solutions to the equation.
Click on the red box named "quadratic equations 2" to begin.

**TOPICS**: quadratic function, graph, roots, parabola, even function,
odd function, x-intercept, completing the square

## DISCUSSION QUESTIONS AND ACTIVITIES

1. Where can you find the solutions to the equation on the graph? Explain how you determined this.
2. How do changes in the value of q affect the graph? How do changes
   in the value of p affect the graph?
3. How does a combination of the values p and q relate to the x-
   intercepts of the function? If p, q, and both x-intercepts are integers,
   is q more likely to be even or odd? Explain how you know.
4. What does the equation $x = -p/2 + -\mathrm{sqrt}(p^2/4 - q)$ represent? How
   do you know if it is true? Prove or disprove this formula.
5. What can the values in the equation tell you about the number of
   times the graph crosses the x-axis? Generalize this claim in terms of
   p and q.

## RELATED INTERNET SITE(S)

See **100. Parabola Defined by Three Points**
See **106. Projectile Motion Applet**

# 111. QUADRATICS: POLYNOMIAL FORM

**URL: http://www.exploremath.com/activities/Activity_page.cfm?
ActivityID=13**

**SUGGESTED LEVELS**: algebra (questions 1–4), advanced algebra
(questions 1–6)

**SITE SUMMARY**: ExploreMath.com has an interactive quadratic
function with graph. Using the function $y = ax^2 + bx + c$, you can adjust
the values of a, b, and c, and observe simultaneous changes in the graph.
You can modify the viewing window of the graph, trace a trail of the
vertex as you modify the parameters of the function, view critical coordinates on the graph, and view a table that describes values of the function on any specified interval. You will need to download the Shockwave
plugin because the activities were made with the tool Macromedia Director. You can see if you have the plugin, or download it, at (1a) http://
www.exploremath.com/about/shockerhelp.cfm.

**TOPICS**: quadratic function, vertex, parabola, graph, symmetry, y-
intercept, x-intercept, coefficient

## DISCUSSION QUESTIONS AND ACTIVITIES

1. Which of the coefficients affects symmetry over the y-axis? Why is
   this true?
2. Which of the coefficients affects the location of the y-intercept? Why
   is this true?
3. Evaluate $b^2 - 4ac$. What does this value relate to on the graph? Why
   is this true? Specify all of the different cases of this relationship.
4. Which of the coefficients affects the direction the parabola opens?
   Why is this true?
5. Determine a relationship between a, b, and the x-coordinate of the
   vertex. Why is this true?
6. Click on "show vertex trail." Examine a vertex trail as you modify the
   value of a. Describe the locus of points and why they form a specific
   pattern. Turn off the trail to clear the locus from the screen. Repeat
   this problem in the two other cases when you modify the values of b
   and c. Explain in each case why they form a specific pattern.

## RELATED INTERNET SITE(S)

See **100. Parabola Defined by Three Points**
See **110. Quadratic Equations 2**

## 112. REALTOR.COM FIND A HOME

### URL: http://realtor.com/FindHome/USMapHome.asp

**SUGGESTED LEVELS**: prealgebra (questions 1–2), algebra (questions 1–4), geometry (questions 3 and 4)

**SITE SUMMARY**: Find current sales in housing markets across the United States. You can specify a certain region in the United States and determine if a relationship exists between the price of the house, the number of bedrooms, the number of bathrooms, and its floor space area. Furthermore, you can investigate how these comparisons change with housing in different parts of the country. To begin, click on the location within the United States where you live. Continue to click and zoom in on the maps until you are able to search for listings within your neighborhood.

**TOPICS**: data collection, data analysis, mean, median, range, linear function, modeling, area of a rectangle, equation of line, slope, y-intercept

### DISCUSSION QUESTIONS AND ACTIVITIES

1. Collect multiple data points that will help you determine the relationship between the number of bedrooms and the number of bathrooms in a typical house in your hometown neighborhood. Explain your solution. Repeat this analysis, but with housing in a different part of the country. Explain any similarities and differences, and possible causes for those discrepancies.

2. How do the mean, median, and range of housing prices compare in the towns around your area? Explain possible causes for similar or different results.

3. Collect data to determine a linear function that describes the price of a house in a neighborhood as related to its floor plan area (in square feet). Once you find a house listing, you may need to click on "More Info" and calculate the area of a house if it is not listed. Explain the real-world significance of the slope and y-intercept of this function.

4. How does the lot size affect the price of a house in a neighborhood? Once you find a house listing, click on "More Info" to view this information for each house listed. Explain your analysis.

### RELATED INTERNET SITE(S)

**Homeadvisor.com**
(112a) http://www.homeadvisor.msn.com/
Search for more property listings across the United States.

**Yahoo! Real Estate**

(112b) http://realestate.yahoo.com/

Find out the value of homes across the United States, a comparison of cities and salaries, and information about buying, selling, renting, and financing a home.

**International Real Estate Digest**

(112c) http://www.ired.com/usa/

This database of state realtors will link you to each individual realtor within a specified region.

**Home Prices**

(112d) http://lib.stat.cmu.edu/DASL/Datafiles/homedat.html

This data file contains sale prices of randomly selected homes in 1993. In addition to the price, the area, age, number of features, location, and taxes are represented in the data set.

# 113. REFLECTIONS OF QUADRATIC FUNCTIONS

## URL: http://www.exploremath.com/activities/Activity_page.cfm? ActivityID=40

**SUGGESTED LEVELS**: advanced algebra (questions 1–4), precalculus (questions 1, 2, 3, 4, and 6), calculus (questions 1–6)

**SITE SUMMARY**: ExploreMath.com has a dynamic quadratic function in the form $f(x) = ax^2 + bx + c$. You can modify each of the coefficients and view immediate changes on the graph. You can also check boxes to see the graphs of $f(-x)$, $-f(x)$, and $-f(-x)$ on the same set of axes. You will need to download the Shockwave plugin because the activities were made with the tool Macromedia Director. You can see if you have the plugin, or download it, at (1a) http://www.exploremath.com/about/shockerhelp.cfm.

**TOPICS**: quadratic function, transformation, symmetry, even function, odd function, minimum, limit, graph, reflection

## DISCUSSION QUESTIONS AND ACTIVITIES

1. Describe the symmetric relationship between $f(x)$, $f(-x)$, $-f(x)$, and $-f(-x)$. Is this also true when $a=0$? Is this also true when $b=0$? Explain why or why not.

2. Under which circumstances does $f(x)$ have the same graph as $f(-x)$? Explain algebraically why this is true. Is there any other pair(s) of functions which have the same graph? Explain why or why not.

3. What is the range of intersections between any pairs of these functions? Explain why this is true.

4. Which two pairs of functions will bound the same area when they intersect? Explain why this is true.

5. When is the area bounded by f(x) and f(−x) a minimum? How do you know?

6. What is the limit of the area bounded by y = f(x) and y = −f(−x) as b approaches infinity? How does this value compare to the limit of the area as b approaches zero?

## 114. RELIABILITY OF SEARCH ENGINES

**URL: http://megasearch.thebighub.com/**

**SUGGESTED LEVELS**: prealgebra (questions 1–4), statistics (questions 1–4)

**SITE SUMMARY**: The BigHub.com is an information source for shopping, news, weather, and business on the Internet. It also contains a metasearch engine, a search engine that is capable of searching multiple search engines simultaneously. The metasearch is capable of providing quick results because they actually organize key word searches ahead of time. That is, the search engines have algorithms that enable them to store addresses and links before you search for them. Since there is a time differential between the engine's organization of word searches and the time you actually search for them, you will occasionally find pages that no longer contain information, have changed information, or are inaccessible. The purpose of this activity is to determine which search engines produce the most reliable results.

**TOPICS**: data collection, data analysis, frequency

### DISCUSSION QUESTIONS AND ACTIVITIES

1. Think of a vocabulary term in your math class. Type that term into the megasearch, check only one of the boxes, and click on Find It! You will end up with ten results on the first page. The name of the search engine that produces each link is listed at the end of the annotation. Click on each of these links and determine if these links are accessible, if they contain information, and if that information relates to the topic you are studying. Repeat the process for the other search engines and determine which search engine produces the best results. Use statis-

tical reasoning in your analysis and provide a data display to support your arguments.

2. How would your results change from question 1 if you search for multiple math terms? Try it.

3. How would your results change from question 1 if you search with multiple search engines simultaneously? Will it make a difference if you check two or three boxes before the searching process? Is there a pattern between the reliability of the return and the number of searches you perform?

4. Perform a megasearch by entering a math term and checking all of the boxes. When you click Find It!, the return will indicate the name(s) of the search engine(s) used to find the link. Which search engine produces the results most often? Is your result the same when you try different words? Use statistical reasoning in your analysis and provide a data display to support your arguments.

## RELATED INTERNET SITE(S)

**Yahoo! Science: Mathematics**
(114a) http://dir.yahoo.com/Science/Mathematics/

**Study Web: Math**
(114b) http://www.studyweb.com/math/

**The Math Forum: Internet Mathematics Library**
(114c) http://forum.swarthmore.edu/library/
    Use the subject tree indices about mathematics and determine the reliability of their links.

**Flags of the World Mirror Sites**
(114d) http://www.allstates-flag.com/flags/mirror.html
    This site has a listing of other sites exactly like it in different parts of the world. This can be a resourceful aid to compare Internet reliability and connection speed to that in a different country.

**Ask Jeeves**
(114e) http://www.askjeeves.com/
    Ask questions about math terms and rate the accuracy of the answers and how well you are linked to the answers.

## 115.  SIGHT VS. SOUND

**URL: http://www.explorescience.com/activities/activity_page. cfm?activityID=38**

    **SUGGESTED LEVELS**: prealgebra (questions 1–2), statistics (questions 1–5)

**SITE SUMMARY**: ExploreScience has created an activity that tests your sight and sound reflexes. When you hear a noise or see a sound, then click on the screen. You will be given your mean reaction time for sight and sound at the end of the experiment. You need the Flash plugin to view this site. If you cannot see the file appear on the screen, then you will need to download the free plugin from Macromedia at (16a) http://www.macromedia.com/shockwave/download/index.cgi?P1 Prod_Version=ShockwaveFlash.

**TOPICS**: data collection, data analysis, normal distributions, mean, median, mode, central limit theorem, hypothesis testing, probability

## DISCUSSION QUESTIONS AND ACTIVITIES

1. Do you have a faster reaction time to sight or sound? How much faster is one reaction than the other type of reaction? Is this always true? Explain your analysis.

2. Does everyone have quicker reaction to the same type of stimulus? Explain how you know. Would a random sight- and hearing-abled person, likely react more quickly to a stop light or an alarm? Explain your reasoning.

3. Plot your reaction means on two different histograms along with the other students' results. Compare the means and standard deviations of the data set.

4. What assumption can be made about reaction time if the distributions were normal? What is the probability that the mean sound reaction time is greater than the mean sight reaction time? Explain your analysis.

5. Are your reaction times significantly better than those of your classmates? Explain how you know.

## RELATED INTERNET SITE(S)

See **(60a) Bop the Mole**
See **29. Circle Zap**

## 116. SIMULATED OCEAN DIVE

**URL: http://illuminations.nctm.org/imath/912/Light/light2.html**

**SUGGESTED LEVELS**: advanced algebra (questions 1 and 4), precalculus (questions 1–4)

**SITE SUMMARY**: NCTM has developed a set of activities in their online i-Standards. This particular activity examines the relationship between light intensity and depth in water. You will collect data using a simulated ocean dive and classroom experiments, and then analyze it using an online data and function plotter.

**TOPICS**: data collection, data analysis, exponential functions, logarithms, difference equations, linear functions, recursive sequence, geometric sequence

## DISCUSSION QUESTIONS AND ACTIVITIES

1. Try the simulated ocean dive. Collect ordered pairs describing the depth and light intensity. What type of function best models this relationship? What type of function best models change in light intensity vs. depth? An interactive graph can be found at the bottom of the page if needed. You can enter your own data, a function, and change the window in the grapher. Explain your analysis.

2. Try the simulated ocean dive. Collect ordered pairs describing the depth and light intensity. Find the log of the light intensity, and graph log(light intensity) vs. depth. An interactive graph can be found at (116a) http://illuminations.nctm.org/imath/912/Light/light3c.html at the bottom of the page if needed. You can enter your own data, a function, and change the window in the grapher. What type of function best models this relationship? Use the equation of the model to determine an equation without logarithms. Compare your results with question 1. Explain your analysis.

3. Try the simulated ocean dive. Collect ordered pairs describing the depth and light intensity spaced apart every ten meters. Find a recursive equation that compares each pair of consecutive data points. What conclusions can you make about the change in light intensity from this equation? Graph change in light intensity vs. light intensity. An interactive graph can be found at (116b) http://illuminations. nctm.org/imath/912/Light/light3b.html at the bottom of the page if needed. You can enter your own data, a function, and change the window in the grapher. What type of function best models this relationship? What does the equation of the graph tell you about the change in light intensity from this equation? Explain your findings.

4. Examine the discrete experiment with plexiglass. Record data relating the distance and light intensity. What type of function best models this relationship? What type of function best models depth vs. change in light intensity? An interactive graph can be found at the bottom of the page if needed. You can enter your own data, a function, and

change the window in the grapher. Explain your analysis. How do your results compare and/or contrast with the experiment in question 1?

## RELATED INTERNET SITE(S)

See **69. Inverse Square Law**

# 117. SLIDING ROD PROBLEM

**URL: http://home.netvigator.com/~wingkei9/javagsp/ladder.html**

**SUGGESTED LEVELS**: precalculus (questions 1–3), calculus (questions 1–5)

**SITE SUMMARY**: A ladder is sliding down a wall with a step of the ladder leaving a trace of its path. This locus of points will help you determine the relationship between the different motion components of the ladder. Click on the refresh or reload button on your browser to clear the locus of points.

**TOPICS**: conic sections, ellipse, related rates, equation, rate of change, optimization

## DISCUSSION QUESTIONS AND ACTIVITIES

1. What type of function is generated by the locus of points? Explain how you know. Generate an equation that describes point R at any given x-value and y-value. Show your work.

2. What would the graph look like if the ladder could move to the left and below the x-axis? Explain your reasoning.

3. How does the graph change as you modify the length of the ladder, PQ? Explain why this happens.

4. What is the relationship between the rate of change between the x-coordinate and y-coordinate? Explain how you know.

5. When is the point R moving the fastest? Explain how you know.

## RELATED INTERNET SITE(S)

See **35. Conic Sections as the Locus of Perpendicular Bisectors**

**ExploreMath Conic Sections**

(117a) http://www.exploremath.com/activities/activity_list.cfm?categoryID=1

These interactive explorations compare the graphs of conic sections to their equations and definitions. You will need the Shockwave plugin on your machine to view these pages.

# 118. SLOPE

## URL: http://www.mathresources.com/slope.htm

**SUGGESTED LEVELS**: algebra (questions 1–5)
**SITE SUMMARY**: This applet from Math Resources allows you to modify two points on a coordinate plane that create a line and view the resulting slope, intercepts, and equation of the line. Click and drag points A and B to change the line.
**TOPICS**: slope, x-intercept, y-intercept, equation of a line

## DISCUSSION QUESTIONS AND ACTIVITIES

1. What is the slope of a line that does not have an x-intercept? Is this always true? Explain.

   What is the slope of a line that does not have a y-intercept? Is this always true? Explain.

2. Where can you find the value of the slope in an equation of a line? Is this true for every line? Explain.

3. What is the slope of a line if it only crosses the intersection of gray grid lines?

4. What is the location of the x-intercept at the moment the slope has the same value as the y-intercept? Explain your solution.

5. Derive an equation that relates the slope, x-intercept, and y-intercept of a line. Why is this true?

## RELATED INTERNET SITE(S)

**Slope of a Line from Its Equation**
(118a) http://www.csm.astate.edu/~rossa/Eqnslope/Eqnslope.html
Identify the slope of a line from a randomly created equation and graph. Input your answer and the computer will tell you if you are correct. If you get an incorrect answer, the computer will respond with a hint and then let you try again.

**Slope Version 2**
(118b) http://www.coe.tamu.edu/~strader/math166H/Cartesian/slope2.html

Illustrates the coordinate method of finding the slope of a line. You can choose any point on a specific line to see that the slope remains constant. You can also modify the slope and y-intercept to view this pattern for any other line.

### Finding the Slope of a Line Segment
(118c) http://www.accessone.com/~bbunge/Algebra/Algebra3-2.html
Plot two points on the coordinate plane and see how the slope of the line determined by those two points is calculated.

### Line Graphing Applet
(118d) http://216.247.77.187/algebra/lines/graph_applet.html
This applet illustrates the relationship between the slope, y-intercept, equation, and graph of a line. You have the option to translate and rotate the graph and see changes in the values of the slope and y-intercept. The applet will also state the corresponding ordered pair where your mouse pointer is located in the Cartesian plane.

## 119. SMARTRAVELER

### URL: http://www.smartraveler.com/

**SUGGESTED LEVELS**: prealgebra (question 1–3), statistics (questions 1–3)

**SITE SUMMARY**: Real-time traffic reports for major highways are available for a dozen large cities in the United States. Data are provided in terms of the speed of traffic on different parts of a highway map. The user has the option of viewing real-time maps, incidents, video, construction closures, weather, and transit.

**TOPICS**: data collection, data analysis, navigation, speed

### DISCUSSION QUESTIONS AND ACTIVITIES

1. Choose a city and locate the most recent traffic incident. How does the time from the most recent incident relate to the speed of traffic? Collect data for multiple incidents in multiple cities. How long does it take for traffic to resume normal speed?

2. Choose a city that displays the entire traffic map. Over a couple of days, analyze how the traffic changes speed with respect to the time of day. Suppose you had a job that required you to be in the city for eight hours each day, and you have the choice of when you would like to start your workday. If you were driving from the suburbs into the city, what time would you leave and which route would you take? Justify your answer.

3. Over a week, examine how the weather and road construction affect driving speeds on the highway. How much more driving time would you expect when these factors vary?

### RELATED INTERNET SITE(S)

**Seattle Transportation—Traffic Flow Data and Maps**
(199a) http://www.pan.ci.seattle.wa.us/td/tfdmaps.asp
    View archived graphical data from 1996 to 1998 that show the varying densities of traffic in different parts of Seattle. Use this information to design strategies for driving through town or creating road improvement plans for the city.

**California Traffic and Vehicle Data Systems Unit**
(119b) http://www.dot.ca.gov/hq/traffops/saferesr/trafdata/
    Examine monthly traffic and freeway ramp volumes since 1972 in the state of California. Use this information to determine where new ramps need to be built, or where construction traffic should be redirected.

**Map Quest**
(119c) http://www.mapquest.com/
    Obtain real-time traffic reports from major cities around the United States.

**Traffic Simulation**
(119d) http://www.jerico.demon.co.uk/java/traffic.html
(119e) http://www.phy.ntnu.edu.tw/java/trafficControl/trafficControl.html
    Explore Java applets that allow you to monitor traffic patterns while adjusting how and when cars stop.

## 120. SMOKING AND CANCER

### URL: http://lib.stat.cmu.edu/DASL/Datafiles/cigcancerdat.html

    **SUGGESTED LEVELS**: prealgebra (questions 1–5), algebra (questions 1–5), statistics (questions 1–5)
    **SITE SUMMARY**: This historical data set compares the number of cigarettes smoked per capita to various causes of death in different states.
    **TOPICS**: data collection, data analysis, data display, percentage, modeling, linear function, confidence intervals, extrapolation, outlier

### DISCUSSION QUESTIONS AND ACTIVITIES

1. Which form of cancer is most related to cigarette smoking? Use the data to explain your answer.
2. Do the data prove that cigarette smoking causes cancer? Explain why or why not.

3. How many more people smoked cigarettes than died from lung cancer in 1960? Explain your solution.

4. If another state reported 4,500 cigarettes smoked per capita, predict the number of deaths in the other categories. Explain your degree of certainty in each prediction. Show your work.

5. Which states have unusually high or low death rates caused by cancer? Explain how you determined this result. What factor(s) might contribute to these values?

## RELATED INTERNET SITE(S)

**Cancer and Mathematics**
(120a) http://www.mste.uiuc.edu/dildine/cancer/cancer.html
This site illustrates how cancerous cells are affected geometrically. Examine the ratio of the perimeter squared to the area of a cell in order to determine if it is cancerous.

See **(102c)** and **(102d) Yearly Consumption of Cigarettes**

# 121. SOLAR SYSTEM DATA

## URL: http://www.seds.org/nineplanets/nineplanets/data.html

**SUGGESTED LEVELS**: prealgebra (questions 1, 2, 5, and 6), geometry (questions 5–7), advanced algebra (questions 3, 4, and 8)
**SITE SUMMARY**: Compare size, distance, orbits, density, and other characteristics of planets in our solar system.
**TOPICS**: exponents, volume of sphere, function, quadratic function, inversely proportional, speed, circumference, data analysis, interpolation, proportion, radius, sphere

## DISCUSSION QUESTIONS AND ACTIVITIES

1. Why are there 365 days in a calendar year? How does the calendar account for the fraction of a day in each orbit? Which planet would have a calendar year that would last a lifetime? Explain your reasoning.

2. Suppose you wanted to build an accurate scale model of the solar system. Place the sun in the center of your classroom and Pluto at a wall in the classroom. Where would the rest of the planets be located?

3. The light intensity of an object is inversely proportional to the square of the object's distance from a source, such as the sun or a light bulb. If the amount of light intensity on Earth represents 1, what is the light intensity on the rest of the planets? Explain your reasoning.

4. The asteroid belt is around four hundred million kilometers from the sun. How long would it take the belt to complete one full cycle around the sun? Explain your analysis.

5. In the physical data link, which planet is about ten times larger than another planet? Explain your analysis.

6. In the physical data link, how is the density of each planet determined? (Hint: density units are sometimes represented as kilograms per cubic meter.) Explain your analysis.

7. In the physical data link, which planet spins around at the fastest rate? Explain how you determined this result.

8. In the miscellaneous data link, what function best models the relationship between a planet's gravity and its escape velocity? Explain your analysis. Predict the escape velocity of a ship from the moon if its gravity is 0.166g. Show your work.

### RELATED INTERNET SITE(S)

See **69. Inverse Square Law**

See **116. Simulated Ocean Dive**

## 122. SQUARING THE TRIANGLE

**URL: http://www.shodor.org/interactivate/activities/pyth/index. html**

**SUGGESTED LEVELS**: geometry (questions 1–6)
**SITE SUMMARY**: The Shodor Foundation has created a Java applet that displays a dynamic right triangle with squares constructed on each of its sides. The display allows you to adjust the lengths of the legs of the triangle to determine the relationship between the legs and hypotenuse of a right triangle. As you modify the side lengths, you are also shown changes in the triangle's angle measures and the area of the squares.

**TOPICS**: sum of angles in a triangle, angle size, triangle inequality, Pythagorean Theorem, area of a square

## DISCUSSION QUESTIONS AND ACTIVITIES

1. Drag the bar to change the side lengths. As you change these lengths, the angle measures will also change. Do all of the angles change? Explain why or why not. Use the data to determine the sum of the angles in a triangle. Explain your procedures.

2. Determine the relationship between the relative size of the side lengths and the relative size of the angles in the triangle. What patterns do you notice? Explain why this might be true.

3. Devise an inequality that compares all three of the side lengths in the triangle. Explain how you determined this result.

4. Modify the lengths of the legs of the right triangle, and watch the changing area of the square that contains side AC. Do you think this measurement is always accurate? Explain possible causes in the changes of decimal place accuracy.

5. How do the area of the squares relate to each other? Use this relationship and determine a formula that compares the lengths of the sides of a right triangle. Is this formula always true in a right triangle? Justify your reasoning. Do you think this formula will work in any triangle? Explain why or why not.

6. Do you think this exploration can be performed only using squares? Explain why or why not.

## RELATED INTERNET SITE(S)

**Investigating Triangles**
(122a) http://forum.swarthmore.edu/~annie/gsp.handouts/investigate/triangle.html
This Java applet gives you the opportunity to compare the side lengths of a triangle and sums of side lengths in order to determine the triangle inequality.
See **108. Proofs of the Pythagorean Theorem**

# 123. STATISTICAL JAVA

## URL: http://www.stat.vt.edu/~sundar/java/applets/

**SUGGESTED LEVELS**: statistics (questions 1–5)
**SITE SUMMARY**: This site offers a variety of applets on statistics. The applet for this investigation is an experiment that compares your reaction times between left and right hands. Click on the home folder, go into statistical application, then experimental design, and select im-

proved design. Select ten students and ten participants, start selection, then randomize, then start applet. Read the applet instruction in the other window to start the activity. This design can be used to compare reaction times from different members in the class, but it also can measure an individual's reaction time through repeated trials.

**TOPICS**: data collection, data analysis, expected value, confidence intervals, hypothesis testing, central limit theorem

### DISCUSSION QUESTIONS AND ACTIVITIES

1. With 95 percent accuracy, how fast does your dominant hand take to click on the target? How about your nondominant hand? Explain your analysis.

2. Is there a significant difference between your agility with your dominant hand than the agility of your nondominant hand? Explain how you determined this result.

3. Share your data with your classmates. Is your dominant hand significantly faster or slower than the dominant hands of your classmates? Hypothesize why or why not. How about the speed of your nondominant hand? Explain.

4. How are the results of the experiment affected when you change the number of trials? Explain.

5. Cover the part of the screen with the red and green starting lights so you are not giving a warning before the start. Repeat the experiment with ten trials. Are the results significantly different without the warning? Explain.

### RELATED INTERNET SITE(S)

See **29. Circle Zap**
See **(60a) Bop the Mole**

## 124. STRAWBERRY MACAW'S 23 MATCHES PUZZLE

### URL: http://207.106.82.89/puzzles/23match/23match.htm

**SUGGESTED LEVELS**: prealgebra (question 1), advanced algebra (questions 1–4)

**SITE SUMMARY**: The Strawberry Macaw's 23 matches puzzle is a game that incorporates an arithmetic sequence in its solution. The objective of the game is to devise a strategy that will leave one match remaining on the screen. Play begins with 23 matches, and the user interacts with the computer by taking at most three matches during each turn.

**TOPICS**: sequence, explicit, recursive

## DISCUSSION QUESTIONS AND ACTIVITIES

1. Play the match game until you feel sure that you can win. Explain a strategy that will help you win the match game every time you play.

2. Devise an arithmetic sequence that incorporates this strategy, and explain what each of the variables represents.

3. How would your sequence change if you started with a different number of matches? Indicate the situations that could prevent you from winning if your turn began the game. Test your new strategy with a partner.

4. How would your sequence change if the players could choose up to a different maximum number of matches during a turn? For example what if they can choose only one or two matches during a turn, or up to four, etc. Test your new strategy with a partner.

## RELATED INTERNET SITE(S)

**Nim Game**
(124a) http://www.darkfish.com/nimskulls/nimskulls.html
   This game is similar to the match game, except there is a different number of pieces at the beginning of the game. Try to determine the sequences that will help you win every time.

**Nim Variations**
(124b) http://www.freearcade.com/Nim.jav/Nim.html
(124c) http://hobbes.la.asu.edu/java/circles/penny.html
(124d) http://www.cut-the-knot.com/nim_st.html
   These games offer different variations of the Nim game, making them more difficult to win.

See **132. Towers of Hanoi**


## 125. SUN OR MOON RISE/SET TABLE FOR ONE YEAR

### URL: http://aa.usno.navy.mil/AA/data/docs/RS_OneYear.html

**SUGGESTED LEVELS**: precalculus (questions 1–5)
**SITE SUMMARY**: This database provides the predicted daily sunrise, sunset, moonrise, and moonset throughout the year. You can enter any

city from the country or world, or a specific latitudinal and longitudinal position. Click on compute table to view the data.

TOPICS: data collection, data analysis, modeling, sinusoidal function, amplitude, period

## DISCUSSION QUESTIONS AND ACTIVITIES

1. Obtain the sunrise and sunset data for a large city near your hometown. Generate two separate functions that model each set of data in the form y=acos(b(x−c))+d. Explain the physical representation of each of the values in the equation.

2. Predict the changes in the general cosine equation if you selected a city north of your location. Explain your reasoning. What would change in the equation if the city were south, east, or west of your location?

3. Where on the earth would you expect the longest days and longest nights? When will this happen? Explain how you determined this result.

4. Where on the graph are the different solstices and equinoxes? Explain why you selected these points.

5. Obtain the moonrise and moonset data for a large city near your hometown. Generate two separate functions that model the data in the form y=acos(b(x−c))+d. Explain the physical representation of each of the values in the equation. How does this equation compare with the results in question 1? Explain why there would be similarities and/or differences.

## RELATED INTERNET SITE(S)

See **95. Normal Daily Maximum Temperature, Deg F**

See **43. Effects of a, b, c, d on the Graph of y = a(sin bx + c) + d**

See **101. Pendulum**

## 126. SYSTEM OF TWO QUADRATIC INEQUALITIES

**URL: http://www.exploremath.com/activities/Activity_page.cfm? ActivityID=30**

SUGGESTED LEVELS: advanced algebra (questions 1–6)

SITE SUMMARY: ExploreMath.com has an interactive pair of quadratic functions with graph. Using two functions in the form $y = ax^2 +$

bx + c, you can adjust each of the coefficients and observe simultaneous changes in the graph. You can set the functions to represent equations or inequalities, and then view their intersections or intersecting regions on the graph. You can modify the viewing window of the graph, view coordinates on the graph and highlighted intersection points, and view a table that describes values of the function on any specified interval. You will need the Shockwave plugin because the activities were made with the tool Macromedia Director. You can see if you have the plugin, or download it, at (1a) http://www.exploremath.com/about/shockerhelp.cfm.

**TOPICS**: graph, quadratic function, linear function, equation, inequalities, system of inequalities, system of equations, union, intersection

## DISCUSSION QUESTIONS AND ACTIVITIES

1. Explain how you would transform the quadratic function into a linear function. How do you know the new result is a linear function?

2. Generate a system of linear inequalities that will have a solution only in the first quadrant. How do you know that the shaded region will not fall into another quadrant outside of the viewing window? Is there another system that will produce this result? If not, explain why. If so, develop a set of necessary attributes that must be present in each of these systems.

3. In a system of inequalities with any combination of linear and quadratic functions, what is the least number of intersecting regions? What is the greatest number of intersecting regions? Provide an example of each case.

4. Generate a system of equations that will produce intersecting points of $(-2,3)$ and $(1,0)$. Verify this solution on the graph and algebraically. Is there another system of equations that will include the same intersections? Explain why or why not.

5. How are the coefficients of two quadratic inequalities related if their solution region is symmetric? Explain all possibilities.

6. Is it possible for the union and intersection to be identical in a system of inequalities that contains different coefficients? Examine both linear and quadratic inequalities. Explain your reasoning.

## RELATED INTERNET SITE(S)

**Linear Programming**
(126a) http://www.exploremath.com/activities/Activity_page.cfm?ActivityID =31

This investigation at Exploremath.com has you experiment with a function in the form $f(x,y) = ax + by + c$ with various constraints in order to optimize a situation.

**Systems of Linear Inequalities in Standard Form**
(126b) http://www.exploremath.com/activities/Activity_page.cfm?ActivityID =29

Graph up to six different linear inequalities in standard form and identify patterns in their intersections.

**Quadratic Inequalities**
(126c) http://www.exploremath.com/activities/Activity_page.cfm?ActivityID =35

This interactive quadratic inequality and graph will show the solution set with one parabola.

# 127. TANGRAM JAVA PUZZLE

## URLs: http://enchantedmind.com/puzzles/tangram/tangram.htm
## http://www.javalovers.com/tangram.htm

SUGGESTED LEVELS: geometry (questions 1–4)
SITE SUMMARY: These identical Java applets provide various polygons so you can complete tangram puzzles. Your goal is to take a set of polygons and use transformations to generate different pictures of animals. Click on the Tangram button to begin.
TOPICS: tangram, polygon, transformation, convex, nonconvex

## DISCUSSION QUESTIONS AND ACTIVITIES

1. Can you find more than one method to complete any of the tangram puzzles? If so, indicate your solutions. If not, explain why.

2. Design a different animal with the tangrams. Challenge your classmate(s) to complete your new design.

3. Generate a design that contains the same area as the other figures, but is impossible to solve with this tangram set. Explain why there could not be a solution.

4. What is the smallest sided polygon you can create using all of the pieces? What is the largest sided polygon you can create using all of the pieces? How do your answers change if the polygons must be convex? Explain.

## RELATED INTERNET SITE(S)

**Interactive Tangrams**
(127a) http://www.mathresources.com/tangram.htm
(127b) http://w0.bonus.com/bonus/card/TangramTangramTangram.html
(127c) http://www.tangram-digital.de/solo.html
    These sites include additional interactive tangram sets that you can manipulate to create figures on the screen.

See **(53a) Patterns Program**

See **(53b) Catalog of Isohedral Tilings by Symmetric Polygonal Tiles**

See **(53c) Tessellate**

**Problem Solving with Pentominoes**
(127d) http://home.planetinternet.be/%7Eodettedm/indexe.html
    Arrange groups of five connected squares in order to create a figure or to tile a plane.

## 128. TEACHER PAY BY STATE

### URL: http://lib.stat.cmu.edu/DASL /Datafiles/teacherpaydat.html

**SUGGESTED LEVELS**: prealgebra (questions 1–3), algebra (questions 1–4), statistics (questions 1–4)
    **SITE SUMMARY**: This data set represents the 1985 average salaries of public school teachers in each state. The data set also shows the average amount of spending on each pupil.
    **TOPICS**: data collection, data analysis, average, modeling, linear function, deviation, outlier

## DISCUSSION QUESTIONS AND ACTIVITIES

1. In which state would you want to look for teaching positions? Explain why.

2. Which region of the country spends the most money on teacher salaries per state? Which region of the country spends the most money on students per state? Explain how you determined this result.

3. Which states have an unusually high or low salary for their region in the country? Which states have an unusually high or low pupil spending for their region in the country? Explain your analysis.

4. Generate a function that will predict teacher salary from pupil spending. Which states are good representations of the line? Which states are not good representations of the line? Explain your analyses.

## RELATED INTERNET SITE(S)

See **(10a) The Pay Gap by Occupation**

# 129. TIME ESTIMATION

**URL: http://www.explorescience.com/activities/activity_page.cfm?activityID=41**

**SUGGESTED LEVELS**: prealgebra (questions 1–2), algebra (question 3), statistics (questions 1–6)

**SITE SUMMARY**: ExploreScience has created an activity that tests your ability to judge a lapse in time. Your goal is to click the screen after you think a certain amount of time has passed. Once you stop the experiment, you are told how close you were to the actual time. You need the Flash plugin to view this site. If you cannot see the file appear on the screen, then you will need to download the free plugin from Macromedia at (16a) http://www.macromedia.com/shockwave/download/index.cgi?P1_Prod_Version=ShockwaveFlash.

**TOPICS**: data collection, data analysis, normal distribution, mean, median, mode, confidence intervals, probability, scatter plot, linear function, line of best fit, histogram, slope, y-intercept

## DISCUSSION QUESTIONS AND ACTIVITIES

1. Which of the time intervals can you predict most accurately? Discuss the criteria you are using to judge which is most accurate. Explain your analysis.

2. Repeat multiple trials using the same time interval. Do your results get closer or farther away from the actual time? Is this result the same if you repeat the experiment with a different time interval? Describe any patterns and conclusions you draw from the data.

3. Try each of the time intervals, and record and plot each of the data on an actual (experimental) time vs. predicted time graph. Create a line of best fit that best represents the data. Explain the significance of the slope and y-intercept of this line. How do these results compare with your classmates' results?

4. Repeat multiple trials using a small time interval. Create a histogram that describes the frequency of occurrence of specific times, maybe equally spaced 0.2 seconds apart. Describe the shape of your distribution. How does the shape compare with that of your classmates?

How would the shape change if you examined a larger time interval? Explain how you know.

5. How likely are you to obtain an experimental result of six seconds when your goal is to estimate five seconds? Explain your analysis.

6. What is the greatest time that would represent an unusual underestimation of five seconds? Explain your criteria and analysis.

## RELATED INTERNET SITE(S)

See **29. Circle Zap**

**Real-time Histogram**
(129a) http://www.explorescience.com/activities/activity_page.cfm?activityID =17

Try to predict every two-second interval of time. A histogram describing your accuracy is built and updated each time you click on the mouse. You need the Flash plugin to view this site. You can download it for free at (16a) http://www.macromedia.com/shockwave/download/index.cgi?P1_Prod_ Version= ShockwaveFlash.

# 130.  TOP 100 EVER ADJUSTED

## URLs: http://www.the-movie-times.com/thrsdir/Top10everad.html
## http://mrshowbiz.go.com/movies/boxoffice/adjusted.html

**SUGGESTED LEVELS**: advanced algebra (questions 2–5), precalculus (questions 2–5), statistics (question 1)

**SITE SUMMARY**: This data set features the 100 movies that have had the highest gross amount of money at the box office based on inflation adjustments. The list also contains the year each movie was released and the total gross that the movie obtained during that year.

**TOPICS**: data collection, data analysis, modeling data, extrapolation, exponential function, proportion

## DISCUSSION QUESTIONS AND ACTIVITIES

1. Which decade has been most influenced by blockbusters? Explain your analysis.

2. What is the average rate of inflation assumed in this data set? Explain how you determined this result.

3. How long does it take for an inflation adjusted gross to be valued at five times the original gross? Explain your analysis.

4. Suppose the largest grossing film is released in 2010. Accounting for inflation, what is the least amount of money it will earn at the box office? Explain your analysis.

5. Predict the gross box office totals of *Star Wars Episode II* that will be released in 2002. Explain your analysis.

## RELATED INTERNET SITE(S)

**The Top Grossing Movies of All Time**
(130a) http://www.imdb.com/Charts/usatopmovies
(130b) http://movieweb.com/movie/alltime.html
The Internet Movie Database and Movieweb have a listing of movies that have grossed the most amount of money in history. The movies are listed in order based on their box office gross, the year they were released, and their popularity with fans. You can also view data about top international grossing films, as well as worldwide sales.

See **142. USA Box Office Charts Archive**

**U.S. Film Average Price from 1935 to 1997**
(130c) http://osu.orst.edu/dept/pol_sci/fac/sahr/movie.htm
This histogram follows the price of a movie ticket for selected years throughout history. The actual prices and inflation-adjusted prices are compared.

## 131. THE TORTOISE AND THE HARE RACE

**URL:http://www.shodor.org/master/interactivate/activities/tortoise/index.html**

  **SUGGESTED LEVELS**: advanced algebra (questions 1–5), precalculus (questions 1–5)
  **SITE SUMMARY**: This race recalls Zeno's paradox, where the animals travel half as far during each stage of the race. The tortoise has the opportunity to get a good lead on the hare at the start of the race. You can look at successive stages, previous stages, and zoom in on the characters' positions throughout the race.
  **TOPICS**: data collection, sequence, geometric series, exponential function, graphing, asymptote, limit

## DISCUSSION QUESTIONS AND ACTIVITIES

1. Graph the total distance of each character as a function of their stage. What pattern occurs in both functions?

2. Devise the equations of the functions that model the total distance traveled for each animal. Can you prove that one function is always greater than the other? Explain why or why not.

3. Who will win the race? Explain how you know.

4. How would the result of the race change if the characters started at different positions? Explain your reasoning.

5. What type of function is modelled by the difference in the distance between the two animals? Explain how you know.

## RELATED INTERNET SITE(S)

See **(64a) Online Encyclopedia of Integer Sequences**
See **64. The Interactive Math Puzzle Archives**

## 132. TOWERS OF HANOI

**URLs: http://www.beavton.k12.or.us/Greenway/games/tower/tower.htm**
**http://www.cut-the-knot.com/recurrence/hanoi.html**
**http://www.teratron.com/applets/towers/towers.html**
**http://ace.ulyssis.student.kuleuven.ac.be/~jeans/study/hanoi/hanoi.html**
**http://www.brainviews.com/abFiles/IntHanoi.htm**

**SUGGESTED LEVELS**: prealgebra (questions 1 and 2), advanced algebra (questions 1–4)

**SITE SUMMARY**: This game is a symbolic representation of the Tower of Bramah, a historical and symbolic representation of the time remaining on Earth given by a Buddhist god. As the story is told, the Earth will crumble and vanish once all of the sixty-four discs from the left needle are moved to the right needle and end up in the same order in which they started. However, the restriction to this game is that you cannot place a larger disc on top of a smaller disc. The goal then, will be to determine the least amount of time this game with sixty-four discs would take. A Java-based simulation will give you a chance to play the game with a fewer and varied number of discs. Once you determine a strategy to win the game, a pattern will appear relating the number of discs and the least number of moves it takes to win the game.

**TOPICS**: sequence, explicit, recursive, data collection, data analysis, exponential function

## DISCUSSION QUESTIONS AND ACTIVITIES

1. Play the game with the least number of discs until you can win. Describe a strategy that will help you win in the least number of turns. One turn represents moving a disc from one needle to another needle.

2. Increase the number of discs and play the game until you can win in the least amount of turns. Describe any necessary changes in strategy.

3. Create a data table relating the number of discs you begin with, and the least number of turns it takes to complete the game. Describe a recursive pattern that allows you to generate the next value in the table. Generate an explicit pattern that allows you to predict any value in the table in the form of a function.

4. According to the Buddhist legend, estimate the least amount of remaining time on Earth if the game begins with sixty-four discs. Explain your reasoning.

## RELATED INTERNET SITE(S)

**Paul Heckman's Java 1.1 Applet for Solving the Tower of Hanoi Puzzle**
(132a)http://members.aol.com/paulhckmn/jHanoi1.htm
    This applet will solve the Towers of Hanoi puzzle and state the specific moves necessary to finish in the least number of attempts. You can modify the number of discs and the algorithm used to solve the puzzle.

**Towers of Hanoi**
(132b) http://www.geocities.com/TimesSquare/Corner/2030/rzhanoi.html
    This Towers of Hanoi Java applet allows you to use up to four needles to place discs. Examine if the strategies and predictions change when you use more needles in the puzzle.

See **(124a) Nim Game**

# 133. TRANSFORMATION GOLF

## URL: http://www.numeracyresources.co.uk/golftrans.html

SUGGESTED LEVELS: geometry (questions 1–7)
    SITE SUMMARY: This activity promotes the use of transformation by playing golf on a coordinate plane. The goal is to put the ball in a hole that is located somewhere on the coordinate plane. You have the option to reflect over each axis, rotate ninety degrees in either direction, or translate in any direction. If you cannot see the file appear on the screen, then you will need to download the free plugin from Macromedia at (16a) http://www.macromedia.com/shockwave/download/index.

cgi?P1_Prod_Version=ShockwaveFlash. This file may take a couple of minutes to load onto your screen because it acts like a piece of software. Once the file is ready, you will be able to interact with the screen without any additional waiting time. Click on Refresh or Reload on your browser to restart the simulation.

**TOPICS**: transformations, rotation, reflection, translation, coordinate plane, coordinate

## DISCUSSION QUESTIONS AND ACTIVITIES

1. What is the smallest possible score on the first hole? Explain your steps.

2. When is it better to use a rotation instead of a reflection? When is it better to use a reflection instead of a rotation? When is it best to use a translation? Explain your reasoning.

3. A point is located at (x,y). Where is its image after a reflection over the x-axis? Where is its image after a reflection over the y-axis? Explain how you determined this result.

4. A point is located at (x,y). Where is its image after a rotation of ninety degrees clockwise about the origin? Where is its image after a rotation of ninety degrees counterclockwise about the origin? Explain how you determined this result.

5. A point is located at (x,y). How many one-unit translations are equivalent to a reflection over the y-axis? How many one-step translations are equivalent to a reflection over the x-axis? Give your answers in terms of x and/or y. Explain your reasoning.

6. A point is located at (x,y). How many one-unit translations are equivalent to a clockwise rotation of ninety degrees about the origin? How many one-step translations are equivalent to a counterclockwise rotation of ninety degrees about the origin? Give your answers in terms of x and/or y. Explain your reasoning.

7. A point is located at (x,y). Devise a method that would use reflections and/or rotations to translate a point z units in a specific direction. Explain as many cases as you can find.

## RELATED INTERNET SITE(S)

See **(23b) Maze Game**
See **(23c) Battleship**

## 134. TRIANGLE'S TREASURES

### URL: http://www.cut-the-knot.com/triangle/EulerLine.html

**SUGGESTED LEVELS**: geometry (questions 1–6)

**SITE SUMMARY**: This applet from Cut-the-Knot is designed to discuss the Euler line and the nine point circle. However, the menus in the applet give you opportunities to investigate a large variety of lines, points, and circles associated with a triangle. You can drag the vertices of the triangle and observe changes in the diagram. Click on "Pop It Up" to begin, and use the drop-down menus to add or remove objects from the screen.

**TOPICS**: circle, angle bisector, incircle, perpendicular bisector, triangle, nine point circle, altitude, Euler line, circumcenter, radius

### DISCUSSION QUESTIONS AND ACTIVITIES

1. The center of the incircle will be the intersection of which lines? Explain how you determined this result. What additional information would you need to verify your prediction?

2. The perpendicular bisectors will intersect outside of what type of triangle? Explain how you determined this result. What additional information would you need to verify your prediction?

3. All of the vertices of which triangle will be on the nine point circle? Explain how you determined this result. What additional information would you need to verify your prediction?

4. If the angle bisectors and altitudes intersect at the same point, then what other sets of lines will also intersect at that same point? Why is this true?

5. Which intersections are on the Euler line?

6. Under what conditions in the triangle will the circumcenter have the largest radius? No radius? The smallest radius? Explain your reasoning.

### RELATED INTERNET SITE(S)

**The Euler Line of a Triangle**
(134a)http: //aleph0.clarku.edu/~djoyce/java/Geometry/eulerline.html
(134b)http: //www.reginacoeli.org/mrspi/geometry/euler.htm

These applets show the collinearity between the circumcenter, orthocenter, and centroid of a triangle. Drag around the vertices and notice that this relationship remains true for any triangle.

**Nine Point Circle**
(134c) http:www.cs.princeton.edu/~ah/alg_anim/version2/NinePtCircle.html
(134d) http:www.nevada.edu/~baragar/geom/Ninept.htm
(134e) http:www.geom.umn.edu/~demo5337/Group2/nineptan5.html
   These applets display all of the characteristics that define a nine point circle.


# 135. TRIGONOMETRIC IDENTITIES

## URL: http://www.sisweb.com/math/trig/identities.htm

   **SUGGESTED LEVELS**: precalculus (questions 1–7)
   **SITE SUMMARY**: This reference list includes a variety of identities and relationships among triangles and functions. The UP link will send you to more tables of mathematical formulas.
   **TOPICS**: right triangle, trigonometry, trigonometry identities, proof, symbolic manipulation, unit circle


## DISCUSSION QUESTIONS AND ACTIVITIES

1. Use a unit circle to verify the opposite angle identities listed below the right triangle trigonometry definitions. Use a diagram in each case to support your reasoning.

2. Prove the three Pythagorean identities (the first one is $\sin^2 x + \cos^2 x = 1$). Why are they given this name?

3. Is $\tan(x+y)$ equal to $\sin(x+y)$ divided by $\cos(x+y)$? Explain why or why not.

4. Explain why the three forms of $\cos 2x$ are equivalent.

5. Use the cosine and sine double angle identities to find $\sin^2(2x) + \cos^2(2x)$. Is there another way to determine this result? Explain.

6. Prove one of the identities about the difference of the sine or cosine of two angles.

7. The table of common tangents evenly divides values by one-fourth. Is it possible to create another table that divides each of the values by a different whole number? Explain why or why not.


## RELATED INTERNET SITE(S)

See **(3a) The Law of Sines**
See **(3b)** and **(3c) The Law of Cosines**
See **38. Dave's Short Trig Course**
See **137. Unit Circle**

## 136. 2 × 2 LINEAR SYSTEMS

**URL: http://www.exploremath.com/activities/Activity_page.cfm?
ActivityID=18**

SUGGESTED LEVELS: algebra (question 1), advanced algebra (questions 1–5)

SITE SUMMARY: ExploreMath.com has an interactive linear system with graph. Using two linear functions in standard form, you can manipulate each of the coefficients and observe simultaneous changes in the graph. You can view the determinant of the system and both equations in slope-intercept form. You can also modify the viewing window of the graph, view coordinates on the graph, and view a table that describes values of the function on any specified interval. You will need the Shockwave plugin because the activities were made with the tool Macromedia Director. You can see if you have the plugin, or download it, at (1a) http://www.exploremath.com/about/shockerhelp.cfm.

TOPICS: graph, system of equations, determinant, matrices, linear equation

### DISCUSSION QUESTIONS AND ACTIVITIES

1. Where is the solution to the system on the graph? Verify your claim algebraically.
2. What do the numbers in the determinant grid represent, and how is the value calculated? Explain how you determined this.
3. How does the value of the determinant relate to the number of solutions in the system of equation? Explain how you determined this.
4. How does the sign of the determinant relate to the two lines? Explain how you determined this.
5. How does the value of the determinant relate to the value of the constant, c? Explain why.

### RELATED INTERNET SITE(S)

See **(126b) Systems of Linear Inequalities in Standard Form**

See **100. Parabola Defined by Three Points**

# 137.  UNIT CIRCLE

## URL: http://www.exploremath.com/activities/Activity_page.cfm? ActivityID=19

**SUGGESTED LEVELS**: advanced algebra (questions 1–5), precalculus (questions 1–8)

**SITE SUMMARY**: ExploreMath.com has an interactive unit circle that will generate graphs of cosine, sine, and tangent functions. You can modify angle measures in degrees or radians. You can modify the viewing window of the graph, modify the center and length of the axes, view coordinates on the graph, and view a table that describes values of the function on any specified interval. You will need the Shockwave plugin because the activities were made with the tool Macromedia Director. You can see if you have the plugin, or download it, at (1a) http://www. exploremath.com/about/shockerhelp.cfm.

**TOPICS**: sinusoidal functions, sine, cosine, tangent, periodic functions, Pythagorean Theorem, degrees, radians, equation of a circle, period

## DISCUSSION QUESTIONS AND ACTIVITIES

1. How many degrees are equivalent to pi radians? Explain how you determined this result.

2. What is the relationship between the x and y-coordinates on the unit circle? Explain in more than one way how you know this is true.

3. Use the reference triangle to generate a formula that describes the relationship between cosine, sine, and the radius of the circle. Explain your reasoning.

4. At what angles during one revolution is the sine value the same as the cosine value? Explain how you determined this result.

5. What is the horizontal length of one cycle of a cosine, sine, and tangent function? Explain why this is true using both the circle and the graph.

6. What is the maximum value of the cosine and sine graphs if they are created with a radius equal to r? Explain your reasoning.

7. What is the relationship between sine, cosine, and tangent?

8. Determine five occasions when the tangent function is undefined. Explain how you determined this result.

## RELATED INTERNET SITE(S)

See **(38a) IES Trigonometry**

# 138. THE UNIVERSAL CURRENCY CONVERTER

**URL: http://www.xe.net/ucc/**

**SUGGESTED LEVELS**: algebra (questions 1–2), advanced algebra (questions 1–4)

**SITE SUMMARY**: The Universal Currency Converter allows you to determine currency exchange rates on a daily basis. Each currency conversion can be written as a linear function. When someone is traveling to various countries, he or she can use composite and inverse functions to explain the process behind multiple currency conversions.

**TOPICS**: function, linear function, composite function, inverse function, slope, y-intercept

## DISCUSSION QUESTIONS AND ACTIVITIES

1. Devise a vacation that will start from the United States, take you to two countries, and return home. Use the currency converter to generate a function that describes the currency exchange traveling from the United States to the first country that you plan to visit. Describe the variables in the function, and explain the significance of the slope and y-intercept.

2. Compare the price of merchandise in the United States and that in the first country that you are visiting. Yahoo has a virtual mall at (138a) http://dir.yahoo.com/Business_and_Economy/Companies/Retailers/Virtual_Malls/Regional/.

3. Devise another function relating the currency from the United States to that of the second country that you are visiting. Show how this function and the inverse of the function from question 1 can create a composite function describing the currency exchange from the first country visited to the second country. For example, if the first country you visit is Spain and the second is France, then show how you can combine f(u) and u(s) to create f(s), where f = French francs, s = Spanish pesatas, and u = United States dollars. Use the currency converter to check your answer.

4. Determine the inverse of the function you found from the first sentence in question 3. Explain what the function represents in a traveling

context. Incorporate the significance of the slope and y-intercept in your explanation.

### RELATED INTERNET SITE(S)

**Currency Converters**
(138b)http://www.wildnetafrica.com/currencyframe.html
(138c)http://finance.yahoo.com/m3?u
(138d)http://kiwishop.com/shop/currency.html
These currency converters will give you updated information about exchange rates for currency when traveling between countries.
See **84. Measurement Converter**

## 139. U.S. CENSUS BUREAU

### URL: http://www.census.gov/

**SUGGESTED LEVELS**: algebra (questions 1–4), advanced algebra (questions 1–4)
**SITE SUMMARY**: The U.S. Census Bureau provides a large array of data about people, business, geography, news, and special topics. This site alone could create numerous opportunities for data analysis and modeling with functions. This exercise examines how you can compare growth rates and predict a population using a mathematical function.
**TOPICS**: data analysis, extrapolation, exponential functions, percentage, rate of change

### DISCUSSION QUESTIONS AND ACTIVITIES

1. Record the U.S. population at the top right of the page. Do you think this number is exact? Explain why or why not.

2. Record the U.S. and world populations at various times of the day, and during different days. Reload or refresh the page to verify that the predicted populations are changing. Based on the data, how fast is the U.S. population growing (each minute, hour, day, month, year)? How does this number compare with the world population's growth rate?

3. Use the data at (139a) http://www.census.gov/population/estimates/nation/intfile1–1.txt to construct a function that will predict the U.S. population for any month after 1980. Using this function, compare the growth rate with your results from question 2. Also, determine the

accuracy of your function with the U.S. population clock. Explain why there might be any discrepancies.

4. In what year will the U.S. population be twice as large as it is now? Explain your analysis.

## RELATED INTERNET SITE(S)

See **(62d) CIA World Fact Book at www.geographic.org**

**Population Tables**
(139a) http://zonedata.com/statistical/Population/popindex.htm
    View data related to longitudinal U.S. population, population and area, immigration, and population breakdowns according to age, sex, race, and state.

**Population Data Sheet**
(139b) http://www.prb.org/pubs/wpds2000/
    Examine demographic and diversity indicators that provide data related to population, growth rate, age, income, race, and occupation of land.

# 140. THE U.S. NATIONAL DEBT CLOCK

## URL: http://www.brillig.com/debt_clock/

**SUGGESTED LEVELS**: advanced algebra (questions 1–5)

**SITE SUMMARY**: This page contains the current size of the U.S. national debt and estimated size of the U.S. population. It is updated continuously by refreshing or reloading the page.

**TOPICS**: data collection, data analysis, exponential function, extrapolation

## DISCUSSION QUESTIONS AND ACTIVITIES

1. How much is the debt increasing each day? Each hour? Each minute? Each second? Explain how you determined these results.

2. Record the time and U.S. debt. Click reload or refresh on your browser, and record the new data. Continue recording data for about ten minutes. Determine a function that best describes the data. Explain your analysis.

3. If the debt continues to grow at the same rate, when will it exceed ten trillion dollars? Explain your analysis.

4. How much is the U.S. population increasing each day? Each hour? Each minute? Each second? Explain how you determined these results. Is the debt or U.S. population increasing more quickly? Explain.

5. Suppose the president created an excise tax on cigarettes so that the additional funding would pay off the national debt in ten years. U.S. cigarette production amounts can be found at (102c) http://www. cdc.gov/tobacco/research_data/economics/consump1.htm. If there are twenty cigarettes per pack, then how much tax should be applied to each pack? How would the answer be different if the president wanted to pay off the national debt in a year? Explain your analysis.

## RELATED INTERNET SITE(S)

**Budget of the United States Government**
(140a)http://w3.access.gpo.gov/usbudget/index.html
   View current and past federal budgets by browsing the supporting documents or searching the database.

See **139. U.S. Census Bureau**

See **22. Cam's Java Web Counter Applet: Dynamic Counter Applet**

# 141. U.S. SENATE VOTES ON CLINTON REMOVAL

**URLs: http://www.amstat.org/publications/jse/datasets/impeach. txt**
**http://www.amstat.org/publications/jse/datasets/impeach. dat**

**SUGGESTED LEVELS**: prealgebra (questions 1–6), statistics (questions 1–6)
**SITE SUMMARY**: This data set represents voting results from President Clinton's impeachment trial. Each senator, his or her votes, political party, degree of conservatism, reelection dates, and state popularity are grouped together. The first URL describes the data set, and the second URL is the actual data set.
**TOPICS**: data analysis, data display, outliers

## DISCUSSION QUESTIONS AND ACTIVITIES

1. Which factor(s) related most strongly to voting in favor of or against impeachment? Explain how you came to this conclusion.
2. Create a data display that best represents the degree of ideological conservatism of the Senate. Which senators, if any, seem to have relatively unusual political views when compared to the entire Senate? Include numerical analysis in your solution. Explain how you determined this result.

3. Which senator(s) in the impeachment vote seemed to conflict with the trend of their party's vote? Use the data to speculate plausible reasons why this happened.

4. How well did the senators' votes relate to each state's popularity of the president? What additional information would be useful to make your argument stronger? Explain why.

5. Based on the data, do you think that any of the votes were based on political loyalty? If so, explain how you could make this argument from the data. Predict the number of Republican seats in the Senate that would have been needed to remove the president from office. Explain your analysis of the data.

6. Create an additional question and solution relating to the data.

### RELATED INTERNET SITE(S)

**U.S. Census Bureau Voting and Registration**
(141a)http://www.census.gov/population/www/socdemo/voting.html
Obtain voting and registration data related to age, sex, ethnicity, region, education, and employment from 1964 to 1996.

See **(107a) Information about Candidates, Parties, and Other Committees**

See **(107b) Politics.com**

## 142. USA BOX OFFICE CHARTS ARCHIVE

### URL: http://www.imdb.com/Charts/usboxarchive

**SUGGESTED LEVELS**: prealgebra (questions 1 and 5), calculus (questions 1–5)

**SITE SUMMARY**: The Internet Movie Database maintains three years of data describing gross box office revenue for movies each week. Each data listing will include the movie's rank in the top ten, its weekend earnings, the number of weeks it has been in the theater, the number of screens it is playing on, its weekend screen average, its cumulative box office total, and its top 100 rank in the Internet Movie Database.

**TOPICS**: data collection, data analysis, modeling, logistic function, exponential function, definite integral, integral, scatter plot.

## DISCUSSION QUESTIONS AND ACTIVITIES

1. Choose a movie that has been in the top ten box office listing since its release, and has been in this listing for at least five consecutive weeks. Record data and create a scatter plot of cumulative box office totals vs. number of weeks released.

2. The data can be modeled with a function g(t), where g(t) = the integral of f(t) dt. Describe what type of function f(t) would be and include units. Justify your answer.

3. Find f(t) and describe how you arrived at your answer. Using this information, find g(t). Graph g(t) with the scatter plot you created in problem 1 and compare the curve with the data. Which points do not fit well with the curve? Explain possible causes for the discrepancies.

4. Suppose you are the manager of a movie theater. Use a function from problem 3 to create a strategy that will determine when a movie would no longer be useful in your theater. Explain your analysis.

5. Generate a strategy that will help you determine how many of your sixteen theaters should be showing the most popular movie during its opening weekend. As the movie plays in several theaters over the next couple of months, discuss how and when you will remove it from each theater until it is no longer playing.

## RELATED INTERNET SITE(S)

See **130. Top 100 Ever Adjusted**

# 143. VECTORS

## URL: http://www.math.csusb.edu/courses/m129/vector.html

**SUGGESTED LEVELS**: geometry (questions 1–4), precalculus (questions 1–4)

**SITE SUMMARY**: This site has a Java applet that gives you the opportunity to discover the relationship between a vector and the translation of a polygon. You can change the coordinates of the vector and vertices of the polygon.

**TOPICS**: vector, translation, origin, coordinate, preimage, image

## DISCUSSION QUESTIONS AND ACTIVITIES

1. Move the tail of the vector to each of the vertices of the preimage, the red polygon. Drag the vertices of the preimage to change its shape.

Based on your observations, what is the function of a vector? Explain your reasoning.

2. What properties of the figure, including its sides and angles, are invariant (stay the same) after a translation with a vector? Explain how you determined these results.

3. If the tail of the vector is located at the origin, make a conjecture about the relationship between the x-coordinate of a vertex on the preimage (red), the x-coordinate of the head of the vector (arrow), and the x-coordinate of a corresponding vertex on the image (blue).

4. Would your conjecture to problem 2 be the same if the tail of the vector were not located at the origin? If so, explain why. If not, explain the difference with a new conjecture.

## RELATED INTERNET SITE(S)

### Vector Cross Product

(143a) http://www.phy.syr.edu/courses/java-suite/crosspro.html

This Java applet is a dynamic representation of the cross product of two vectors. As you modify the angle and length of the vectors, you will see changes in their cross product.

### Graphing Vector Calculators

(143b) http://www.frontiernet.net/~imaging/vector_calculator.html

(143c) http://comp.uark.edu/~jgeabana/java/VectorCalc.html

(143d) http://www.pa.uky.edu/~phy211/VecArith/index.html

Sketch and manipulate vectors on a graph to see the relationship between two vectors and their sum or difference. The calculator will also show you the co-ordinates associated with the resulting vector and its length.

### IES Vector Directory

(143e) http://www.ies.co.jp/math/java/vector/index.html

This series of applets uses vectors to investigate the area of a parallelogram, inner products, dot products, Cramer's Rule, Cerv's Theorem, and more.

### Vector Land

(143f) http://members.tripod.com/~Paul_Kirby/vector/VectorLand.html

Investigate vectors in three dimensions by viewing applets associated with dot products, cross products, distance to a plane, the great circle, and more.

### Vector Addition

(143g) http://www.phy.ntnu.edu.tw/java/vector/vector.html

This applet shows how to add two vectors. When you plot the two vectors, you will see an animated transformation that represents the sum.

# 144.  VOLTAGE CIRCUIT SIMULATOR

## URL: http://jersey.uoregon.edu/vlab/Voltage/index.html

**SUGGESTED LEVELS**: algebra (questions 1–5)
**SITE SUMMARY**: This applet investigates the relationship between

voltage, current, and resistance in a circuit. The goal of the activity is to find the appropriate pairs of voltage and resistance to turn on a light bulb. The bulb will break if you place too little resistance on the current in the circuit, and the bulb will not light if you place too much resistance on the current in the circuit. Begin by placing voltage and resistor sources onto the circuit and flip the switch to see the outcome.

**TOPICS**: data analysis, data collection, modeling, linear function, slope, y-intercept, equation of a line

## DISCUSSION QUESTIONS AND ACTIVITIES

1. Find multiple ways to turn on the light bulb and state the possible outcomes. Explain how you found these solutions.

2. Using the data that will turn the light on, graph voltage as a function of resistance on a piece of graph paper. How do the two variables relate? Generate an equation that describes the two variables. Explain the meaning of the slope and y-intercept in your equation.

3. Suppose you went shopping for batteries that exceed twenty-four volts. What type of resistors would you need? Explain.

4. Compare the voltage and resistance of circuits that light the bulb at (144a) http://jersey.uoregon.edu/vlab/Voltage/volt1.html. How is this relationship similar to and/or different from the circuit in problem 2? Explain.

5. What types of batteries and resistors would you need to handle a circuit with twenty amps of current? Explain.

## RELATED INTERNET SITE(S)

**Voltage and Current**
(144b) http://www.mste.uiuc.edu/murphy/LightBulb/default.html
   This applet shows the variation of current flow through a circuit as you modify the voltage source.

**Voltage Circuit Simulator**
(144c) http://www.javasoft.com/applets/archive/beta/Voltage/index.html
   This site is very similar to the applet used in the activity above.

## 145. WHO WANTS TO BE A MILLIONAIRE?

**URL: http://abc.go.com/primetime/millionaire/mill_home.html**

**SUGGESTED LEVELS**: prealgebra (questions 1–3), probability (question 4), statistics (questions 1–3)

**SITE SUMMARY**: Play simulated games of the television game show *Who Wants to Be a Millionaire?* You can use a data display to discuss your performance, as well as that of your classmates. Moreover, the outcome of the game can lead to issues related to measures of center, such as mean, median, and mode.

**TOPICS**: simulation, data collection, data analysis, data display, mean, median, mode, average, probability

## DISCUSSION QUESTIONS AND ACTIVITIES

1. Start playing the game using lifelines, and keep track of how many questions you answer correctly. If you miss a question, do not continue, and play another game. Play up to five games total. Predict the order of questions answered correctly, from largest to smallest, of the class mean, median, and mode. Explain your reasoning. Now combine your data with that of your classmates. Use a data display and measures of central tendency to describe the performance of your class. Evaluate your prediction and discuss important factors that affect the different measures of center.

2. Start playing the game without using lifelines, and keep track of how many questions you answer correctly. If you miss a question, do not continue, and play another game. Play up to five games total. Predict the order of questions answered correctly, from largest to smallest, of the class mean, median, and mode. Explain your reasoning. Now combine your data with your classmates. Use a data display and measures of center to describe the performance of your class. Evaluate your prediction and discuss important factors that affect the different measures of center. How does your result compare with problem 1? Explain why there are similarities and/or differences in the results.

3. Start playing a new archived game and keep track of how many questions you answer correctly and incorrectly. If you miss a question, continue the game until you complete the one million dollar question. Predict the order of questions answered incorrectly, from largest to smallest, of the class mean, median, and mode. Explain your reasoning. Now combine your data with your classmates. Use a data display and measures of center to describe the performance of your class. Evaluate your prediction and discuss important factors that affect the different measures of center. How do your results compare with problems 1 and 2?

4. What is the probability that you will win one million dollars if you guess the answers to all of the questions? Give an example of a situation where the probability of winning one million dollars is 1 out of 100. Explain your reasoning.

## RELATED INTERNET SITE(S)

**The Station**
(145a) http://www.station.sony.com/
  Play interactive online games such as Jeopardy, Trivial Pursuit, Wheel of Fortune, and more. Some of the games provide real-time statistics. Determine your accuracy and how well you match up with others.

## 146. WORLD-WIDE TRACK & FIELD STATISTICS ON-LINE

### URL: http://www.sci.fi/~mapyy/tilastot.html

  **SUGGESTED LEVELS**: prealgebra (questions 1–4), algebra (questions 1–5), advanced algebra (questions 1–6)
  **SITE SUMMARY**: This site contains data related to the men's and women's world record times in Olympic track and field events. You can view the progression of times or marks and their associated years each time a world record is broken for over twenty-five different events. Click on the WR progression links to view each set of data.
  **TOPICS**: data collection, data analysis, graphing data, function, modeling, system of equations, linear function, exponential function, extrapolation

## DISCUSSION QUESTIONS AND ACTIVITIES

1. Is this website from a machine in the United States? Besides the URL address, what indicator(s) on the page supplies this information?

2. Have all of the times been measured and recorded with equal precision? Explain how you know.

3. When you look at the records, how often are they broken? Which records are most likely to be broken in the next summer Olympics? Explain your reasoning.

4. In the same track event, is a female or a male more likely to break the world record this year? Explain how you came to this conclusion.

5. If you graph the world record vs. the year it occurred, what function would best model the data? Would you use the same type of function for all events? Explain.

6. In the same track event, in what year will women begin running faster than men? Is this result consistent among all track events? Explain how you determined these results.

## RELATED INTERNET SITE(S)

See **(14b)** and **(14c) Sports Statistics**
See **(14d) Sports Statistics on the Web**
See **(14c) Major League Baseball Statistics**


# 147. XFUNCTIONS XPRESSO I

### URL: http://math.hws.edu/xFunctions/

**SUGGESTED LEVELS**: advanced algebra (questions 1–6), precalculus (questions 1–6)

**SITE SUMMARY**: This function grapher is capable of graphing multiple functions, evaluating a function, modifying a viewing window, animating a varied coefficient or constant, graphing a derivative, calculating Reimann sums, graphing 3D plots, and more. Scroll down the page and click on Launch xFunctions to begin.

**TOPICS**: step function, graph, system of equations, polynomial function, x-intercepts, factoring, quadratic functions, symmetry, roots, degree


## DISCUSSION QUESTIONS AND ACTIVITIES

1. Click on the menu and make sure you are on the main screen. How does the floor function evaluate? Why does the graph have steps? How is this function different from the round, trunc, and ceiling functions? Generate an example of how each of these types of functions can be applied in real-world business and industry.

2. Click on the menu and make sure you are on the multigraph utility. How many real number solutions exist for $2^x = x^2$? Explain how you know.

3. In a polynomial function, what happens to the x-intercepts if you reverse the leading coefficient and the constant term? Explain how you determined this result.

4. Click on the menu and make sure you are on the animate utility. Graph and find an appropriate window of $y = k* \times {}^\wedge 2 + k*x$. Click Go to animate the graph. Explain why you think this window is appropriate. What characteristics of the graph remain constant as k varies? Why is this true?

5. Describe the symmetry of all functions in the form $y = x^{2k-1}$, where k is any natural number. Why is this true? State another series of functions with the same symmetry in terms of k.

6. How does the greatest number of roots of a polynomial function relate to its degree? Explain how you determined this result.

## RELATED INTERNET SITE(S)

**Multimedia Activities at ExploreMath.com**
(147a)http://www.exploremath.com/activities/index.cfm
   ExploreMath.com has a series of dynamic functions that allow you to adjust each of the coefficients of the equation of a function and observe simultaneous changes in the graph. You can modify the viewing window of the graph, modify the center and length of the axes, view coordinates on the graph, and view a table that describes values of the function on any specified interval. You will need the Shockwave plugin because the activities were made with the tool Macromedia Director. You can see if you have the plugin, or download it, at (1a)http://www.exploremath.com/about/shockerhelp.cfm.
**See (74c)–(74j) Function Graphers**

# 148. XFUNCTIONS XPRESSO II

## URL: http://math.hws.edu/xFunctions/

   **SUGGESTED LEVELS**: calculus (questions 1–6)
   **SITE SUMMARY**: This function grapher is capable of graphing multiple functions, evaluating a function, modifying a viewing window, animating a varied coefficient or constant, graphing a derivative, calculating Reimann sums, graphing 3D plots, and more. Scroll down the page and click on Launch xFunctions to begin. Click on the menu and make sure you are on the Derivatives Utility. The first graph will represent the function, the second graph will represent the first derivative, and the third graph will represent the second derivative.
   **TOPICS**: function, graph, increase, decrease, tangent line, derivative, relative minimum, relative maximum, extrema, slope, domain, second derivative, continuity, differentiable, third derivative

## DISCUSSION QUESTIONS AND ACTIVITIES

1. Enter a function that increases and decreases over a specified domain in the graphing window (you can change this). What function did you enter? Click and drag on the graph to see the tangent line and corresponding value of the derivative. How does the tangent line relate to the value of the derivative function? What component of the tangent line relates to whether the function is increasing or decreasing?

2. Enter a function that will have a relative maximum and minimum.

What function did you enter? What are the slope of the tangent line and the value of the derivative at a maximum or minimum? Generate a hypothesis that will help you predict when a function has a relative minimum or maximum without viewing its graph.

3. Find a function that is never decreasing, but has a derivative equal to zero at a point in its domain. Explain your answer.

4. Find a function that has a second derivative equal to zero for some value in the domain. What happens to the function and its derivative when the second derivative is equal to zero? Explain your analysis.

5. Find a function that is continuous at x = c, but the first derivative at x = c will not exist. Generate a hypothesis about the tangent line of the function when its derivative does not exist. Test the hypothesis with a few more cases. Explain your analysis.

6. Generate a graph of the third derivative of y = sin(x). Explain your procedures.

### RELATED INTERNET SITE(S)

See **(9a)** and **(9b) Derivative Puzzles**

See **(9c) Derivative Definition Java Applet**

## 149. XFUNCTIONS XPRESSO III

URL:http://math.hws.edu/xFunctions/

**SUGGESTED LEVELS**: calculus (questions 1–4)
**SITE SUMMARY**: This function grapher is capable of graphing multiple functions, evaluating a function, modifying a viewing window, animating a varied coefficient or constant, graphing a derivative, calculating Reimann sums, graphing 3D plots, and more. Scroll down the page and click on Launch xFunctions to begin. Click on the menu and make sure you are on the Riemann Sums Utility. If you Clear Intervals, you will start with one rectangle. When you Divide Intervals, you will end up with twice as many rectangles. The menu in the lower right-hand corner allows you to change the view between the six different types of geometric shapes that will be used to approximate area.
**TOPICS**: function, area of rectangle, area under curve, area of trapezoid, limit, integral

## DISCUSSION QUESTIONS AND ACTIVITIES

1. Enter a function and set the window so that the top of the rectangles can be seen. State your function and window. Divide the regions until you have four intervals. Which approximation is best for the area beneath the curve? Is this true for any function? Explain.

2. Click on the menu and make sure you are on the Riemann Sums Utility. For which type of functions will the rectangular approximations represent exact areas? For which type of functions will the trapezoidal approximations represent exact areas? Explain your solutions.

3. Click on the menu and make sure you are on the Riemann Sums Utility. Devise a strategy that will decrease the variability in the different area approximations. Test the strategy with multiple functions and explain your findings.

4. A factory worker manufactures toys at a rate of $p(t) = 25(2)^{-t/6}$ toys per hour, where t is the number of consecutive hours worked. In a nine-hour work day, the worker is given one hour for lunch and two twenty-minute breaks. As a manager, devise a schedule that would maximize the workers' productivity. Explain your analysis.

## RELATED INTERNET SITE(S)

See **50. Finding the Area Under a Curve**

See **(50a) Minimum Value of Integral of Function**

See **(51a) Problem of Area**

See **(50b) and (50c) Evaluating Integrals**

## 150. YAHOO! FINANCE

**URL:http://finance.yahoo.com/?u**

**SUGGESTED LEVELS**: advanced algebra (questions 1–4), statistics (questions 5–6)

**SITE SUMMARY**: This site will give you information about stock companies, updated quotes, and up to a five-year history of the trend of stock prices.

**TOPICS**: data collection, data analysis, modeling, function, linear function, exponential function, logarithms, confidence intervals

## DISCUSSION QUESTIONS AND ACTIVITIES

1. Click on Dow to view a graph of the stock index over the last year. What type of function does the Dow Jones Industrial Average (DJIA) look like over the last year? Go back and compare this to the Nasdaq index. Explain any similarities or differences in the functions.

2. Click on a five-year big chart of the DJIA. How are the values on the y-axis spaced out? What type of function does the DJIA look like over the last five years? If the y-values were spaced out evenly, what type of function would the DJIA look like over the last five years? Go back and compare this to the Nasdaq index. Explain any similarities or differences.

3. Use the five-year big chart of the DJIA. Collect data from the graph and derive an equation that will predict the value of the index. What do the numbers in your equation represent? Show your calculations and reasoning. Assuming the growth model continues, when will the DJIA reach 100,000? How did you determine this?

4. Use the five-year big chart of the Nasdaq. Collect data from the graph and derive an equation that will predict the value of the index since five years ago. What do the numbers in your equation represent? Show your calculations and reasoning. Assuming the growth model continues, will the Nasdaq index ever be higher than the DJIA index? If so, when? Explain your reasoning.

5. Ameritrade (AMTD) and Etrade (EGRP) have very similar price fluctuations. Examine their yearly charts and use the ratio of the stocks' prices to devise a method that will help you determine when it is better to buy one stock over the other. Explain your analysis. Find two other stocks in any particular sector that have similar price fluctuations. Which pair of stocks would be better to invest in? Explain your reasoning.

6. Choose a stock that you think has been steadily growing over the last five years. How well has this stock grown compared to both of the stock indices? Explain your analysis.

## RELATED INTERNET SITE(S)

**Stock Market Simulations and Games**
(150a) http://www.smg2000.org/
(150b) http://www.santacruz.k12.ca.us/jpost/projects/TS/TS.html
(150c) http://library.thinkquest.org/3088/
(150d) http://www.ichallenge.net/
(150e) http://tqjunior.advanced.org/4116/Investing/stock.htm

These simulations of the stock market allow your students to trade shares, familiarize themselves with the industry, and compete against other people.

See **(24a) Stock Exchange Game**

# 151. YAHOO! SHOPPING

**URL: http://shopping.yahoo.com/**

**SUGGESTED LEVELS**: prealgebra (questions 1–5), statistics (questions 1–5)

**SITE SUMMARY**: Yahoo! Shopping gives you the opportunity to find a product online and compare its prices with products from other companies. You can search for a product, look at gift ideas, or browse hot products. Search features will return merchants, categories in Yahoo, and products for sale. In the products results, you can sort the return by relevance, increasing price, or decreasing price.

**TOPICS**: data collection, data analysis, data display

## DISCUSSION QUESTIONS AND ACTIVITIES

1. Search for an item that can be found at multiple stores (less than $250) that you would like for your birthday. Which companies are offering the item at an unusually inexpensive or expensive price? Explain your analysis.

2. What factor(s) contribute to the relevance and order of the findings that appear in the search? Test your hypothesis several times and use data to support your answer.

3. Search for multiple items that can be found in three or more of the same stores. Design a shopping guide for a friend who would like to visit these stores. Discuss what type of products are good buys at the various stores, and how you determined this information. Include a statistical analysis in your findings.

4. How do you think the companies that sell their products appear in the search results? Are all possible retailers shown in the search return? Explain criteria that lead to being on a search return.

5. Is it better to buy an item online? Explain why or why not.

## RELATED INTERNET SITE(S)

**Other Comparison Shopping Sites on the Web**
(150a) http://shopping.altavista.com/

(151b) http://www.buy.com

(151c) http://www.iwon.com/home/shopping/shopping_overview/0,11722,,00.
html

Search for retail items by an assortment of categories, including apparel, groceries, computers, office supplies, toys, and more.

# 152. YOUR WEIGHT ON OTHER WORLDS

## URL:http://www.exploratorium.edu/ronh/weight/index.html

**SUGGESTED LEVELS**: prealgebra (questions 1, 2, 4, and 5), algebra (questions 3–5)

**SITE SUMMARY**: Compare your weight on different solar bodies. Input your weight into the text box, press the Calculate button, and view the data on the screen.

**TOPICS**: linear function, data collection, data analysis, proportion, extrapolation

## DISCUSSION QUESTIONS AND ACTIVITIES

1. On which planet will you weigh the most? On which planet do you weigh the least? Is this true for everyone? Explain why or why not.

2. On which planet is your mass the greatest? On which planet is your mass the least? Is this true for everyone? Explain why or why not.

3. Graph weight on Earth vs. weight on Mars using the range of the weights of students in your class. What type of function is represented by the data? What do each of the numbers in the equation represent? How much would an elephant weigh on Mars? Explain your analysis.

4. Look at the solar system data at (152a) http://www.seds.org/nineplanets/nineplanets/data2.html.

    What is the relationship between the gravity value and weight? Explain how you determined this result.

5. How much stronger is the gravitational pull on a neutron star compared to on the Earth? Explain your reasoning.

## RELATED INTERNET SITE(S)

See **121. Solar System Data**

# 153.  ZIP FIND CENTRAL

## URL: http://link-usa.com/zipcode/

**SUGGESTED LEVELS**: advanced algebra (questions 2–6), statistics (question 1)

**SITE SUMMARY**: This calculator and database will tell you the number of zip codes available within a specific distance, the population within that radius, and the population density within that radius. You can enter two zip codes and find the distance between their corresponding cities, as well as find the zip code for an unknown city.

**TOPICS**: data collection, data analysis, modeling data, function, expected value, confidence intervals, exponential function, quadratic function, extrapolation

## DISCUSSION QUESTIONS AND ACTIVITIES

1. Predict the distance between two cities that have zip codes which differ by one digit. Explain your analysis. What range of distances would you provide if you wanted your prediction to be 95 percent accurate? Explain.

2. How does the number of zip codes relate to the radius, or distance, from a particular zip code? What type of function is modeled by the data? Explain your analysis.

3. Search for different sizes of cities around the country. Record the population of the city and the number of zip codes it has. Graph the population of a city as a function of its number of zip codes. What type of function best models this data? Explain your reasoning.

4. The population of a city with 500,000 people is growing at a rate of 2 percent each year. How often should the city obtain additional zip codes?

5. In what year will the U.S. Postal Service need to add an additional digit to its zip codes? Monthly U.S. population estimates over the past twenty years can be found at (153a) http://www.census.gov/population/estimates/nation/intfile1–1.txt. Explain your analysis.

6. Is there any relationship between the price of a package and the distance it is travelling? Is there a function that can predict this comparison? Shipping costs can be found at the USPS site (103. http://postcalc.usps.gov/). Explain your analysis. Does this relationship change if you use UPS (103. http://wwwapps.ups.com/servlet/

QCCServlet) or Federal Express (103. http://www.federalexpress. com/us/rates/) to ship the package? Explain your analysis.

## RELATED INTERNET SITE(S)

See **139. U.S. Census Bureau**

**Langenberg.com**
(153b) http://zip.langenberg.com/
  Obtain a variety of zip code information relating to distances, location, position, and population.

**United States Postal Service**
(153c) http://www.usps.com/ncsc/lookups/Lookup_zip+4.html
  Obtain zip code information, locations of post offices, and postage rates from this national mail carrier.

# Appendix: Web Sites by Topic

## ALGEBRA

## GEOMETRY

## ADVANCED ALGEBRA

## MATH HISTORY

# Index

## About the Author

EVAN GLAZER is a Ph.D. candidate at the University of Georgia in the Department of Instructional Technology, and a former mathematics teacher at Glenbrook South High School in Glenview, Illinois. He has designed and developed curriculum for the Intermath project and has completed writing projects on the subjects of mathematics and instructional technology in the classroom.